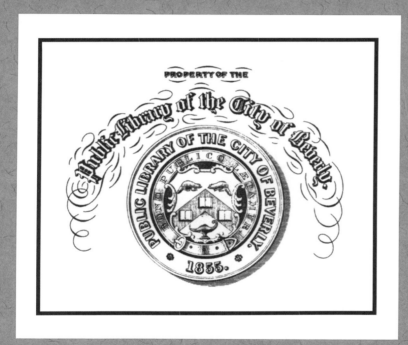

EARLY NANTUCKET
AND ITS WHALE HOUSES

Early Siasconset was a medieval British village of whale houses of small scale. Back of the hollyhocks is *Auld Lang Syne;* beyond is *Nauticon. Photo, author.*

Early Nantucket

AND ITS

Whale Houses

By HENRY CHANDLEE FOREMAN

Ph.D. (Fine Arts), A.I.A.

Drawings and Photographs by the Author where Noted

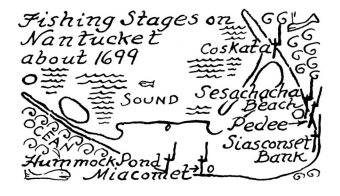

HASTINGS HOUSE   *Publishers*   NEW YORK

To
Charles E. Peterson
of
Philadelphia, Pennsylvania

Loyal Friend

Contents

	Acknowledgments	IX
I	At the Sandy Land Far Out to Sea	1
II	The Indian-American Island	5
III	The Proprietors' Early Town	21
IV	Rise of the Whaling Stations	29
V	Pioneering with Love and Skillets	47
VI	" 'Tis Tu I Can't, and Tu I Ken"	63
VII	The 'Sconset Baulk and Whale House	79
VIII	More About the Whale Houses	95
IX	The Two Oldest Known Buildings on Nantucket	111
X	Whale Houses and Lean-Tos on Lower Broadway	131
XI	Whale Houses on Middle Broadway	149

XII   *Upper Broadway Whale Cottages.*   173

XIII   *Lanes Through the Old Pump Square*   195

XIV   *First Buildings in Nantucket Town*   221

XV   *Transitional Lean-Tos and Gambrels in and About the Town*   243

        Notes   265

        Selected Critical Bibliography   277

        Index   283

Acknowledgements

The writer wishes to thank all those persons and organizations which gave assistance to, or supplied photographs for, this work, including the following:

The late Mr. Donald Craig, Mr. David Gray, Mr. Robert Deeley, the Nantucket Historical Association, the Nantucket Whaling Museum, *The Nantucket Inquirer and Mirror.*

Also, Miss Mildred Burgess of 'Sconset, Miss Alma Robbins, Mr. William Lyne Wilson, of Lynchburg, Va., Mrs. Julia Macy Urann, Miss Grace Brown Gardner, Mr. J. Marshall Whiting, of Guilford, Conn., the Nantucket Athenaeum Library, the Historic American Buildings Survey (HABS), the Society for the Preservation of New England Antiquities.

In addition, the late Mr. James Hamar, of Summit, N. J., Mr. and Mrs. George Selleck, Mr. Edouard Stackpole, Mrs. Robert Medlicott, Mr. Earl Ray, Mr. Theodore Whittlesey, of Bryn Mawr, Pa., Mr. Josiah Barrett, Mrs. M. W. Boyer, Mr. Jesse Eldridge, Mrs. Donald E. Callender, Mr. R. Hammond Gibson, of Easton, Md., Dr. Walter Boyd, of Washington, D.C., Miss Gladys Wood and Mrs. Caroline Lippincott Forman.

I

At the Sandy Land Far Out to Sea

1 – "The World Forgetting by the World Forgot"

NO MATTER WHERE the early settler went or what he did on Nantucket, there was just over the hummock or down the lane the booming sound of the great sea waves breaking over the wide, sandy beaches. Upon this spacious sand-bar, about fifteen miles long by three wide, one can never get very far from the salty smell of the ocean. The Island was well named by the American Indians *Natocket,* meaning "At the Land Far Out at Sea."

So apart from the wide world was Nantucket in its early days that February there was especially known as "trumpery" month, that is to say, "rubbish" month, because by that bleak season the Islanders had nothing left in their répertoires to discuss but what happened in their small, closed, insular circle.

In addition, the Island has been so isolated that in 1873 *Scribner's Monthly Magazine* declared that it was currently reported on Nantucket that the first news received from the "States" after the American Revolutionary War had ended in 1781 at Yorktown, Virginia, reached that Island months later *via London, England*. It happened that this news, which meant much to all Americans, had been printed in newspapers in Great Britain and had been brought by a British ship that had stopped off the shore of Nantucket for water and provision.

They say that the early Nantucketer was much like the ancient Chinese map-maker, who drew a circle touching the four sides of his paper for China and placed the remainder of the earth in the four corners. Even when the Island became fa-

1

ınous as the whaling capital of the world in the 1840s, the inhabitants still clung to their ingrained, island ways — pretty much as their ancestors had done as far back as they could remember. The charm and fascination of Nantucket Island has been that it has always resisted the worst elements in change.

So quaint and archaic are some of the written records of the Island that the first page of volume one of the County of Nantucket — which includes the whole great sand-bar itself — begins for the year 1699 in this way: "Roland Gardners Shop Book. The rattling tounge [tongue] of saucy and audacious eloquence. Our old dog has broke his leg eating skin milk cheese." Then there follow the usual prosaic County entries and items.

You could well sum up early Nantucket in these words: "The quiet perfume of antiquity and conservatism hanging round both homes and persons was like the scent of dried roses in a long-closed cabinet, or of box-plants in a still, summer noon as one saunters through the old, old garden of a deserted country home."[1]

2 – Coofs and Pretty Girls

Now that word conservatism strikes the keynote, because this Isle has tended for centuries to maintain its own conservative British customs, idioms and thinking in the face of "modernism" and "progressivism" emanating from the mainland — called "America" or "the continent" by these Islanders. And besides, mainlanders since the early days were often known as "coofs."

The sweet appellation of "coof" or "couf" — rhyming with "hoof" — was, it has been said, the Nantucketer's way of being polite to strangers. However that may be, the stigma of being called "coof" must not have sounded very agreeable to Off-Islanders, who perhaps would have preferred another term, especially after they had learned that the word is one of derision and came from the ancient Scottish expression for "fool," "lout" or "coward."

In spite of its attitude toward "foreigners" — those who were not lucky enough to have been born on the Island — Nantucket was a friendly place. For generations every door stood open, or at most with the latch-string hanging out, as the old saying goes. And on the Island there were literally thousands of latch-strings. No one ever bothered to lock up anything. Every man, woman and child felt a friendly interest in every other. Whatever misfortune happened to his own house or family, nobody went homeless or friendless. It has been told that since the seventeenth century Nantucket has been the kind of place which many would like to live in, but which few attain. Besides, on the great sand-bar there was always a drawing card. The Island girls were universally pretty, graceful, shapely and, most of all, unspoiled by the great world. They are reported to have looked fresh as the sea breeze tinting their cheeks, and to have had a simple ease of manner and sincerity of tone seldom found in urban drawing rooms. Small wonder that many of those sea-girt damsels were snatched up in wedlock as young as sixteen years of age. Way back in the seventeenth century on that Island one Ruth Gardner, a maiden scarce fifteen, married a Coffin.

On the other hand for generations there was an unfortunate taboo against any well-born Island girl, pretty or otherwise, wedding with a "coof," no matter how fine a man or a gentleman he was.

3 – What This Book is About

In a nutshell this volume concerns the Nantucketer's peculiarly seventeenth- and early-eighteenth-century type of British civilization, medieval in some aspects, like town planning and building methods, which persisted, it may be noted, in more or less degree down to the Victorian era. For the most part this work is a tale *not* of the great whaling epoch of the 1830s and 40s, nor about the Town's Main Street mansions built on whale oil — a period widely known; but of humble beginnings, Indian antecedents, fishing and sheep-shearing economies, sailboat voyaging, rain-barrel water supplies and the like. It is about space-saving furniture where space was at a premium, medieval boat's crew cottages and homey lean-to dwellings, and nautical ways of doing things and of thinking. It is a story not about the rich sea captains and affluent merchants, but mostly about the plain islanders who formed the very backbone of Nantucket Island.

More than half the book deals with the buildings which Nantucketers constructed and continually changed at their pleasure. There is much about the Medieval and Transitional Styles of architecture and something about the early Georgian. By "medieval" we do not mean, of course, the medieval period of history, but a manner of building which lagged in both Old and New England down to about the year 1700, and which therefore had ample time to flourish on Nantucket.

The village of Siasconset, or 'Sconset, for short, has been emphasized over Nantucket, known as "Town," because it represents an earlier stage in the development of the Island than does the Town. Consequently there is presented in the following pages the portrait of a medieval village — with as exact and complete a record, historically, chronologically and visually, as possible. Street by street, house by house, and we may even state "flake" yard by "flake" yard, we have made a record for posterity of this village, the first summer resort in America. By chronological drawings and charts we have sought to stress how building on the Island was never static, but largely one of change, growth and peripatetic aspect.

4 – Singularity of Siasconset

There seems little doubt that 'Sconset about the time of the American Revolution was the most unusual village in New England and perhaps in the United States. The only settlement which may have resembled that village was the Sesachacha (Ses-ák-a-cha) Beach hamlet, also on Nantucket Island; but by 1776 Sesachacha had already gone downhill and had dwindled in size in favor of 'Sconset. To this writer's knowledge, on the mainland there was no other village even remotely resembling 'Sconset.

Its principal street, Broadway, was once undoubtedly the most picturesque thoroughfare in the United States. The copyrighted restoration drawings of this lane (pp. 68-75) were made possible chiefly because of discoveries, as this work progressed over eleven years (1950-61), concerning the typical early dwelling in the village. *For the first time in this country a hanging-loft or baulk building has been recognized, identified and described in this book about Nantucket.* Not only has a type of structure, not known in the United States until this writing, been added to the history of American architecture, but also the history of American whaling has been augmented *because the hanging-loft house was used on Nantucket as a whale house* — something the writers of the whaling histories have not yet recorded.

When the author came to finish this account of the early life, customs and structures, he had been acquainted with Nantucket Island for over half a century; in addition, six generations of his family had been loyally summering there. And when he wrote of carrying water from rain barrels in the seventeenth and eighteenth centuries, he had spoken from his own experience, because as a small boy he had to carry water home in buckets — only by that time the 'Sconset rain barrels had been replaced by a town pump and street water faucets. In 1965 he made a special trip to Wales to study hanging-loft or baulk buildings.

On this Island, then, there lived in the early days "an unmixed English breed" on the edge of a vast wilderness. But before those colonists were others, many others, who upon that great sand-bar continually fought for survival against isolation, an angry sea and starvation. Some account of them is given in the next chapter.

Nantucket Harpoon
Very old "Two flue iron"

The Indian-American Island

1 – The Finding of Nantucket

THE ISLAND, it appears, has had two chief discoveries by white men, and possibly a third.

For years it has been said that the "Vinland" of the old Norse sagas was named for grapes, or was Martha's Vineyard; but that is not so, for "Vinland" was named for grassy or grazing lands, and has lately been tentatively identified at a location in farm lands in northern Newfoundland at a place called the "Bay of the Meadow," near St. Anthony. There Leif Erickson and his fellows from Norway about the year A.D. 1000 — five centuries before Christopher Columbus — constructed houses, of which nine layered turf foundations still exist.[1] In one of his exploratory sailing journeys southward from Newfoundland Erickson probably sailed past or even landed on Nantucket Island.

The second finding was by Bartholomew Gosnold, an Englishman, and his men, who in 1602 debarked at Sankaty Head, Nantucket, while on the way to the Elizabeth Islands to establish — on Cuttyhunk — the first known white settlement in New England. Moreover, it was Gosnold who "in a short five years [after the settlement on Cuttyhunk] perished in the terrible first Jamestown summer of 1607 in Virginia."[2]

The third discovery does not concern this work because of its lateness; for the Island of Nantucket was "found" again by "Off-Islanders," who in the 1870s sought rest and recreation.

5

Most early Nantucket history had already passed when Gosnold landed at Sankaty. If history is a catalogue of the forgotten, then there is relatively little about the first owners of Nantucket, the American Indian. Light-brown men with brown or black eyes and straight, blue-black hair, they also possessed "the continent" — the incipient United States of America. Of the million or more of them estimated to have lived in this country in the seventeenth century, relatively few are left; and none survives on Nantucket.

Now America is believed on good authority to have been continuously inhabited by man — that is, by what we generally call the American Indian — for at least 100,000 years. In Massachusetts traces of *Folsom* spear points, with a flute or channel on each face, and dating somewhere between 25,000 and 13,000 years ago, have been discovered[3]; but not one genuine spear point of that kind has come to light on Nantucket.

The first known group of Indians to live in the Nantucket area were the *Archaic* peoples, generally divided into Early Archaic and Late Archaic by the time — about 5000 years ago — when Nantucket was separated from the mainland and became an island in the sea.

The pre-Island Early Archaic aborigines hunted with the spear and with the throwing stick — known in Mexico as the "atlatl." They also employed a slate knife with a semi-circular edge sharpened for cutting — an example of which has been found in Polpis Harbor on Nantucket.[4]

On the other hand, the persons of Late Archaic vintage used bows and arrows, smoked pipes and introduced durable soapstone pottery.

Finally, the last group of Indians to occupy Nantucket was the *Woodland* people — more specifically, the eastern Algonquian-speaking group of the Eastern Woodland area. The Woodlanders were agriculturists who cultivated corn, squash and beans, used some pottery cooking vessels, went about in canoes and lived in wigwams or houses.

2 – Contributions of the Aborigines

In the seventeenth century the American Indian was culturally about halfway between the natives of Central Africa and the English who came to America. Generally speaking, the white man made war on the "poor" Indian for four centuries. Such a situation never encourages an objective appreciation of the good values and high skills of an enemy.

Even though he had some barbarous customs, he was not really a savage, popular beliefs notwithstanding. He had no Buchenwald concentration camps nor any power as terrible as the capacity to wipe out a great city in the twinkling of an atom flash.

Nantucket Indian Mortar & Pestle

H.C.Forman

dia. 6¾"
Fair St. Mus.

The ordinary Indian in this country, including Nantucket, was more advanced in the arts and crafts, and had a finer artistic sense, than the *average* American today. The aboriginal civilization also reached a goodly level in religion, philosophy and ethics, music and dancing. In architecture — at least in the Eastern United States — he never passed the rudimentary stage of development. Except for the Cherokees in the South with their printing press, newspaper and English-Cherokee dictionary, and perhaps the Nantucket Indians with their translation of the New Testament into their own language, the American Indian was continually handicapped by having no written language. What he had to speak or think was mostly handed down by word of mouth over a hundred generations and more.

Because he contributed to this earth the products known as tobacco, corn, potatoes, tomatoes, squash and a number of other foods, which the average American now takes for granted when wheeling a shopping cart around a super-market, it should appear that the Indian would popularly be given credit for some of his chief contributions to modern civilization.

When an old map of Nantucket Island is examined carefully, one cannot help knowing that "the Indians were there." There are more aboriginal names than English. In the southeast portion of the Island — 'round about where the Siasconset cliffs meet the edge of the sea — lay the territories of the Sachem or Chieftan Wanackmamack, a tongue-twister pronounced "Wan-ack'-ma-mack'." The northeast and central sections of the Island comprised lands of the Sachem Wauwinet. Next, in the area to the South of Nantucket Town and west of Surfside extended the domain of Chief Autopscot. Finally, the western part of the Island, including Tuckernuck Isle, was encompassed by the lands of Sachem Potcone.

Even though Indian names remain everywhere, traces of the Indian occupation, except for museum relics and underground remains, have just about vanished.

But the names indicate much. Siasconset, for instance, is probably derived from "Missi-askon-sett," meaning "Near the great whale bone." Miacomet, also "Mya-comet" or "Maa-yea-komuck," was an Indian village with a council chamber which stood at the head of the pond of the same name, and means "At the meetinghouse or meeting place." A circular burying ground is reputed to have existed there. And so it goes — each Indian word usually has a quaint or unusual meaning.

How fortunate that Nantucketers have preserved many of the picturesque names: Nauma, the sandy point now called Great Point; Coskata; Podpis, now Polpis; Shimmo; Pocomo — pronounced "Pah'-co-mo"; Quaise, "the reed land"; Quidnet, also Aquidnet; Nobadeer; Pochick, the bluff south of 'Sconset; Sankaty, from "Sankatank," rhyming with Virginia's "Piankatank"; Sesachacha, name of the widest pond on the Island.

Then there are Weeweeder, forming two pools near Miacomet; Wannacomet, "the pond field"; and Tuckernuck, formerly pronounced "Toockernook," and meaning a "loaf of bread" — for even the poor Indian had bread. One of the most interesting Indian localities was Nopque, the landing place on Smith's Point where canoes were hauled up after coming from Martha's Vineyard. This point once formed a long peninsula which extended all the way westward past Tuckernuck Island.

At the time of the white settlement of Nantucket in 1659 there were at least six Indian villages on the Island. Near the east end of Gibbs' Swamp in the direction of 'Sconset stood a hamlet called Occawa or Agawam. The other places have been located on the following map.

Furthermore, the Shawkemo Chapter of the Massachusetts Archaeological Society has excavated a site in the Ram's Pasture near Hummock Pond which appeared to have been a settled village.

The Indians liked best the ocean shore between 'Sconset and Wauwinet, and as may be seen, there were three villages between those points. Fishing must have been excellent, and vegetable gardens flourishing, in that area. Also another favorite place was "Siasconset Roots," the swampy lands to the south of 'Sconset where grew a kind of ground nut which was pulled out of the earth and eaten.

3 – Island of Praying Men

Before the time of the white settlement Christian missionaries had established (1642) religious meetings among the tribes on Nantucket under the leadership of Thomas Mayhew, Jr., and his Indian convert, Hiaccomes, preacher for Martha's Vineyard. That evangelical movement had begun in England where God had helped some upright Christians to advance a considerable sum of money for encouraging and propagating the Gospel in New England, including Nantucket and Martha's Vineyard. The aborigines on Nantucket spoke Nattick and according to accounts they comprised about 300 families. Those who had been converted to Christianity were spoken of as "praying Indians," and their conversion was much assisted by the translation of the New Testament into their language, as has been indicated. Of the Indians who became teachers, two went to Harvard College and afterward found hard luck. The first, Joel, son of Hiaccomes, was murdered by members of his own race when he came home in 1664 on vacation. The second, Caleb Chee-shah-tean-muck, graduated in 1665 from Harvard only to die of tuberculosis the following year.

One of the English missionaries was mentioned in Cotton Mather's *Magnalia*. He was Peter Foulger, or Folger, whose grandson was Benjamin Franklin, of Philadelphia. Peter, stated Mather, was employed on Nantucket to teach the Indian youth reading, writing and the principles of religion by catechisms. Mather further noted that Peter was well learned in the Scriptures and able to assist young people in what might be needful. At the times of religious worship on the Island the Indians showed, it was said, solid devotion. Their service was described as a mixture of the Presbyterians' and the Friends' or Quakers'. When church was over, they would get out their clay pipes and in rotation smoke the peace pipe and say "tawpoot," which meant thank you.

It has been told that Chief Wauwinet of Nantucket liked the English so well that by 1665 he had all his people take the pledge of allegiance to the King of England. The early relations of the English and aborigines were happy, as they were in Maryland and Pennsylvania at first.

4 – Of Indian Architecture

When the Indian villages, like Miacomet, were Christianized, the old and rounded council chambers must have given way slowly to simple and plain churches of English style of construction. Accounts of some of the missionaries

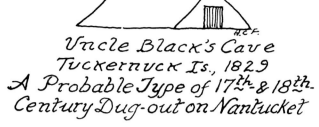

Uncle Black's Cave
Tuckernuck Is., 1829
A Probable Type of 17th- & 18th-
Century Dug-out on Nantucket

on the Island usually referred to Indian habitations as "mere wigwams," not really amounting to much, but to the community church as an "English house" — that is, one of British construction, usually timber-framed. Such a church was to be found in every sizeable Indian-praying village.

The Indians on the Island lived in wigwams, which were native houses, not fragile tents. In case anyone should doubt the former existence of wigwams on Nantucket, some maps show the following: the Wigwam Ponds just south of Altar Rock in Saul's Hills; Wigwam Pond three miles east of Surfside; and another of the same name near 'Sconset. The court records also mention wigwams. In 1704 Sabo, an Indian, was indicted for murdering his wife in their wigwam. Even though there were four Indians on the jury at that trial, Sabo was sentenced to be hanged by the neck.

To our knowledge no picture of an Indian wigwam on the Island has been found. The last three houses of that category are believed to have been extant at Squam as late as the year 1796, but there is no description of them. Excavations at Squam from 1938 to 1941 by the Massachusetts Archaeological Society revealed greasy deposits and miscellaneous post-holes which may have represented wigwam floors. The Nantucket wigwam probably conformed to the two general types of sapling structures prevalent in the Eastern United States: roughly circular "beehive" huts; and "arbor" houses, in general shape like the quonset hut. The round dwelling had a domed roof, and the "arbor" one was arched in the form of a tunnel vault with slightly battered walls. The English in this country called them "arbor" because they were reminded of their own Medieval and Elizabethan garden arbors in the Old Country.

There was also a third kind of wigwam — a conical construction, called a "tipi," built on frameworks of two sets of poles — an inside set of supports and an outer.

One of the features of the wigwam was its sidewall mats or skins which could be rolled up in the manner of the flaps of a circus tent in order to give more ventilation in warm weather. But the natives of Nantucket are reported not to have used skins, which were rare on the Island.

Throwing more light on their shelters is a contemporary account generally describing some fifty wigwams on the adjacent island, Martha's Vineyard. They were said to be of a temporary type and made of small poles like an arbor and covered with mats. In the middle of each hut was a fireplace with an outlet in the roof for smoke. As on Nantucket, skins were scarce enough not to be used for a wall covering.

It is interesting that the British themselves in the very early days had built in England a *prehistoric* type of hut, something like the Indian "arbor" house, called a "tan." It was built up by two parallel lines of saplings set firmly in the ground and tied together at the top to make arches, and the walls were covered with cloth, canvas, thatch, or any suitable material at hand. In more recent history "tans" often formed the home of gypsies.

Because of the bitter winds which lash Nantucket in winter, some of the Indian shelters were probably dugouts — crude abodes half inside the ground. One such dwelling, built probably by an Indian in imitation of English work, was sketched in 1829 by Eliza Gardner on a map of "Tookanook Island," preserved by the Nantucket Historical Association. She labeled the structure "Uncle Black's Cave." This one seems to have had a chimney and a door at one end (p. 10). Of course dugouts were familiar to the Indians long before the white men came to America. At the Ocmulgee Mounds near Macon, Georgia, for instance, the Indians built a council chamber or earth lodge half sunk in the ground. That the Nantucket aborigines had dugouts is a reasonable theory.

Certain of the more ingenious Indians on the Island sought to imitate English construction, generally the timber-framing method. In 1747, almost ninety years after 1659, an Indian Sachem by the name of Samuel Chegin left by will to one Chapman Swain "my English built dwelling house at Squam where my father lived."

Also, when Crèvecoeur[5] visited Nantucket in 1772, he noticed that the aborigines lived "together in decent [that is, "fair, English"] houses along the shores of Miacomet Pond." Of the people themselves he made note that they were an industrious and harmless race, as expert and as fond of a seafaring life as their fellow inhabitants, the whites.

Sometimes an Indian would help an Englishman build his house for him, or vice versa. Thomas Story, Quaker, related in his Journal that in 1704 a great company of Indians helped to raise for John Swain of Polpis on Nantucket a timber house — that is, timber-framed. Again, in 1698 Captain John Gardner procured from the Indians a timber-framed meetinghouse or church which they were building.

How large were some of the Nantucket wigwams is not known; but often, as in Virginia in the seventeenth century, the public buildings of the Indians had a larger floor area than that of the wealthy mansions of the English. In New England the more capacious Woodland lodges were constructed up to 200 feet in length and thirty in width.

5 – The First American Whalers

On Nantucket the English settlers adapted Indian trails to their own use as cart paths. The *old* road from Nantucket Harbor to Siasconset evidently followed approximately the footpath of the aborigines. Chester Street, believed to be the oldest English thoroughfare on the Island, ran from the heart of the first English town, Sherburne, located near Capaum Pond, to Nantucket Harbor and was derived from an Indian trailway.

Even though the Indians possessed no wheeled vehicles, they did have a lot of canoes, some of which must have been fairly sizeable to keep from upsetting in the ocean swells. In the early days it was a crime to secrete a canoe during the fishing season. Wo-so-ah, for instance, complained in 1681 that a colleague of his took and carried away his canoe at the fishing time — a real calamity. The brown-skinned natives were great fishermen; and the English on Nantucket, when they came to stay, were during the first 200 years fundamentally not much more than that.

In the first place the Indians were offshore whalers long before 1659, when the first party of white settlers came. Consequently it is difficult to believe, as one authority has it, that Indian whaling did not commence until 1673. Much the reverse was true: the English learned a lot about whaling from the Indians, even though there had been some Britishers who had earlier practiced that art off the coasts of Great Britain.[6]

In fact as early as 1605 Weymouth in his "Journal of a Voyage to America" told in detail how the American Indian caught whales by first getting fast to the mammal by means of a bone harpoon attached to a bark rope, and then killing it by arrows. And the harpoons were nothing but stone-headed spears.

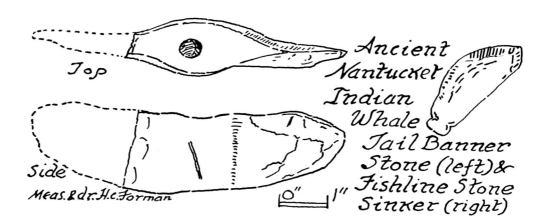

Top

Side

Meas. & dr. H. C. Forman

Ancient Nantucket Indian Whale Tail Banner Stone (left) & Fishline Stone Sinker (right)

0"   1"

According to immemorial custom all dead whales cast on Nantucket beaches belonged to the Indians — thus declared the English Court on the Island. In 1676 the Court ordered that no "Rack [wrecked] whale" which came ashore on the Island in the territory of any Chief should be cut up until the masters of the shares which belonged to that whale were present. About the same time Jeptha, an aborigine, complained to the Court that Nickanoose and Wauwinet hindered him from getting his share of the whale at Coatue which he formerly enjoyed. In 1692 a whalebone was stolen by two Indians on the Island, and a third took away a parcel of blubber and was reported to have sold the oil from it.

As far back as 1642 Thomas Mayhew, Jr., and his companions had observed the Indian doing his off-Nantucket-shore whaling in fragile canoes. The Indian-Americans were the first whalers in America, and had an appreciation of the value of blubber and oil.

On Nantucket the best "yum-yum" seafood came from the shoals off the South Shore, the sand-bars of which formed bulwarks to protect the Island from tremendously large deep-sea waves. There the natives caught bluefish, cod and other varieties of fish. On the beaches they gathered clams— soft-shelled, hard-shelled and great sea clams — which were as much free food as they could carry home.

On the shores of the Island the Indians erected fishing stages, which were, as far as we know, small wigwam shelters and elevated platforms or lookouts from which to spot whales. The aborigines on the mainland had been familiar with raised platforms in cornfields and vegetable patches for generations and generations, so that it is logical to believe that the Nantucketers had their eyries for whaling. Later, the English must have done little more than elaborate upon the Indian fishing stages.

One of the interesting cooperative ventures between the Indians and English occurred in 1665 when the Court agreed to have a trench dug to drain the Long Pond. In regard to a weir for catching fish and also for making a meadow, half the work was to be done by the Indians and the remainder by the English inhabitants or owners. As long as an Indian attended carefully and honestly to the weir, he was to have half the catch — so proclaimed the Court.

6 – An Industrious Race

The aborigines made the usual clay pots and bowls; woven mats of fine design; ropes; beaded belts; and tools — like bevel-edged stone knives; stone scrapers, drills, adze blades, awls, axes and hoe blades. They manufactured stone weapons,

Offshore whaling and retrieving dead whales flung up on Nantucket beaches had been the custom of Indians and whites for hundreds of years. Two views of the 1880s.

such as tapered-stem arrow points and spear points. Their native mills comprised mortars and pestles (p. 7) for grinding corn. They had seine sinkers (p. 12), sharpening stones and flint strike-a-lights.[7]

One sharpening stone used for giving keen edges to chisels (p. 17) is of particular interest because it has the incised name of a Christian Indian, together with the date, as follows: "P Johm 1731." Another curious object is a ceremonial stone known as a whale's tail, which was carried in processions when a whale came ashore.

Some of these useful objects were mentioned in the Court records, such as the cook pot which Sese-panu in 1682 claimed that a squaw Cuddu-sue had taken from him and not returned. Sometimes the Court defended the rights of the Indians, as when it ordered that they should have freedom to gather flags and other beach grass to make straw mats on Nantucket.

7 – Black Monday

When Thomas Mayhew, Sr., of Martha's Vineyard sold in 1659 the Island of Nantucket to the original ten purchasers, thereby paving the way for the English settlement of the Island, it was a fine day for the whites, but a Black Monday for the Indians. That purchase was the signal of their doom, although fortunately at that time they did not know it. Thomas Macy in the autumn of 1659 embarked with his family and three other persons from Salisbury, Massachusetts, in a sailboat for Nantucket. They wintered at Madaket at the west end of the Island. It has been told that the Indians kindly received them, and helped set up winter quarters, but in the long run the aborigines found that as far as their own civilization was concerned, they had taken in an asp. For them it was the beginning of the end.

The English, even though they had been granted the Island in which to live, had to buy it over again in stages from the Indians who were the real owners. At first the whole plain from Madaket to Hummock Pond was sold to the whites, and then in 1671 a new Indian deed was given for the land west of Nantucket Harbor, including the area of later Wesco and Nantucket Town (see map p. 22). There were also smaller tracts sold by the Indians to individual Englishmen, as the one purchased in 1680 by John Swain at Polpis. In 1701 Indian chieftain Henry Britten sold to the "Inhabitants" a tract bounded by the Atlantic Ocean, Miacomet Pond, the Town fence and gate on the north, and the existing boundaries of the English on the west and northwest. In like manner all Indian lands passed to the whites. But the Indian deed sometimes reserved rights to half of the drift-whales found on the sandy beaches.

This is the wedge-shaped square along Front Street, 'Sconset, where the lookout mast may have stood. BELOW: Stone for sharpening chisels, property in 1731 of the Christian Indian, P Johm Nu Poo, of Nantucket. *Photo, author.*

The Court records, like any court records, are filled with offenses committed; few good things which the Indians performed are written there. These are some of the bad things, almost all of which happened in the seventeenth century. No-watten complained against Birdkeeper for being drunk and hurting an old woman. Tatak-amuck was convicted of stealing beef out of the Town storehouse.

But theft was not the least of these crimes. One Indian lass complained against John, the "fisherman's son," for non-performance of his covenant with her. The Court showed that the maid had been promised marriage by him and that he had told the Court that he had wedded her. But such was not the case, it seemed. Whereupon the Court ordered that if he did not marry the girl to whom he was promised, he should be whipped twenty stripes and pay the girl thirty shillings. One wonders where an Indian would get hold of the goodly sum of thirty shillings.

Another Indian girl by the name of Patience had worse luck, for she accused with some justification another of her race, Gentleman Son, of getting her with child, with the result that she was ordered to be whipped fifteen stripes and to pay Court costs after the baby came, and he had to be whipped or pay a twenty-shilling fine. Adultery, too, was severely punished, the partners being whipped with great lashes on their bare backs.

One of the most unjust law cases was that of an Indian woman who complained to the Court that she had been whipped for gathering gooseberries. The natives did not seem to understand the English practice of the rights of private property.

Next, came a fateful sign: instances of selling liquor to the Indians, whose bodies could not stand alcohol any more than German measles, smallpox or influenza. In 1694 a white man was convicted of selling rum to Indians. Even to sell cider to an aborigine was against Nantucket law — which nonetheless was broken.

The 300 families believed to have been living on Nantucket when the first white settlers came began to dwindle. Slowly but surely the little native villages, the tiny fishing stages, the small outlying farms and the encampments declined. Fewer Indians went fishing or hoed their cornfields. Those whom Crèvecoeur had called members of an industrious and harmless race found fewer nut-brown maidens to marry, so that for a century and a half decimation was the order of the day. At the end of the first hundred years of English settlement the Indian population had dropped to 358 persons. Then, in 1763, a plague swept away 222 more of them. It was a strange fever which the English who nursed them never caught.

The last chieftain was Benjamin Tashma, who died in 1770 — only six years before the outbreak of the American Revoluntary War. He was a Christian Indian, grandson of the Sachem Autopscot; but even better than that — he was a very nice man in the era in which he lived. Preacher for the meetinghouse northwest of

Siasconset at Accawa, already mentioned, he lived in a dwelling long known as "Tashmy's House," located at the foot of Bean Hill between the fifth and sixth milestones on the 'Sconset Road. Every summer these recent years thousands of bicyclists coast down that same Bean Hill without knowing of the Indian chief's house which once stood there. Before the front door of his home was a stone weighing some 1800 pounds, which in 1917 was placed in front of the Fair Street Museum of the Nantucket Historical Association. His daughter, Dorcas Honorable, was thought to be the last full-blooded Indian to live on Nantucket, and she died in 1822. The missionary efforts of Thomas Mayhew, Sr., and his son of the same name, and of Peter Folger, bore bitter fruit. The physical antipathy of the English and the Americans to the aborigines helped to cause their annihilation. The last native passed away, leaving the Island wholly to the whites, a few Negroes and mulattoes.

In the Island records are ancient words and sentences of which the meaning has long been forgotten. That sentence about Sachem Nickanoose is typical: "Noon Nekanoosee wana noon nanomet nononk nuttun nunnummowannan yacob noshamum akke." But the sound of such words is no worse than those still in use today like "nonantum, nauma, wanackmamack, myacomuck, nauticon, wauwinet, nobadeer."

Nantucket Town was built largely as a Georgian settlement. Some Georgian homes, two stories high front and rear, with off-center front door and walk on roof, are seen in this old view of Vestal Street. BELOW: A four-wheeled Nantucket box-wagon with springs.

III

The Proprietors' Early Town

1 – Seaside Generations

AT FIRST a part of the Colony of Maine, then of New York, and finally of Massachusetts, the great Nantucket "sandbank," lying about thirty miles seaward, was settled in 1659, as has been told, by a party of English from the mainland. By establishing such a colony on the Island the ten original proprietors, such as Thomas Macy, Tristram Coffin and Thomas Barnard, together with their ten partners, including Edward Starbuck and Thomas Coleman, turning their backs on oppressive Puritan restrictions in their home towns, determined once and for all that generations of Island children would be born by the "Sea-side" and would hear the roaring of its waves as soon as they were able to listen. It is the first noise with which they become acquainted, as Crèvecoeur related, and by plunging into the ocean at an early age they acquire that boldness, that presence of mind and dexterity, which make them ever afterward such expert seamen.

Always at Nantucket the sound of the great waves upon the wide, sandy beaches is carried through the silent fog to the inner recesses of the moorland — up over the ponds and bogs to the little glaciated valleys between the hills and among the hummocks. From almost every spot on the Island there is a view of water — ocean, sound, harbor or pond. Until the Victorian era the sea largely shaped the life of, and supported, Nantucket people. It forms a nautical island, and all the children figuratively have salt in their blood from generations of mariners. Every-

21

where, in Town or on moorland, is the influence of the briny deep. In fact the Island male could be recognized at a distance by his peculiar gait, said to be the result of whale oil in his joints.

Thus it was that Thomas Macy's sailing vessel, loaded with his wife and children, his household belongings and his friends, Edward Starbuck, Isaac Coleman and James Coffin, landed at Madaket. They built temporary shelters, like dugouts, puncheon sheds — that is, those having vertical planks for walls stuck in the ground — and wigwams. In the spring of 1660 Starbuck and Macy each took up a hoe and went to look for better homesites. Starbuck chose the locale at the north end of Hummock Pond; the other went further, to a place called Wannacomet, beside the Reed Pond, just east of Capaum Harbor on the sound.[1]

2 – The Building of Sherburne

Little by little from 1660 onward the first English settlement developed by extending southwestward in a crescent from Reed Pond, past Wyer's or Maxcy's Pond, to the western arm of the U-shaped Hummock Pond. Later the north arm of this crescent was extended to Wesco — meaning The White Stone — on Nantucket Harbor, as the map on p. 22 indicates.

In the literal sense that colony was no town. It possessed as far as we know today no streets of settled, row houses and shops, no market square, no alleyways, parks and sidewalks. Instead, it was only a spread-out country village, arranged in helter-skelter fashion, where the average dwelling lot comprised about twenty acres, and the roads were nothing but sand ruts and paths through the grassy hummocks and woods. At the end of thirteen years this rural neighborhood was named (1673) Sherborne or Sherburne, called the first town on the Island. With due grains of allowance today's settlement on Tuckernuck Island resembles in several respects the layout of Sherburne.

In the half-moon belt of house lots extending from Wesco, past Capaum, to Hummock were erected the homes of the settlers. Presumably all the structures were wood and most of them timber-framed, that is, put up with studs, sills and posts. There the pioneers hewed the trees from the Island forests or brought their timbers with them from the mainland to assemble in pre-fabricated style — each structural piece marked with a Roman numeral for facility in fitting it with another. There the colonists carried their furniture up from the sailing boats and led their little sons and daughters by the hand to their chosen hummock and clearing. There stood the finished medieval cottages and outhouses, of which no picture has yet been found. There were plowed the first fields, enclosed mostly by neat, straight cedar posts and rails. There arose the first gardens, surrounded by fences of palings or wattles or other materials.

On the map the habitations have been approximately located by this writer. Besides those belonging to Starbuck and Macy already noted, there were the homes of Tristram Coffin on the southwest side of Capaum Harbor, now a pond, where a stone marker stands today. Coffin and his wife Dionis had previously served as tavernkeepers in Newbury, Massachusetts. On Nantucket he possessed (1676) upon his house lot an old dwelling "down the hill" and a new one "up the hill." At one time he was chief Island magistrate. Other households were John Coleman's, located west of the existing *Elihu Coleman House* (1722), which is marked by a star on our map; Peter Folger's, the site of which is identified approximately today by the memorial fountain and seat in honor of Peter's daughter, Abiah Folger, the mother of Benjamin Franklin; and Robert Barnard's, near Upper Cambridge at the Head of Hummock.

Then, to get a little more complete picture of the settlement, there was a string of homesteads and properties to the west of Wyer's Pond, which included those of Thomas Mayhew, Sr., the gentleman who made the sale of the Island with certain reservations; Captain Christopher Hussey, a man who was reported to have had no house on Nantucket and to have been eaten by cannibals in Florida; and John and Richard Swain.

3 – The East End of Town

Toward Nantucket Harbor there also arose dwellings. There were the *Jethro Coffin House* (p. 230), built in 1686 or soon after, still extant on Sunset Hill, and Bunker's domicile beside No Bottom Pond. William Gayer's abode on Centre Street, described in 1683 as being located near the *"Verandah House,"* was another early home. Mr. Gayer, it may be noted, married the daughter of Edward Starbuck and is reported to have been one of the few settlers in Massachusetts who was entitled to bear a coat of arms.

The most noted of the public buildings in Sherburne was known as *"Parliament House,"* Nathaniel and Mary Starbuck's home, commodious for those days. In 1665 it was still standing on Lower Cambridge, lying just northwest of Head of Hummock. Mary Starbuck was the daughter of the senior Tristram Coffin and was founder of the Friends' Meeting on the Island. The large assembly room in *Parliament House* was described in 1701 by John Richardson, a Quaker visitor to Nantucket, as "the bright rubbed room . . . set with suitable seats or chairs." When

Friends' Meeting was held there, he noted that "the glass windows were taken out of the frames," so that persons outside could hear, and that "many chairs were placed without very conveniently."

The first Quaker meetinghouse on the Island was in existence as early as 1711 in the Friends' burial ground to the southeast of Wyer's Pond. Some think that this structure, marked on our map, was the first house of worship on Nantucket, even though before that year the Indians had had religious meeting places for centuries.

On a hummock north of No Bottom Pond were built a Town house, school-house and jail (c. 1676), which was kept by William Bunker. It was that prison which figured in the story of Peter Folger's incarceration there. Peter, it appears, in default of twenty pounds' bail, was placed in the jail for hiding or destroying a Court record book. Behind barred windows he wrote at the time that the prison-house was a place where no Englishman had ever been jailed before and where the neighbor's dog had lain the previous night in bitter-cold frost and deep snow. The jailor told Folger that he might sleep upon wood boards, but then relented enough to bring him a little straw.

On the whole, throughout its long history the Island had infrequent use for its prison, of which much fun was made. A typical story is that of the jailor who once was asked how he made sure at night that all his prisoners were locked in, and who replied that all that he had to do was to shout through the heavy door, "Boys, are you there?" — to which question there always came a muffled response, "Yes, we're here."

In Sherburne there were a large number of warehouses, such as Tristram Coffin's one at Wesco, shown on the map, and of outhouses, like barns, stables, fish sheds, boat houses, necessaries, sheep pens, tents, booths and shops. Surrounding these structures of one kind or another were the usual fences, gates, yards, enclosures and pounds. In 1669, for instance, a pound four rods square was ordered built for stray animals near Capaum Harbor, and in 1672 all house lots between that place and Richard Swain's were specified to have fences around them.

In this settlement there was last, but not least, the first grist mill, run by water, built in 1666 at Lily Pond, Wesco. There followed a tidal mill (1673), equipped three years later as a fulling mill for the purpose of fulling, pressing, shearing and dying cloth.

The rutted roads in Sherburne (p. 22), which grew up like Topsy, owing more to use than design and planning, in the medieval way, were given street names. First there was Chester Street — now Westchester — which was mentioned as early as 1671, running from Capaum and Wannacomet to Nantucket Harbor. It seemed that there was a ditch along a portion of that highway which drained the Lily

Pond, but that the water moved so slowly in the little canal that the grist mill (1666) upon it was bound to fail. Then there were Duke Street and Crooked Lane, both of which had many early homes fronting upon them. Duke passed between the existing *Elihu Coleman House* and the Thorn lot, of hawthorn fame. Main Street — the Madaket Road — was probably an open way before 1700, and was not called "Main" until years later. It ran from the Harbor out past the *Parliament House* on the Cambridge Farm.

4 – The Problem of Wood Supply

In some minds there has been a question whether or not the Island had sufficient wood on it for all the needed construction work. Whereas the Island today is one of moorlands with relatively little timber, such as a hidden copse in the pockets of the hills or deciduous trees planted in the settlements, in the seventeenth century Nantucket abounded in trees. For as early as 1663 the Island trees came into mention: the townspeople were not to cut timber on the neck of land known as Coatue "except for building houses." Then, in 1668 the Nantucket Court ordered that no more green wood should be felled in the Long Woods near Hummock Pond except what was taken for rails and fences. A deed of 1678 mentioned the "timber wood" on the Island. And about the same time Stephen Hussey was sued for trespass because he had cut down and carried away certain timber from a neck of land called Maskotuck.

Further, in 1701 the Quaker, John Richardson, visiting the *Parliament House,* as has been mentioned, could not sleep at night and therefore walked to and fro in the "woods" until meeting time in the morning. It is interesting, too, that the newly-planned Friends' meetinghouse in 1709 was located eastward of Nathaniel Starbuck, Jr.'s land, "whereon ye timber now lieth."

At the same time the Islanders imported wood from the beginning of their settlement. We find that in 1670 pine boards were brought from "the continent" by Nathaniel Barnard. Gradually through the eighteenth century the great forests were depleted, and the Island became largely denuded as we know it today. For instance, John Woolman, noted Friend, in 1760 reported "The timber so gone, that for vessels, fences, and firewood they depend chiefly on the buying from the Main [land]." In recent years the discovery of large ancient oak-tree stumps in a peat bog at Quidnet on the Island proves the former existence of trees.

5 – The Move to Wesco

Around 1700 a change came over the town of Sherburne. For one thing, Capaum Harbor had become blocked and formed a pond. Besides, the Wesco Lots on Nantucket Harbor had been laid out in 1678, and the Harbor itself was a better landing place than ever Capaum had been. So it was that the inhabitants began moving their homes to Wesco or building new ones there. Soon after 1720 the transmigration was in full movement. Then the name of the town, Sherburne, was superceded by the term, Nantucket, in 1795, by which it is known today.

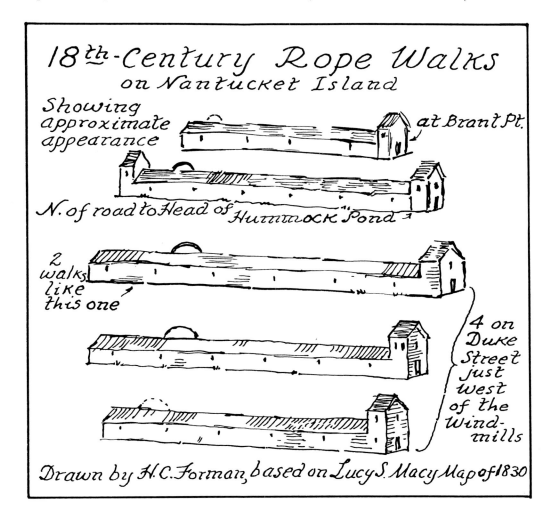

18ᵗʰ-Century Rope Walks on Nantucket Island. Showing approximate appearance. at Brant Pt. N. of road to Head of Hummock Pond. 2 walks like this one. 4 on Duke Street just west of the Wind-mills. Drawn by H.C. Forman, based on Lucy S. Macy Map of 1830

Now 1720 and soon after are the years when English Georgian architecture began to flourish on the mainland and on Nantucket; consequently the Wesco portion of Sherburne became largely a Georgian town (p. 20). The architectural characteristics of buildings in that style are large scale, high ceilings, wide sash, ornamental and classical doorways, cornices, mantels and stairs. Of course it is well to remember that interspersed with those Georgian edifices were buildings of the older style, the Medieval, a fashion of building already mentioned in the first chapter.

A section of Sherburne was devoted to Negroes and mulattoes. The Friends were the first persons on Nantucket to free their slaves — for even Nantucketers kept slaves; and when Crèvecoeur visited the Island in 1772, he found not one slave there, but at the same time noted that slavery prevailed all over the mainland. At a place called "New Guiney," located south and east of the Nantucket windmills, where Pleasant Street today crosses York, lived the blacks and the mixtures. It is interesting that in the eighteenth century the Town gave land in "New Guinea, where the Black People live near New Town" to Negro Thomas Gardner, mulatto Daniel Gardner and Indian James Dyer. Not far from that area of Sherburne once stood the New Town Gate, which formed a barrier across the highway to Siasconset at the first milestone, in order to keep out sheep and other animals. Immediately adjacent to that gateway is believed to have been the Gallows Field, whereon stood a gallows as late as the year 1840.

Having made some acquaintance of the Proprietors' early town, we proceed to the other settlements on the Island, the fishing villages.

IV

Rise of the Whaling Stations

1 – Off-Shore Hunts

COINCIDING WITH THE BUILDING of Sherburne in the seventeenth century, there arose a group of men on Nantucket Island whose work was the chasing and despatching of live whales off the shore. They created whaling stations, which were fishing stages, along the ocean beaches; and it is with these same outposts that this work is chiefly concerned.

Nantucket was not the first English settlement to initiate offshore whaling. Cape Codders are believed to have been the first in America to try for whale fishing, although in a desultory manner. It remained for the settlers on Long Island, New York, in the 1640s to be the first to make whaling a business.

There were two kinds of whale which men went after in those days: the blackfish, which is a small cetecea averaging twenty-five feet in length; and the right whale, a *Mysticeta,* having a large head with long and narrow whalebone plates in its mouth and yielding the most oil of any species. Both these varieties of whale had their feeding grounds inshore, and the best time of year to kill the beast was between November and April.

As we have already seen, the American Indian went after whales in their flimsy canoes and with primitive weapons. The English colonists and their descendants used whaleboats, which were at first intended to be rowed, but which later possessed sprits — sails stretched by small spars — and centerboards (p. 30). The usual whaleboat was about twenty-eight feet long and six feet wide, and had sharply pointed prow and stern.

29

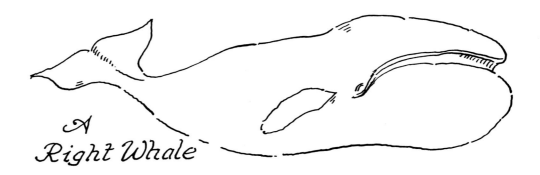

A Right Whale

Five men rowed the whaleboat, the sixth standing up to steer with an oar about twenty-two feet long. The five seats for rowers were named as follows, commencing at the prow: the harpoon, the bow, the amidship, the tub and the afterthwarts. When attempting to kill a whale, the harpooner stood upright in the bow with a thigh fitted into a large notch of a plank to keep himself steady. The small foredeck, known as a warp box, was sunk about eight inches below the gunwhales in order to make a place to take in slack line attached to the harpoon. At the stern was the cuddy or small pantry for provisions, as well as the loggerhead, a post around which the line was turned in order to slow down the speed of the harpooned whale.

When whales became scarcer during the seventeenth century, small sloops (p. 240), either towing or convoying one or two whaleboats, were pressed into service, so that the hunters could sail further afield for their prey. In that way a couple of whales could be taken within a couple of weeks or even a month, and the blubber could be stowed in casks and brought back home to be tried out on shore. At suitable spots along the coast the blubber was boiled in large iron kettles in brick furnaces known as tryworks.

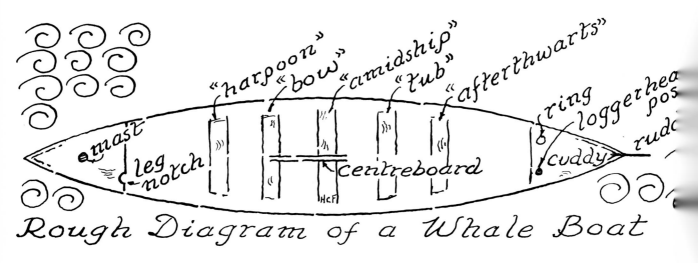

Rough Diagram of a Whale Boat

On Long Island in the 1640s and 50s the fishing stages were for the purpose of spotting drift-whales from shore. According to accounts they comprised *lookouts* — tall spars climbed by means of wooden pegs fitted into them and with elevated seats for scanning the ocean; and thatched-roof *shelters,* open to seaward, through which the wintry wind whistled at will. This trade must have developed into a flourishing business because whole whaling companies were organized, and whales were allotted by law.

2 – First Nantucket Whale Houses

At first not one of the Nantucket settlers was reported to be a whaler, but they soon learned the business. One Ichabod Paddock organized those fishermen who thirsted after whales by roughly dividing the south and east shores of the Island into four districts, each said to be about three and a half miles long, and by putting six men — a whale boats' crew — into every beat.[1] Although physically separated in groups, all stations carried on their whaling business in common. The first four whaling stations appear to have dated from the 1660s-70s and are shown on the map on the title page of this work. They were located near Hummock Pond at a place now called Cisco; between Miacomet Pond and the Weweeder Ponds; at Siasconset Bank (c. 1676); and at Sesachacha Beach (c. 1670). Inasmuch as there was a wider space between the second and third station, the districts were by no means equal in length.

At the center of each location a whaling hut was constructed for the shelter of the crew during stormy weather. Beside it a tall spar was erected, from the top of which a lookout could scan the ocean for the spouting of the whales in a wide range of vision during the daytime and on moonlight nights. A man could climb the tall mast by means of wooden pegs or pins stuck into its surface, or by ladder rungs as on shipboard. Also around the hut stood fish racks and other paraphernalia.

As time passed, the existing four whaling stations were enlarged, and new ones established on the sand dunes. At Hummock Pond the stage grew into a great number of whale houses, and the second station, Miacomet, showed a whole "parcel" of them. Also the number of tall masts for lookouts increased.

A fifth whaling station stood at Pedee, a tiny village just south of Sesachacha Beach; a sixth at Quidnet (c. 1700); and a seventh at Coskata, located at the base of Nauma, or Great Point. These three were situated on the east coast where the fishing was "allowed" to be better.

There must have been also a number of small, private fishing stages. There is record, for example, of stages at Sesachacha belonging in 1682 to John Swain of

Polpis and Richard Gardner of Sherburne. The latter's stage covered an acre of ground. William Worth later owned a "Fishing house" at Aquidnet Point on the Ocean.

To help to visualize what an early whaling station looked like in the 1670s, we have made a conjectural diagram showing the tall mast, taken from an eighteenth-century sketch of the village of Siasconset (p. 33); the fish racks, of which there are still photographs extant at Nantucket; and a section through a whale hut showing where the boat's crew slept — an arrangement obtaining in several existing whale houses on the Island.

Of the seven known whaling stations, only two appear to have left traces of their original appearance: 'Sachacha and 'Sconset, as they were known for short. Some stations probably grew out of Indian encampments, like Sesachacha Beach; but Siasconset and Quidnet (p. 263) seem to have commenced their careers as English fishing stages independent of Indian settlements.

By 1760 the industry of offshore whaling seems to have been abandoned, because even as early as 1712 it had been discovered that sperm whaling far away from Nantucket Island, even beyond Hatteras, was more profitable. In short, the whaling stations folded up or were used for small fisheries.

3 – Largest Fishing Stage on the Island

The station known as Sesachacha Beach stood on the Atlantic Shore just a little southward of the 'Sachacha Pond sand-bar at a spot known locally as Quannata Beach. For a time Sesachacha was said to be the largest fishing stage on Nantucket, and was also the first white settlement of any size outside Sherburne. Since it had become by 1676 a hamlet of thirty cottages — whale huts — covering six acres of ground, its founding probably was about 1670. It continued in existence for two and a half centuries. In the height of its prosperity, so it has been told, it had more buildings than early Siasconset. From Sesachacha a rutted road led off across the moorland to Sherburne (map, p. 38). Nevertheless, by 1820 most of the dwellings in the village had been moved one way or another to Siasconset. Photographs of the 1880s and 90s show sparse remnants of the depleted hamlet of Sesachacha. By 1888 only three or four of the ancient homesteads still remained.

The transmigration from 'Sachacha to 'Sconset has been graphically described by Mr. Edward F. Underhill[2] — in this work called "Underhill" — in the following words: "For some reason there was a drift of life to the southward. Whether the fishing off 'Sconset was better, or the beach, even in those days, wider, or the site more desirable — whatever the cause — most of the fishermen who had grouped their homes around the old 'Sachacha well, took their houses down and put sides and roofs and floors aboard Nantucket box carts, put helms astarboard, steered around Sankaty Head and set them up complete, or added them to others already built on this more favored spot." Underhill then relapsed into this sentimental couplet which perhaps has some historical truth in it:

> "What was 'Sachacha's grievous loss,
> Was 'Sconset's joyful gain."

18th-Century Schematic View of Siasconset

4 – The Whaling Village of Siasconset

For our purposes the chief value of 'Sconset is that it forms the only example on Nantucket Island of a surviving settlement of the period of the founding fathers — that is, the seventeenth century. And early Sherburne and Sesachacha have gone.[3]

With the founding of 'Sconset about 1676 — one hundred years before the American Revolution — we have, too, our foremost exemplar of what early Nantucket Island was like before the prosperous sperm-whaling era of the 1830s and 40s. Also 'Sconset can give a pretty good picture of the hamlet of Sesachacha, since at least half the early cottages came from Sesachacha.

Like the Indians, the English found fine fishing off Siasconset Bank, as the place was first called, especially opposite the Pochick Rip, where cod, blackfish or tew-tag, sea bass, smelt, perch, shadine and pike were caught. There is a tradition which persists that early 'Sconseters regarded the ocean as a large stew-pond.

Perched on a bluff directly above the sea, the village lay within a great fenced field known as Siasconset Lot. To the northwest was another large enclosed area known as Plainfield.[4] How large a settlement there was at 'Sconset within its first three decades can only be guessed. At first it may have been only one whale hut and a mast for a lookout — soon to be increased to a dozen cottages. At least it appears that the older portions of the domiciles named *Auld Lang Syne* (c. 1675), *Rose Cottage* (c. 1675), and *Shanunga* (c. 1682)[5] — and perhaps *Nauticon Lodge* as well — were in place by the year in which William Penn laid out the great city of Philadelphia.

Now those four whale houses were erected on the west side of a thoroughfare in 'Sconset later called Broadway — a street which was in those days the third one over from the edge of the Bank or Bluff. Some idea of the layout of early 'Sconset may be obtained from the map of the village on page 39. Undoubtedly there must have been other cottages of the same vintage as *Auld Lang Syne* on Front Street, which *then* was not "front" at all, and on the Highway along the edge of the Bank near the spot known as Middle Gulsh or Gulley. At any rate *that small cluster of whale houses, the early fishing stage, formed the nucleus of the colonial village.* The tall mast probably stood in the wedge-shaped "square" or open space along the Bank edge, clearly seen on the map.

Thus in the very early days of 'Sconset there were only three "highways" — if you could dignify as such the spaces where there were no dwellings but only meandering ruts. As time progressed, one of those thoroughfares began to diminish: the highway along Bank edge. Great ocean waves of storms, notably in the late eighteenth century, in October of 1835 and of 1841, undermined the Bank, except for a small piece of road at the North Gulsh or Gully opposite *Nauma, Nickanoose* and the *Robinson House*. The net result of the collapse of the highway into the sea was that the next road inland became Front Street. Broadway, the third thoroughfare, was named about two centuries after the establishment of 'Sconset, whether for the chief street in old New York or for the famous village in the Cotswolds in England is not known.

Ever since the 17th century, this was the way the retired whaling captains lived along the Nantucket coast. These old views show Cap'n Fred Parker, the "hermit of Quidnet," taking it easy. Note slatted fishrack and driftwood salvage.

The atmosphere of the early Siasconset fishing stage is well shown by these old views: 'Sconset Bank looking north to Middle Gulley. At left is probably *Headache House*. BELOW: Looking down Middle Gulley, the original main entrance-way to the village.

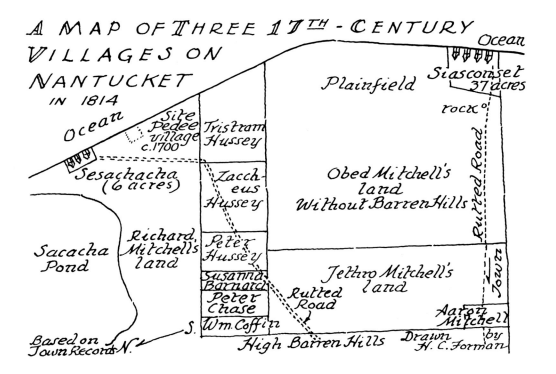

A MAP OF THREE 17TH-CENTURY VILLAGES ON NANTUCKET IN 1814

All the whale houses faced the Atlantic. It is not true that the inhabitants built one lane of buildings as a "weather row," with their backs upon the sea, as one authority has it. But it is correct that the gable-ends were placed together so close that housewives could easily converse with each other out the gable-end windows.

5 – Visiting an Early Fishing Family

About a century after the beginning of Siasconset Crèvecoeur told something of its primitive life. His forceful and colorful words may scarcely be improved:

"I . . . arrived at last at Siàsconscèt. Several dwellings had been erected on this wild shore, for the purpose of sheltering the fishermen in the season of fishing; I found them all empty, except that particular one to which I had been directed. It was like the others, built on the highest part of the shore, in the face of the great ocean, the soil appeared to be composed of no other stratum but sand, covered with a thinly scattered herbage."

Which cottage did he visit? In those days the dwellings had no name signs, except perhaps those used as taverns, so that there was no occasion for him to identify the place. Next he brought out a fact of much interest and then lapsed into romanticism as follows:

"What rendered this house still more worthy of notice in my eyes, was, that it had been built on the ruins of one of the ancient huts, erected by the first settlers, for observing the appearance of the whales. Here lived a single family without a neighbor; I had never before seen a spot better calculated to cherish contemplative ideas; perfectly unconnected with the great world, and far removed from its perturbations. The ever raging ocean was all that presented itself to the view of this family; it irresistibly attracted my whole attention: my eyes were involuntarily

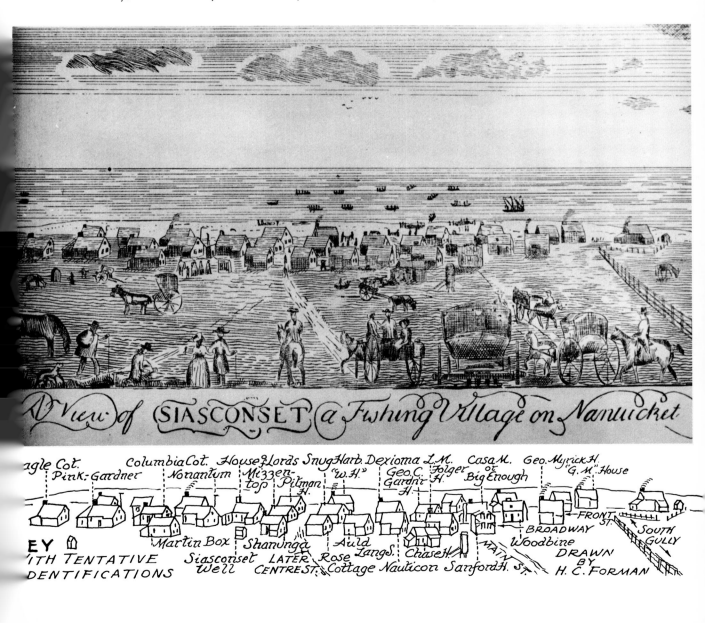

directed to the horizontal line of that watery surface, which is ever in motion, and ever threatening destruction to these shores. My ears were stunned with the roar of its waves rolling one over the other, as if impelled by a superior force to overwhelm the spot on which I stood."

Crèvecoeur was probably wrong when he declared that the house he visited had been constructed on the ruins of one of the ancient huts. Because they had no foundation other than stone boulders, 'Sconset buildings were not erected on the ruins of others. What he meant perhaps was that the abode had been *extended* from the original fisherman's whale house.

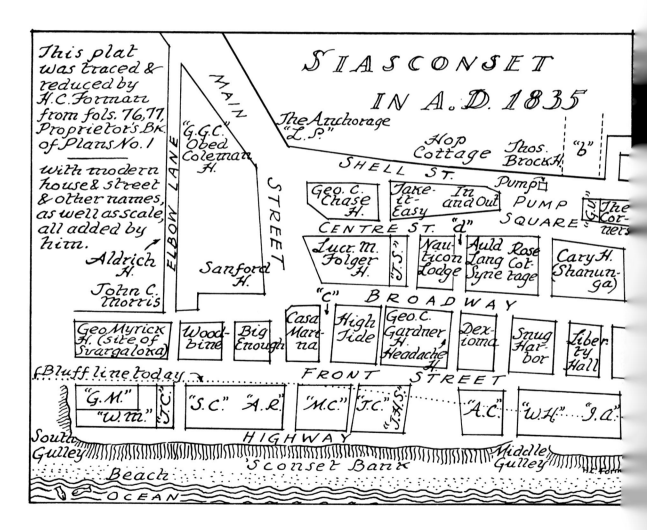

6 – Eighteenth-Century 'Sconset

In 1758, some eighty-two years after the establishment of 'Sconset, the Town of Sherburne voted an impossible gridiron type of plan for the village. It ordered that "Siasconset Bank" be laid out into twenty-seven shares, beginning at the South Gulsh, or Gulley, to the southward of the "South Well" and extending northward along the bluff. Each lot was to be three rods, or forty-nine and a half feet, by

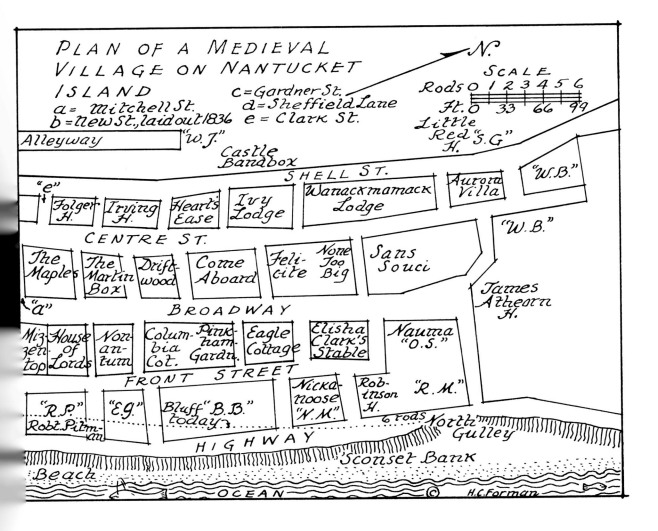

eighteen rods, or 297 feet, in size. But anyone at that time could have told you that lots of that area were too large to fit around the existing whale houses, which were packed closely together. It is not surprising that the Proprietors' order was almost at once countermanded. The record does leave us with knowledge of the existence of the South Well, which obviously stood somewhere north of the South Gulley.[6]

No one knows exactly when the other two thoroughfares in the village were added — that is, Centre and Shell streets. The time was probably about 1790 or 1800. Except for Elbow Lane, the cross streets — if they should be called "streets" at all, as they ranged on an average less than thirty feet long — were merely spaces between the cottages where the grass grew. Some cross lanes were short and squat, others long and narrow — say, three feet wide and sixteen in length. Underhill correctly called Siasconset a village unique in the arrangement of its streets and lanes and byways.

In the first year of the Revolutionary War the villagers were too far removed from the great world, as Crèvecoeur put it, to pay much attention to what was happening in the "continent." As Underhill wrote somewhat facetiously, the representatives of the rebellious colonies assembled in 1776 in Philadelphia were able only to declare their independence of King George III, while the 'Sconseters on Nantucket in substantial form achieved their independence of hogsheads placed under their gutters to catch the roof rainfall and passed around the hat for a new source of water supply, the "Siasconset Well."

This well was the ancestor of the existing Town Pump, which today stands in Pump Square more for looks than anything else (p. 199). Perhaps by 1776 the South Well had dried up and new water was needed. However that may be, the list of donors of the "Revolutionary" well is preserved on a paper of 1776 at the Fair Street Museum of the Nantucket Historical Association, and gives the names of 160 subscribers with the amount of English money donated by each.[7] The first three names are representative, as follows:

	£.	S.	d.
Sylvanus Folger		2	6
Tristram Hussey		3	6
Benjamin Chase		6	6

Altogether, the equivalent of sixty-seven American dollars was contributed for the project, which made the villagers independent of rain-barrel supplies.

7 – The Invaluable Copper Plate

One of the finest source materials about the Siasconset whaling station is an engraving from a copper plate which is supposed to date from 1791, over a century after the founding of the settlement. The drawing (p. 39) is small and crudely done. It was formerly a Coleman heirloom from Elizabeth Coffin of Nantucket, and there are two copies in the Fair Street Museum there.

The bird's-eye view is to the eastward from 'Sconset hill. In the distance is the Atlantic Ocean with nearly a dozen boats containing from two to six men. One boat has its sails set.

The writer has tentatively identified (p. 41) the thirty cottages shown in the engraving. It will be noted that most of them have the characteristic "warts" or projections of the typical early fisherman's hut — a feature which will be dwelt upon at length in a later chapter. It is to be noted likewise that there are no Centre and Shell streets, nor a Pump Square, and that the buildings along the Bank or Bluff highway are visible. Not a structure bearing the appearance of a pretentious style of dwelling is to be seen.

The date, 1791, is about correct for the scene in the engraving. One of the curious features is the representation of a building in the process of construction, showing studs, rafters, diagonal braces and window frames. Was it the *Frederick C. Sanford House,* no longer existing on Broadway? The other twenty-nine structures conform pretty much to the state of development which could be expected about 1790, and are described individually later. What the tall, square, thin structure tied with ropes to the ground, immediately to the left of the dwelling under construction, represents has not been determined. Was it the South Well or a corn crib or the remains of a lookout mast? One thing it was not: a water tower.

8 – The 'Sconset Plan — Organic and Medieval

Redrawn from the Town Records is what is probably the first map of Siasconset showing house lots (p. 40), together with the writer's own topographical notations for the sake of clarity. Although the map dates from 1835, it preserves the seventeenth- and eighteenth-century village plan as well as the early flavor of the whaling station. In the quaint manner in which the Proprietors' records are often written, the story is told how the map came into existence, in this way:

"This book was bought the 12 mo, the 13 1808 by the Proprietors of the Island of Nantucket to record their doings in that they think ought to be recorded in their records."

Then turning the folios of the volume to number 205, we find these words written on the map: "At a meeting of the Proprietor's of the Common and Undivided Land on Nantucket, held at the Town House 23d, 5 mo., 1835, Voted that the Map of the Village of Siasconset exhibited at this meeting by the Committee appointed for that purpose be accepted and the Clerk is directed to lay it on file in his office, for the inspection of all concerned therein. Obed Macy, Prop[rietors'] Clerk."

A surprising feature of the map is that the owners of the lots were so well known on the Island that their initials, not their names, were inscribed on the properties. Where the names were known to this delineator from the initials given, they have been duly written in their squares.

'Sconset streets are of the meandering type, the buildings having been erected along their sides wherever their owners wanted to put them, before there were such things as yard boundaries. Of the five thoroughfares running more or less parallel to the Bank, Broadway is the widest and the principal one. How cleverly the villagers placed a house at each end of the broad section of that avenue: at the north was *James Athearn's home,* now replaced in whole or in part by *Sea Spray,* the former dwelling of Fred Pitman, and at the south, where Main Street crosses

Shanunga (Phase IV)
West Side

Broadway, was the *Frederick C. Sanford abode,* now gone. Whichever way you look down Broadway, there was, like the Duke of Gloucester Street in Williamsburg, a building to stop the vista.

At the site of the *Sanford House* Broadway narrows and makes a small jog in the direction of the ocean, and then continues southward a short distance until it is stopped by the South Gulsh or Gulley, the southern limit of the village.

Not the Pump Square, but the wedge-shaped area on the Bluff, was, as has been mentioned, the probable site of the tall mast in the nucleus of the settlement. At any rate that was the place where for generations the villagers used to assemble to buy freshly caught fish. In the very early twentieth century *Cash's Fish Market* stood on the north side of this area, and was probably a continuation of earlier market shops for cod, mackerel and other fish. From the time of earliest photographs there have been wooden steps leading down from this wedge-shaped "square" to the squatters' Codfish Park on the beach below (p. 36). Just north of the area a cart path ran down Middle Gulley, thus allowing vehicular traffic in the center of the village bank.[8]

Under their pseudo-Greek and pseudo-Gothic trappings the 17th-century lines of the early Siasconset cottages can still be discerned. This view, looking north on Broadway, shows *Nauticon* with rain barrel in foreground. *Wyer Photo, 1881.*

Of further interest in the plan are the bowling alley, which in 1835 was located on one of two lots belonging to George B. Elkins — a place not yet identified — and some lots with fish *flakes* upon them. A flake was a frame or rack, or even brush or hurdles, upon which fish were dried.[9] As late as 1835 there was a "Flake yard" upon Thomas Barney's 'Sconset property. One "Flake lot" belonged to Timothy M. Gardner, and another was owned by George B. Elkins, of bowling-alley fame.

Most of the whale houses in 'Sconset formed small plantations in themselves, for beside the homestead, they had "7 x 9" barns, peat houses for fuel supply, fishing-tackle houses, boat houses, the inevitable "necessaries," fish racks or flakes and flower and vegetable gardens.

The village plan of Siasconset was organic and medieval: it mostly just grew up, in the pack-donkey's way, with little aforethought. It was the result of use, not design. It fitted the hamlet into the landscape, it kept to crooked and meandering rutted roadways, and it was full of walks for pedestrian purposes. It had, as we have seen, two open spaces — village greens, if you will — and a bowling alley, that feature of the old villages of Great Britain. It possessed also small-scaled buildings in true English medieval *village* fashion (frontispiece).

Lastly, the medieval plan and layout of 'Sconset reflects in several respects early Sherburne and Sesachacha — but more the latter place since it, too, was a fishing stage, which Sherburne was not.

V

Pioneering With Love and Skillets

1 – Life with Rain-Barrels

FOR A LONG TIME the life of the unmixed English breed which colonized the Island was a rough, outdoor one. Nantucketers from colonial times until fairly recently had to deal continually with adverse circumstances — real character-builders. They had no electricity, gasoline, fuel oil, gas, steam or any of those generators of power which are necessities today. They had no running water — as many of the old photographs plainly show.

You cooked out of doors over wood or peat fires, where the big, iron pot on crotched sticks swung in the wind, or inside on clay or brick hearths, where the drafts were almost as strong as those outdoors. Smoke blackened your rafters and ceilings so that sometimes the soot became an inch thick upon them. Usually you slept in unheated places, such as a loft gained by a stepladder or a little space on the first floor known as a "stateroom." In winter the ink sometimes froze on the paper as you wrote. If your family lived in Sherburne and was fortunate enough to possess an upstairs fireplace, a fire was not lighted there unless you were ill.

At night the family gathered around the warm hearth and watched the sparks rising up the chimney. The bright glow of the fire was sufficient for the enjoyment of the social intercourse of the household, even when neighbors lifted the latch and took their places in the circle for a quiet chat. It was only when members of the family desired to read that a bayberry candle or a whale-oil lamp (p. 50) was lighted. You did not do much night writing or reading, and besides, books were scarce.

47

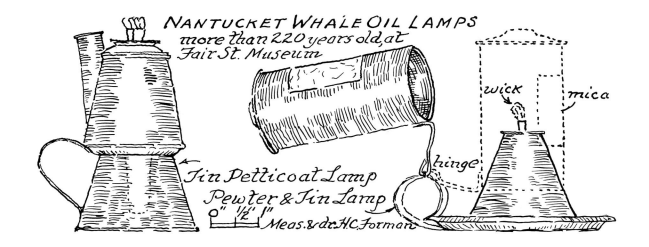

NANTUCKET WHALE OIL LAMPS
more than 220 years old, at
Fair St. Museum

Tin Petticoat Lamp

Pewter & Tin Lamp

0" ½" 1" Meas. & dr. H.C. Forman

wick — *mica*

hinge

The kitchen was the most important room in the house. There you ate your meals on wooden trays or platters called trenchers or on pewter plates or on anything which you could find, even wood shingles. And you used iron two-tined forks, iron or steel knives, and spoons of wood, pewter or latten. At Squam in the excavations of 1938-41 a spoon of latten, a brass-tin alloy, was discovered with initials *I P* on the back of the bowl and a rounded stem having a finial representing what appears to be a blackberry. For fish chowders and stews there was employed an iron skillet (p. 49) or saucepan, and for meat and fish fries an iron spider with three long legs.

For soft soap you made your own mixture of ashes and kitchen grease boiled together *à la* Indian. You carefully treasured all ashes from fireplaces; and when the time came to make soap, you placed these ashes carefully in a leach or vessel outdoors, and poured water over them. As the water percolated through the masses of ash, it absorbed the potash and slowly dripped from the bottom of the vessel into a tub. Then a friendly neighbor was called in for help in filling a try-kettle with lye and kitchen grease and in stirring the thickening, boiling mass.

After a few months of that kind of existence you found that household chores took up most of the day: cutting wood, digging peat, making clothes on spinning wheels and looms, or laundering in a wooden tub. You got your water for drinking or other purposes from rain-barrels or hogsheads set under roof gutters at a corner of the dwelling to catch any rain that happened to fall. Washstands were a rare extravagance. When your guests arrived, you stood in the front doorway, pointed out the barrels, and hinted that the company might remain with you while the water lasted. You perhaps heated the guests' shaving water by flame of a candle (p. 161).

Underhill described getting started in the day in this way: "In the morning the members of the household went, one after the other, to the pewter wash basin or wooden bowl in the main room, or kept on a bench outside, and washed their faces and hands in rain water, using home-made soft soap, when soap was needed, and dried themselves with a flaxen towel made on the island and used in common by the household. They arranged their hair with a family comb before the only mirror, a little one, mounted in an antique frame and hung in the living room. Their raiment was not more than sufficient to fill a small chest. An extra gown for the women made of wool grown, sheared, washed, carded, spun and woven on the island, and a few articles of underclothing, for a change, sufficed."[1]

Make no mistake about your life on the colonial island of Nantucket. You pioneered on the edge of a wilderness.

Because isolation was your customary condition, you were usually self-sufficient. You went to Cape Cod or the mainland by slow sailing vessels, and frequently the water was too rough to navigate the open stretches where the ocean poured into the Sound in roaring waves. The Quaker records of Nantucket cite instances

English Skillet
brought to
Nantucket
in 17th Century

bowl dia. 5 3/16"

of Friends who had been appointed to attend Quarterly Meeting on the mainland, but who could not go there because head winds prevented them. Sometimes you got little to eat because for weeks at a time the weather was too inclement for fishing.

There were no newspapers, telephones, radios or televisions to give news. Instead of the little over an hour it takes to go to New York City from Nantucket today, it took a whole week or more. On the Island you might learn some news item comparable to Peary's discovering the North Pole, but at the same time the tidings would be stale by a year. To give an idea of how remote was this Island from news facilities in time gone by, the story is told of a certain young man named Folger who went off for four years on a Pacific cruise. On his return to Nantucket he found his father in the parlor with a good-looking but strange lady. "Where's Mother?" asked the youthful Folger, to which question his father replied that Mother had died two years before, and that the woman standing beside him was his second wife. Poor Folger in one instant had to take in the facts of his mother's death and burial and the establishment of a stepmother in his home. Instead of blaming the lack of quick communications, he suddenly wished himself back in Tahiti.

2 – Furnishing the Early Homestead

"This island," declared Crèvecoeur," has nothing deserving of notice but its inhabitants; here you meet with neither ancient monuments, spacious halls, solemn temples, nor elegant buildings; not a citadel, nor any kind of fortification, not even a battery to rend the air with its loud peals on any solemn occasion. As for their rural improvements, there are many, but all of the most simple and useful kind."

He did strike the keynote of early Nantucket with these words, "simple" and "useful." Whether it was their homes, pleasures or making a living, Nantucketers conformed with few exceptions to those two basic words. A cottage of the poorest Islander did not have much in the way of furnishings: three-legged stools, "formes" or benches and a table made of common boards and perhaps hinged to the wall to save space. Possibly there was a chest (p. 233) or box for spare clothing. Twig hooks or pegs in auger holes on the wall also served as closets. There was no table linen. There were few beds: only folding canvas X-cots (p. 51) and bunks. There was no plumbing of any kind, and sometimes there was no "necessary" house but the great outdoors or the primitive Indian arrangement.

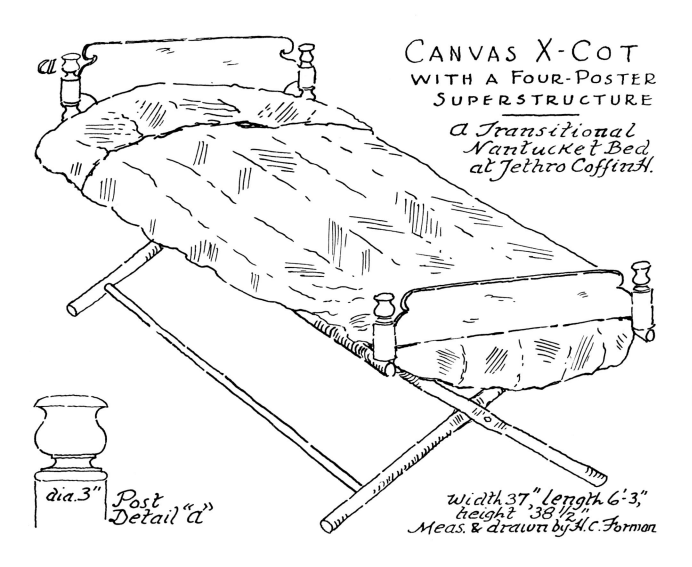

CANVAS X-COT
WITH A FOUR-POSTER
SUPERSTRUCTURE

A Transitional
Nantucket Bed
at Jethro Coffin H.

dia. 3" Post
Detail "a"

width 37," length 6':3,"
height 38 1/2"
Meas. & drawn by H.C. Forman

3 – First Hall-and-Parlor Houses

On the other hand the well-to-do Nantucket home of the 1680s was comparable to that of the plainer yeoman in England. On the west side of Wyer's Pond in the heart of Sherburne stood the farmhouse of Nathaniel Wyer (map, p. 22). The inventory of his estate was written (1681) in the rustic, badly spelled idiom of those days; nonetheless it presents a good picture:

First, Wyer owned a dwelling house and outhouses upon ten acres of land. The abode had but two rooms — a "Hall," which was the Great Hall or Great Room where the family lived, cooked and ate; and a bedchamber, or inner bower. The Hall was not a passageway, as it has become today. The chamber was apparently furnished with two pairs of "half-worn" sheets and a pillowcase, plus a flock bedstead — a flock being a wool mattress. In addition there were an extra pillow, a blanket and two old coverlets to protect against March winds. In the Hall were a small "table board" — evidently a trestle table — three chairs and some kitchen equipment, as follows: an iron pot, two old brass kettles, a skillet, a frying pan, an iron kettle and a trammel or pendant hook in the fireplace.

Then there were a fire shovel for scooping up hot peat, fire tongs and a lamp — the only one in the cottage.

Wyer's dish compartment supplied but six milk trays and four little trays, four trenchers for eating upon, three old pewter dishes, two porringers — used for porridge — and one salt cellar. Finally there were a pint pot, a saucer and a butter churn. No china or glassware is mentioned in the list.

In one of the two Wyer rooms lay two old chests, two boxes, an old Bible as well as five other books, and five yards of woolen cloth, which had been fulled at five shillings a yard. Those were all the interior furnishings which Wyer held at his death upon that Island outpost.

He also owned the necessary farm stock and implements, such as two steers, a cow, a heifer, a yearling, plus seventeen small cheeses, wheat, Indian corn, malt, and — what luxury! — a twentieth weight of bacon, valued at five pence — then worth about a dime — for each pound.

Sometimes the bedchamber was called the "Inner Room," as in the home of Samuel Beckford in Sherburne, where, unfortunately, in 1678 one Katheryn Innis, "the Scot," was "got with child" by one Denny Manning, not without later punishment meted out by the Nantucket Court.

4 – Richer but Later Seats

By 1715 some homesteads on the Island had become plush — that is, by insular standards. We learn, for example, that John Swain's estate at Polpis then comprised furnishings worth £ 310 sterling — a goodly sum — and included a silver tankard, a Bible and a china platter. There was, too, a "fashionable" table — presumably not the timeworn medieval-type trestle table. Still, the Swain domicile had little similarity to the great Georgian mansions of the same age, such as *Westover* (1730) in Virginia or the *Isaac Royall House* (1732) in Massachusetts.

Frequently the bedroom was called by the name of its orientation: East, West and the like. A case in point is the house of William Gayer, who in 1710 left to one of his former Negro servants, Africa, the "East" chamber of the dwelling where he lived and also the "lean-to" room for life.

The household in which Crèvecoeur stayed in 'Sconset for two days could not have had much in the way of furnishings. The family had numerous children of all ages and lived entirely by fishing — "the plough," as he quaintly put it, "having not yet disturbed the parched earth." They ate clams, fish, bacon and Indian dumplings, which simply were large lumps of boiled cornmeal. The noise of the spinning wheels revealed to him the industry of mother and daughters — one of whom was bred a weaver. The loom, by the way, was the entire means of clothing the whole family. Although there was little time for reading, their library had copies of *Josephus, Hudibras,* a few school tracts in the Nattick Indian and English languages and a Bible. Crèvecoeur was astounded to find that this lowly fisherman's family frequently read *Hudibras,* Samuel Butler's satirical poem against the Puritans, and could repeat passages from it by memory.

The reference to the spinning of flax on Nantucket calls to mind the time during the American Revolution that the father of a family on Tuckernuck one day hid his beautiful and luscious daughter under a heap of flax in his garret because an English warship loitered in nearby waters.

5 – Wholesome Young Islanders

The early Nantucketer usually married young. A man, it seems, could take a wife almost as soon as he chose her. Because their daughter's education, good health and customary "outset" were all that a father could normally afford, no marriage portion was required. The fortune of a young bride comprised chiefly her potential, skillful management, her modesty and her economy in financial matters. When a young chap went as harpooner on his second or third voyage, he almost always took with him the true promise of one of his early playmates to be his wife as soon as he came home. Once married, a woman customarily became a good financial investment, because in the long absence of her husband it was she who transacted the family business and looked after the young ones. She became an astute tradeswoman.

Besides, the average early Islander was healthy. It is told of one Nantucket woman that she lived so healthily and long that when she died, she had ninety-eight grandchildren. Temperance — the lack of strong drink — the control of passions, frugality and continual exercise kept the Islanders invigorated and preserved unimpaired that constitution which they had received from parents as wholesome as themselves; parents, who in the unpolluted embraces (Crèvecoeur again) of the earliest and chastest love, conveyed to them the soundest bodily frame which nature could give. The meaning is clear: having healthy and robust young wives, the men did not go cheapening themselves with other women.

Therefore it came to pass that these sober, orderly and industrious parents, constantly following some useful occupation, never guilty of riot, dissipation or other irregularities, naturally trained their children in the same way. Until twelve years of age the young boys learned to read and write a good hand. Then they were usually apprenticed to a cooper — a man who made barrels. At fourteen they were sent to sea, where in their leisure time they were taught navigation.

It was unfortunate that consanguine marriage did exist on Nantucket, with resultant cases of mental defects, insanity, feeblemindedness, deafness, blindness and so on. Tuberculosis was reported common in the period when Crèvecoeur visited the Island, but he did not mention it.

There is no doubt that the Islanders whom he met were brimming with health, and if some had infirmities, they were confined and out of sight. He did describe one girl whom he escorted to a "house of amusement" at Polpis. Now Polpis was the kind of place where farmers were "Polpisy" — having straw sticking out of their collars might be one definition. The place of entertainment there was nothing like the present Island hot spots, nor even like the dens which Crèvecoeur must have known in Paris. It was a building in Polpis, he explained, given over to rural and rustic amusements which were conducted upon the same plane of moderation as those in Town. Some pastimes were simple enough to be scarcely described: the pleasure of going and returning together, of chatting and walking about, of throwing an iron bar, of heaving stones and such like. Those were the diversions which Islanders knew.

The girl who accompanied him was one of many beauties there. According to him she was dressed in a bewitching attire of charming simplicity, and like the rest of the company, she was cheerful without loud laughs and smiling without affectation. In fact the whole crowd appeared gay without levity. Never in his life had he seen so much unaffected mirth, mixed with so much modesty. The pleasures of the day were enjoyed with the greatest liveliness and the most innocent freedom. There were no disgusting pruderies nor coquettish airs tarnishing the gathering. They behaved according to their native dispositions, the only rules of decorum with which they were acquainted. What, he asked, would a European visitor have done at that house of amusement in Polpis without a fiddle, a dance or cards? The gentleman from across the Atlantic would have called the place *an insipid assembly,* and ranked the outing among the dullest days which he had ever seen.

You can well size up a people by their recreations. On Nantucket amusements were simple and modest. No loud laughs or shrieks from the girls, yet mirth everywhere.

6 – Going on Squantums

Early Nantucket was a place where families did things together. The chief activity for relaxation was going on a squantum, which means an outdoor feed. The party usually comprised merry lads and lassies, with a couple of parents along as guides. There were a boat, a bushel of clams, a bag of cold chicken, a lot of roasting-ears of Indian corn, potatoes, hardtack, cold coffee and baskets crammed with tasties. There were ten hours' sail, more or less, and a great deal of mirth — not to say mild flirtation. Wood shingles, like the earlier trenchers, served as plates, and fingers as forks. Everyone sat on the sand, for aluminum beach chairs had not been invented.

The clambaking stage involved digging a hole large enough to hold a cask and then paving the hole with cobblestones, upon which a substantial fire of driftwood was lit. After the embers had died down and while the stones were red hot, a quantity of wet seaweed was thrown in, and a bushel or more of fresh clams was emptied upon the seaweed. Quickly on top of the clams were laid several chickens cut open as if to broil, potatoes pared and cut in half, and green corn in the husk. Then more seaweed was thrown in, topped by an old sail or a few boards to hold in the steam. No wonder in later years one Nantucket visitor named his cottage "N'Yum N'Yum Hut."

Upon a cloth on the sand were laid the many cakes, pies and sweets to supplement the goodies from under the old sail or planks. And how those firm-limbed, lipstickless Nantucket girls could cook. It is not surprising that many married early: the men were all for them.

At parties in Town the young people would assemble in private houses, for then there were no alcoholic Purple Swans or Rope Walks to visit. Drawn together by neighborhood or social ties, they combined into "gangs" — utterly unlike the East Side variety. At any rate each little society kept very much to itself and frequently met in the evening, not as couples dating, but as family groups. Instead of cards, music or the dance, the boys told stories of their sea voyages and the foreign lands where they had been — tales which in their utter simplicity and naiveté would to us seem absurd. One goes like this: "The island of Catherine in Brazil is a very droll island; it is inhabited by none but men; women are not permitted to come in sight of it; there is not a woman on the whole island. Who among us is not glad it is not so here [on Nantucket]?"

Much tittering followed — the girls laughing most of all. After the stories came puddings, pies and custards, to take up the time eating. Since inebriation was unknown, and music, singing and dancing were held in disapprobation, the young persons sat and diverted themselves by laughing and talking together. When the father and mother of the household entered the room, the party was over.

It is told that the young folks kept their chat to a whisper — a conversation known as a "gam" — because of parents being in the house. But the stifled bursts of laughter soon gave notice to the old folks.

If there was bundling on the Island, as one historian indicated, it must have been a custom no different from the one in other parts of New England.

7 – Under Quaker Influences

The first religious body to be organized by the Nantucketers was the establishment in 1708 of the Religious Society of Friends. These particular ones were very stringent Quakers indeed. From about 1670, when the first Friends reached the Island, until the 1840s, when they began to lose their hold there, a great deal of severity prevailed. Plainness of dress and language was the order of the day. Originally, of course, the whole world talked with "thous" and "thees," but the Friends have continued the custom into later times. It was only on First Day, Sunday, that Islanders were permitted to wear garments of *English* manufacture. The rest of the week they put on homespun clothing. Further, all clothing, wherever made, was of the gravest colors or had no color at all. There was no difference in dress because they were all clad alike. The women wore the coal-scuttle bonnet during the nineteenth century, but before then used a hat which was wide and flat.

In the 1791 engraving of Siasconset (p. 41) are men and women in Quaker garb, the exception being a person thought to be a Dr. Tupper, who is dressed in a cocked hat and a bag wig.

So strict were the Friends on Nantucket that one of them in 1678 was fined by the Island Court for being away from home on First Day. Another was censured (1792) for permitting suppers for a gathering of children to be cooked in his own dwelling house. If you painted portraits in your home; if you played music or had a spinnet placed by your hearthside; if you allowed young folks to dance in the parlor; or if you married one of the world's people — that is, Presbyterians, Methodists, Episcopalians and their ilk — you were put out of Friends' meeting. Indeed, one Thomas Coffin was ejected from membership in the meeting for permitting some young persons to kick up their heels in his 'Sconset cottage.

Once there was a Quaker bride who secretly marked with a rose the grave of her freshly buried husband, so that she would be able to distinguish the place where he lay. For that deviation from Friends' disciplines she was removed from membership. Of course those Quakers had no fancy things like gravestones, so that the poor girl's flower was the only marker visible.

That the Friends in the eighteenth century comprised two-thirds of the magistracy of Nantucket Island means that they were for all practical purposes the pro-

Dorcas and Deborah walk to Meeting in Nantucket on First-Day

prietors and rulers combined. On the other hand, the Island allowed on its territory no fort, soldier, governor; no pageantry of state or ostentatious magistrates; and no public executions or humiliating punishments, except the gallows.

8 – Methods of Going About

The wealthiest and most respectable inhabitants went to meeting for worship or to their farms in single-horse box-carts, sometimes with awnings for shade, but without springs or fixed seats. The driver usually stood upright and his passengers sat in kitchen chairs, as shown in the aforementioned 1791 engraving of Siasconset (p. 41). On squantum or sheep-festival trips the young men occasionally would unfasten the hooks which kept the cart in a horizontal position, and the girls and those who were not forewarned would suddenly find themselves sliding out of the box-cart onto a well-chosen spot of soft grass or smooth sand (p. 60). From excursions like those the box-cart came also to be known as the jaunting-cart, spring-cart or tip-cart. What fun it was, and how well the vehicle took the deep sand ruts of Nantucket.

The Islanders had an ingrained distaste for ostentation, luxury and frippery. So it happened that when a couple of single-horse *chairs* or chaises, gaudily painted, were imported from the city, they caused such resentment on Nantucket that the owner of one wisely sent it back to the "continent." The buyer of the other vehicle stiffened in the face of hostile criticism and hung on to his importation.

By the end of the eighteenth century there were many *four-wheeled* box-*wagons* (p. 20), having seats and occasional covered tops bulging outward — true aristocratic conveyances. They were roomier and smoother to ride than the simpler box-carts. The number of seats was usually two; the back one was often removed, and low chairs or rockers put in its place.

9 – Nautical and Insular Idioms

The early Nantucketer spoke somewhat differently from the way we do today, and in many respects unlike his contemporaries in the rest of New England. That isolating expanse of salt water was always a factor to be dealt with, and seafaring terms were frequently popping up in the Islander's speech. The word "gam," hitherto referred to, meant originally a school of whales; then came to mean the visiting of crews among ships. Today it can mean a get-together on Nantucket to compare old family trinkets and valuables.

On the way to a shearing pen (after a painting of a single-horse colonial box-cart, also called a spring or shearing cart). BELOW: A box-cart being driven in the 1890s to Quaise Shearing Pen. Shearing song, " 'Tis Tew I Can't," is tacked to the cart.

A NAI

FROLIC.

Nantucket youths, driving a group of young people in a box-cart to a squantum or a sheep festival, would often pull out the hooks of the cart and tip it for fun. *Scribner's Monthly, 1873.*

It has long been a tradition that an Islander never sits at a window, but always under a window, because portholes are high up from the floor. A Nantucketer does not throw away trash, but always "heaves it overboard." In giving his rival a licking, he speaks of it as "taking the wind out of his sails." And according to him a "slatch" is a spell of good weather. To be on deck means, of course, to be prepared.

A woman of the Island does not arrange a table setting, she "rigs it up." A man never ties up an object, he merely "splices it." If a girl is "pernickity," she is extremely particular. If an insular belle "flaxes around," she is simply gadding about; on the other hand if there is any shade of contempt or derision about her movements, then she "traipses about." If you "wilcox" on the Island, you have a bad night there. If you find "strams" running between your legs as you walk, they are only small children who impede your progress. Sometimes in the early morning you might take a fancy to go after "diddleders," which means that you desire to get pine needles for a fire. If you go to a "huddle," like Arabella Coffin Macy's famous huddle, you attend a dance.

In the building trades on the Island there are nautical names for things. Right-angled braces to strengthen the framework of a building are called "ship's knees." When clapboards were employed on walls or roof, the dwelling was termed "clinker-built," that is, using the external planks of a ship. A platform on the roof of a house is called a "captain's walk," or a "widow's walk," usually reached by a scuttle or trapdoor next to the chimney.

If you could speak naturally some of these salty expressions, you needed no passport to Nantucket; you could well make your way among the retired mariners sitting around swapping fish stories and whaling reminiscences. You would not be considered a "coof."

One thing the sea captains would do as their voices droned on and on by the hour was the cutting, etching or carving of a variety of boxes and pretty toys out of wood, bone or whale teeth. They would make kitchen-knife handles — handy for the little woman — or ship models or patriotic emblems. There were "wick picks" to take up wicks in whale-oil lamps, busques for the front of ladies' corsets, fly swatches, jagging wheels, sets of napkin rings and harpoons. There was no limit but the imagination to what could be made. These things were called scrimshaw.[2] The art has continued from the seventeenth century.

Nantucket Sea Captain
Owen Wyer

VI

"'Tis Tu I Can't, and Tu I Ken"

1 – A Rich Wool Trade

As has been indicated, the chief resource of the early Nantucketer, both white and Indian, was fishing. This livelihood included offshore whaling, which reached a climax in the 1710s, followed by sperm whaling, which brought great wealth to the Island from the 1820s through 1843, Nantucket's peak year. So fond of whaling were these Islanders that the people on Cape Cod called them "scrap-eaters," meaning that they liked eating brown pieces of blubber after the oil had been extracted at the tryworks.

The principal land industry of Nantucket from the white colonization to the time photographs were being widely taken was "sheeping," the wool trade. For wool as well as whale oil could bring wealth — witness the rich wool merchants of Chipping Camden in the Cotswold Hills of England: they could afford handsome, cut-stone residences with bay windows and oriels.

Thus on this Island in the seventeenth century it came to pass that there slowly grew up on the grassy moorland a number of sheep-raising and shearing establishments. Most of the moors became sheep pastures. A "sheep's common" meant either the right to pasture one sheep or the possession of a tiny piece of land which represented a fraction $(\frac{1}{19440})$ or a whole tract held in common. Further, a distinction was made between the common, or undivided, land and the "dividend land," which was a division of property, private and usually fenced.

63

On Nantucket, farms have always been few because there are not many places which can be cultivated without fertilizer, which must be transported from the "continent."

In later times the sheep's common became so subdivided that it was usual for a girl to have no other marriage portion but her outset, or beginning outfit, plus four sheep pastures or the privilege of grazing a cow. Four sheep pastures on the Island, it turns out, were considered equal to one cow. Two cows could be counted as one horse. The whole business was very arithmetical.

A typical arrangement for laying out a sheep's pasture is given in the Town Records of 1701. It was voted to lay out the land which had not already been surveyed in the neck called "Long Woods," within the arms of Hummock Pond, to every freeholder, according to his proportion. Every whole-share man was to have liberty to place in that neck twenty sheep in order to fatten them at the time the rams were taken up.

The estate of one Nantucketer, Benjamin Aston (d. 1680), revealed that there were other ways of making a living on the Island than fishing, and presented a list of his belongings as follows:

"21 sheep, 7 lambs, a cow and calf, 1 mare, 5 pecks of wheat, and 60 weight of wool."

Three of the largest shearing pens were located at these points: on the east side of Miacomet Pond; beside the appropriately named Washing Pond; and at a little distance west of Wyer's or Maxcy's Pond. It is said that ticks are thicker today in those areas than in other parts of the Island — even though almost a century has passed since sheep shearing ended. The finding of such insects is supposed to remind one of the gay times which took place upon those sites.

Nantucket SheepShears (12" long)

For generations the sheep shearing was the one big fiesta time of the year for the Islanders to enjoy. This is an old view of the Miacomet Sheep Pens. The sails shaded the workers or caught fleeces on the ground.

2 – Going to a Shearing Festival

At shearing time around the twentieth of June, before the "hot" weather commenced, thousands of sheep would be rounded up from the furthermost reaches of the Town commons. You can be sure that washing and shearing by hand 10,000 to 20,000 sheep in two consecutive days was no light work. For over a

These 19th-century Nantucketers at a sheep-shearing picnic must have looked very much like their forebears of the 17th and 18th centuries. The drink was milk. BELOW: Town building once standing at end of Commercial Wharf resembled a 'Sconset whale cottage.

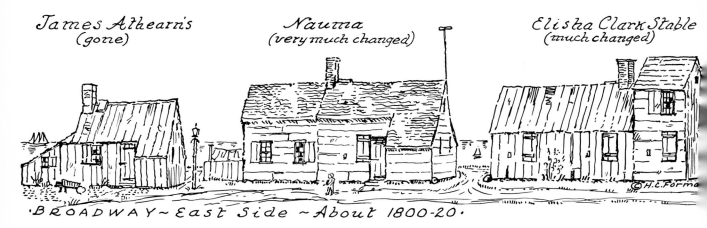

hundred years Nantucketers made out of this hard work a Shearing Feast or Festival. At the very first streak of dawn the Islanders would bring out to the sheep pens their sails and tents to catch wool and make shade. Their food hampers would be stuffed to the tops; and little booths would be set up crammed with pies, tarts, cakes and jams for everyone to buy. Old photographs (pp. 66, 210) show what an unceremoniously good time was had by all — young and old alike. In these views one can almost smell the aroma of the rose-impregnated butter, the Maine salmon, the West Indian candy, the salty Nantucket quahogs or the East Indian tea, for those products were almost invariably at a Shearing Feast. The photographs do not, as far as can be seen, show the little pieces of wool which blew about the shearing grounds and which the poor people present pounced upon with eagerness.

In connection with the annual festival a poem called "The Harper," written in 1844, became a popular song for nearly half a century on the Island, and reflects the customs of an earlier day there. This is a portion of the composition:

> "The harper seats him 'neath a tent
> Made of mainsail patched and rent;
> The curious folk, of every hue,
> Looked on as though they'd look him through.
> He signifies his mad intent
> To drink — of the limpid element;
> He eats a large three-cornered bun,
> And then, his slight refection done,
> He takes his harp, and plays again
> The same mysterious wild refrain:
> 'Tis tew I can't, and tew I can,
> All the way to the shearing pen!' "

·*Author's Reconstruction of* AMERICA'S QUAINTEST STREET·

This poem then goes on to relate that three maidens clad in spotless white did "reel it strong" with three nice young men. Finally everybody went home, the harper himself going to "coofdom." In the last sentence the word "tew" or "tu" is Scotch and dialectical for work hard or fuss. The word "can" should perhaps be "ken," to understand.

3 – Handling the Sheep Business

The Island records are full of items about sheep. In 1696, for example, a tax of 140 pounds of sheep's wool was levied upon the estate of Stephen Hussey. At another time it was voted at a Town Meeting that a committee be formed to keep the sheep out of the Town, and to demand that the "Lamb Marker," as he went about dutifully marking lambs, should turn the animals from the Middle Pasture into the Southeast Pasture, to abide there until time to wash them. On still another occasion the sheep were to be kept in the Winter pasture, where they were to be guarded against killing.

Among the archives of Nantucket is a book, written by hand and entitled "Earmarks of the Inhabitants of Sherborn on Nantucket." The marks were made on sheep. The first entry reads thus: "The earmark for John Swain ['s sheep] a half penny under the right ear."

One time twenty-six men were individually asked to stand at the gates of a stair at shearing time in order to take account of all the sheep which had been put in small pens, and to place the animals among the rightful owners. Upon finishing that job, the men were then to turn over the sheep to the clerks of the yard, who perforce had to enter the beasts in the sheeping record books. Another year it was forbidden to set up any tents or booths at shearing time inside the Middle Pasture fence.

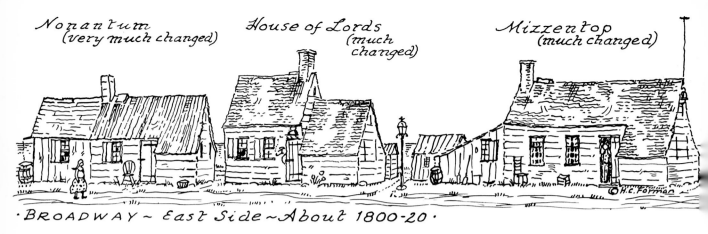

Nonantum (*very much changed*)   *House of Lords* (*much changed*)   *Mizzentop* (*much changed*)

·BROADWAY ~ East Side ~ About 1800-20 ·

There was even a committee formed to skin dead sheep and to relieve the live ones when needed. The owners kept three-quarters of the sheep, and the remainder went to the committee. There is an instance of a young lad being hailed into Court in 1686 on the complaint of having pulled wool off a sheep's back; he admitted the charge.

A story is told about a time in early Nantucket when the sheep were permitted to wander at will through the Town. Once a prisoner sent word to the jail authorities that if the prison was not mended immediately to keep the sheep from coming in, he would get out.

4 – A Landscape of Mills

Closely akin to the gathering of the wool was the fulling of it by mill work; and milling was another way of making a living on Nantucket. There were not only fulling mills to full, press, shear and dye cloth, but other kinds, like grist mills, for grain. The power for these mills came from wind, steam, tide or horse.

In the seventeenth century the principal fulling mill, it seems, stood at Polpis. In October, 1677, John Swain, who had a house in Sherburne, was licensed by the Town to operate a fulling mill near his new home at Polpis, and he worked it by a water wheel driven by a rivulet called Stony Brook which flowed into Polpis Harbor. In the immediate neighborhood of the water mill (1666) for grain at

Liberty Hall—formerly London Tower (very much changed) · *Snug Harbor (much changed)* · *Dexioma (slightly changed)* · *Headache House: (gone)*

Author's Reconstruction of AMERICA'S QUAINTEST STREET

Wesco Pond was, in 1673, a tide mill, which three years later was equipped as a fulling mill. In the eighteenth century at Squam was another fulling mill, watered by a small stream.

The picture of early Nantucket included a landscape of busy mills, grinding and turning on their wooden machinery. An old wind-driven mill stood in 1717 near Daniel Russel's homestead on the Island. At the time of the American Revolution there were four windmills on Mill Hills back of Nantucket Town, then a part of Sherburne. In order from west to east stood Benjamin Whippey's mill, Uriah Bunker's, Barnabas Bunker's and Timothy Swain's — known today as "The Old Mill," which was built in 1746 (see map, p. 122). It is said that this last mill was constructed by Nathan Wilbur, a Nantucket sailor who had visited Holland and who designed the structure upon an octagonal plan with four wind-driven arms, each thirty feet long. After various periods of neglect by owners, this mill in 1897 passed into the possession of the Nantucket Historical Association. The building is unusual in that the grindstones are not on the ground floor, but on the second story.

On Mill Hills there was also a fifth one, called the "Round-Top Mill," which was located on the present New North Cemetery and remained in use until 1873.

Soon after the English settlement of the Island, the Town agreed to construct a horse mill, but a little later thought better of the scheme and abandoned it. Perhaps insular horses were too rare and valuable for treadmill service. A tide mill instead of a horse mill was built.

George C. Gardner House
(slightly changed)   High Tide (Phase III)   Gardner   Casa Marina
(forever ebbed)   St.   (very much changed)

©H.C.Forman

·BROADWAY ~ East Side ~ About 1800-20·

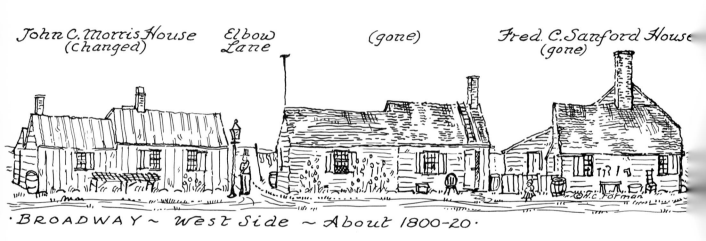

John C. Morris House   Elbow   (gone)   Fred. C. Sanford House
(changed)   Lane   (gone)

©H.C.Forman

·BROADWAY ~ West Side ~ About 1800-20·

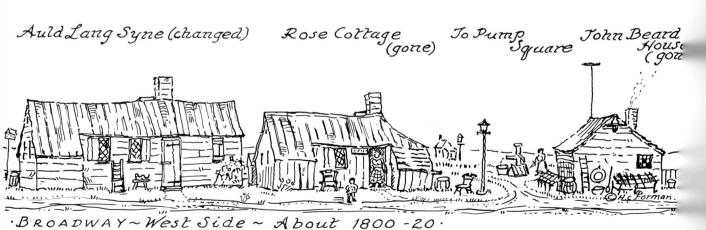

Auld Lang Syne (changed)   Rose Cottage   To Pump   John Beard
(gone)   Square   House
(gone)

©H.C.Forman

·BROADWAY ~ West Side ~ About 1800-20·

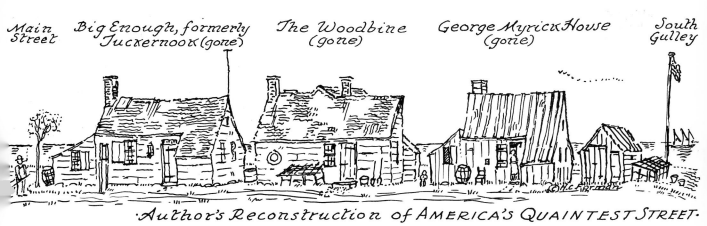

Main
Street
Big Enough, formerly
Tuckernook (gone)
The Woodbine
(gone)
George Myrick House
(gone)
South
Gulley

·Author's Reconstruction of AMERICA'S QUAINTEST STREET·

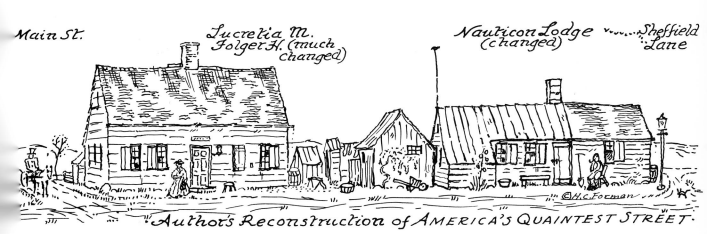

Main St.
Lucretia M.
Folger H. (much
changed)
Nauticon Lodge
(changed)
Sheffield
Lane

·Author's Reconstruction of AMERICA'S QUAINTEST STREET·

hanunga-formerly
Betsy Cary H.
Mitchell St.
The Maples-formerly Eliza Mitchell H.
(much changed)

·Author's Reconstruction of AMERICA'S QUAINTEST STREET·

The Martin Box ~ called "The Parfect Rope Walk" (much changed)

Driftwood, formerly Clifton Cottage (very much changed)

Come Aboard, formerly Nonquit (very much changed)

·BROADWAY ~ West Side ~ About 1800-20·

5 – Of Gardens, Pounds and White Gloves

There appears to have been on the Island plenty of Indian corn for grist. Yet in 1675 the Nantucket Court commanded that no corn could be taken off the Island except to the Province of New York, of which it was then a part. The ears, of course, were much smaller in size than those which are grown today. Sometimes the Town voted to lay out a "cornfield to plant corn." That pests hampered corn growing is evidenced by the bounty which the Town offered for killing crows.

Plots like the Gallows Field, the Smoking Field or the "Place called Oblong" were planned by the Town for growing turnips, wheat, rye, barley and other vegetables. Occasionally it was ordered that the common grass within Siasconset Pasture, a fenced enclosure, should be mowed by the first of August.

Because of the sterile and sandy ground in the Wesco section of Sherburne, there were only a few gardens and arable fields there; but by means of tireless perseverance the Islanders brought in a variety of manure, and by cow-penning they were able to enrich their plots.

That the early settlers attempted gardens at first is indicated by at least one reference — the garden of Thomas Macy's house (1664) near Reed Pond.

It was the custom for the Town to employ a poundkeeper and a cowkeeper. Stephen Coffin, for example, was instructed (1669) to keep the pound for stray animals near Capaum Harbor "when once there is a lock to it, and he is to have two pence a time for turning the key to lock or unlock the pound." About that same year a cowkeeper by the name of Will and another man were indicted by the Court for breaking open Mr. Coffin's warehouse at Wesco, and for stealing cloth and corn from it. In the eighteenth century there were 500 cows from the Town which were led daily to pasture upon the Tètoukemah Lots at the second milestone on the 'Sconset Road and in the evening driven back into the settlement.

Félicité
(very much changed)

None Too Big
(very much changed)

Sans Souci (changed)

End
of
Broad
way

© H.C.Forman

·Author's Reconstruction of AMERICA'S QUAINTEST STREET·

Another Town job was that of the caretaker of the Island beaches, who had the right to impound any creatures which were found there.

Hogs, another Island staple, figured in the Court case (1675) of Stephen Hussey, a hot-tempered gentleman, charged with contempt and presumption for his rude speaking to Captain John Gardner. While the good Captain was talking to one Edward Carter and asking him to keep his hogs from rooting up the Town Commons, Hussey blurted out: "Meddle with your own business. I give him leave for his hogs to do so."

That the liquor business flourished on Nantucket from the beginning is the record. As has been indicated, the whisky commerce was one of the chief factors in eliminating the Indians from the Island. Jack Never, one of the aborigines, for example, confessed (1679) that in the middle of the night he had gone into Captain John Gardner's home and taken five shillings out of the jacket by the bed, and had also opened a case and carried away a bottle with a pint of liquor in it. The sentence was twenty stripes to be laid on Jack's naked body. Sam Cook, another Indian, was branded on the forehead with the letter "B" on account of his breaking open Richard Coffin's ship and stealing about five quarts of rum. Among the white settlers, John Swain, it seems, in his will left the "still house" to his wife.

It might seem to the casual reader that the early history of Nantucket has been full of criminal cases — when such cases actually have been rare. An ancient Island custom, established in England several centuries ago, was employed on occasion in the Superior Court for Nantucket County — an area comprising the Island: the presenting of a pair of white gloves to the presiding justice to signify the purity of a court having no criminal cases on the docket. After a long lapse this custom was revived on Nantucket in the early 1890s.

6 – Mother Cary, a Colonial type

In the middle of the nineteenth century there was a "lady" on the Island who dispensed liquor and became famous for it; the story is told because it echoes almost perfectly an incident as it might have occurred during colonial days on the Island. Certain visitors, it appears, came to the home of Mistress Betsy Cary in 'Sconset — the place later known as *Shanunga* (p. 92). Getting out of their carriage, they made such shouts that the door of the "tenement" — for the cottage looked little more than that — opened wide, and an old cripple issued forth. "Just go in there," he said, indicating with his cane the low door of the cottage from which he had emerged, "and Mistress Cary will entertain you as nice as need be."

Thereupon the travelers entered the Cary inn or public house and found themselves in a cuddy — which means a small cabin in a boat. This one measured eight feet by ten and served as both reception room and general store. Looking about, they could discern dried codfish, bottled beer, sugar candy, fishing lines and hooks, eggs, whisky, sugar cakes, opodeldoc — which is camphorated soap liniment — pork, cigars, cheese, "Radway's Relief," tobacco, ship biscuit and "Pain Killer." There were also jackknives, lucifer matches and costume jewelry.

Suddenly from a side door entered the little old Cary woman with a motherly aspect tinged with vinegar. She greeted her guests in this way: "What have you got to sell?"

"Nothing at all," they replied.

"Then take your traps and tramp," she ordered in her 'Sconset dialect.

"We have been informed that you could entertain us," spoke up the visitors.

"What's your orders?" she thereupon asked.

They at once proceeded to give orders for large amounts of food and drink, and the clink of their silver coins soon smoothed the wrinkles from the old lady's face. Next thing she knew, a glass of rum was pressed upon her, whereupon she declared agreeably:

"I like to deal with liberal-minded, polite gentlemen. Why, there are people that come here who would spend the day skinning a clam rather than pay five cents for a good dinner."

It was after that interview that a caricature of Mistress Cary appeared. It is a particularly graphic picture (p. 77), down to the dried codfish hanging on the wall and the barrels of rum. This view is the kind of *genre* which had obtained on the Island for two centuries before the Mother Cary engraving was made.

Siasconset, by the way, was America's first week-end place and, in a time when Saratoga was unknown, the country's first summer resort. From about 1676 — *100*

MOTHER CARY.

Elizabeth Cary in the cuddy of her inn, later called *Shanunga*, 'Sconset, 1860. *Harper's Magazine* caricature.

years before the American Revolution — week-enders and summer-resorters from Nantucket Town spent time at 'Sconset — a spot in which to kick up their heels. Especially captains and mariners staying in Town would get restless, fill their wagons with pieces of salt pork, a pound or two of hardtack and some bottles of rum, and then drive off to their fishing village across the Island — Siasconset Bank.

VII

The 'Sconset Baulk and Whale House

1 – Two British Architectural Styles

REFLECTING IN PART the early civilization of Nantucket are the fishing, sheeping and farming already described; but more important for a study of how the Islanders lived is their architecture. For if nothing else, architecture is a social art and forms a careful record of a culture. Consequently we come to our most significant chapter, the one which has the most to contribute to the story of the early Island.

What will the reader think when it is here declared that the average early Siasconset whale cottage was a hall-and-bower or but-and-ben structure, with a baulk, a heck, a speer, a stee and a marsh? Except for the speer, for which there is only the slightest evidence, the other features did exist there.

To commence this account, we should turn to consider Great Britain in the sixteenth and seventeenth centuries, because all the architectural styles, other than Indian, on Nantucket before the American Revolution were British styles — English, Welsh and Scotch. The early white inhabitants of the Island were overwhelmingly British, many of them having been born in the Mother Country. For example, Peter Folger, the missionary to the Nantucket Indians, was born in England, as already noted, and came in 1635 to Massachusetts Bay before settling on Nantucket.

At Siasconset there flourished two building fashions brought over from Great Britain in the seventeenth century and after. The second is a continuation of the first.

79

1. *The Medieval Style* flourished through the seventeenth century and was marked on Nantucket by plain wood or brick structures of small scale, usually only one room deep and one-story-and-loft high, and characterized by small windows or wind-holes, shutters, batten doors, chimneys of wood or brick, vertical board partitions, stepladders and winding staircases, and interior post-and-beam construction.[1]

This style continued in a somewhat weakened manner throughout the entire eighteenth century, and most of the nineteenth. For convenience this infiltration and persistence of the style into later years is called:

2. *The Hangover Medieval Style.* This fashion of building thrived on Nantucket from about 1700 until about 1890, and was characterized by the aforementioned medieval features, watered down by the introduction of occasional pseudo-classic details, like ornamental mantelpieces and large sash windows, some of fifteen panes.[2]. Even so, this style does not include the Gothic Revival and the Victorian Gothic, which are imitative Gothic styles of the 1830s through the 1890s.

As far as present research has disclosed, all but two of the early 'Sconset abodes in this work conformed to either the Medieval or the Hangover Medieval. The two exceptions, *Svargaloka* and the *Lucretia M. Folger House*, are discussed at length in a later chapter.

2 – Fire in the Great Hall

The usual 'Sconset whale house of the seventeenth century was therefore medieval, of English, Welsh or Scotch derivation. It was timber-framed, that is, constructed by means of a prefabricated framework of oak posts, sills, studs, beams and rafters, which were mortised and tenoned together into place, so that the frame could not be wrenched apart by storms. An edifice of timber-framing was called "a fair English house." In England the word "timbran" meant to build.

Underhill stated the matter correctly when he wrote that the beginning of each of the ancient Siasconset dwellings was but a single room — a rude, boarded enclosure. This one room, as we shall see, was boarded off to make two staterooms, named for tiny ship's cabins. The main room formed the "Hall," "Great Hall" or "Great Room." It was the "fier-house"[3] where the bonfire was kept for warmth. In 'Sconset the main room averaged only eleven feet by thirteen in size, a little more, a little less. Now "Hall" may seem a grandiose name for such a small apartment, but that is what it was called in England and in certain parts of this country, such as Virginia and Maryland. Nothwithstanding the fact that this room is not known by that name on Nantucket today, it has usually been labeled on the floor plans of this work as "the Great Room" — the technically correct terminology.

The wee 'Sconset "fier-house" was open to the rafters, exactly like the lofty medieval halls of Great Britain, which moreover possessed usually a central hearth. The popular small house through the greater part of the sixteenth century in England had an open-timbered roof and central bonfire,[4] but on Nantucket we have so far found no evidence of a central fireplace — nevertheless, that does not mean it was not used there.

3 – The Whale House and its Prototypes

The early lodging in 'Sconset, as has been indicated, was a whaling shelter for a six-man boat's crew. The men were fitted snugly into the house like sardines in a can. That was done by screening off the Great Room by a partition, usually of vertical boards, which in England was called a "parclose" or "heck," in order to make twin staterooms, each about six or seven feet square. The partitioning was placed in the cottage either at the time of original building or slightly later. It seems to have been the custom to make only two staterooms, always located at the south end of the hut for warmth.

Such an arrangement of space may be seen in the floor plan (p. 82) of *Shanunga* (I) — the "I" meaning the original or first phase of development of the cottage. In each stateroom slept two men on narrow bunks or cots only a few inches apart. At *Nauticon Lodge* (p. 144), also in 'Sconset, each stateroom has only a five-foot-eight-inch space for two sleeping men. Such a cubbyhole has been well named stateroom, because while sitting on your cot you could reach practically everything hanging on the walls. Besides, the whale houses were built by fisherfolk, and it was natural for them to call their rooms by that name.[5]

The fifth man, and the sixth when he was not on duty up the mast or lookout, climbed up the Great Room board partition by means of either a series of cleats or a removable stepladder or "stee" to a tiny *piece* of garret over the twin staterooms. There they slept on narrow, folding canvas "X"-cots or on truckle beds, the rafters with cobwebs, bats and insects close to their noses. There was no space in which to stand up, and there was continual danger of rolling off the garret floor, actually a balcony without a railing, into the Great Room below.

The precarious method of reaching this balcony sometimes later developed into a set of rudely built steps as steep as those in the companionway of a small coastal schooner.

The twin-stateroom or -bedchamber "bower" scheme at the end of the Great Hall was English medieval, as well as Welsh and Scotch, and is illustrated on the comparative floor-plan diagram (p. 82) of a Lancashire cottage and *Shanunga* (I).

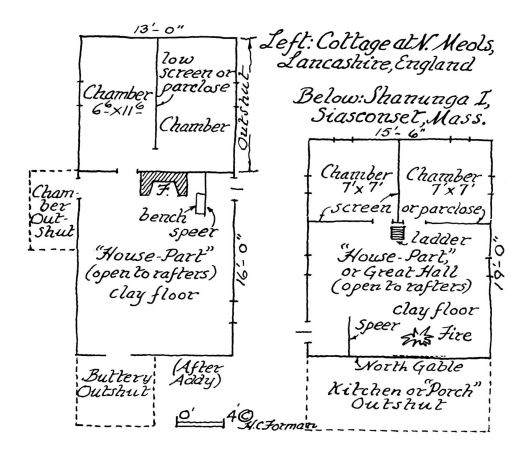

Left: Cottage at N. Meols, Lancashire, England

Below: Shanunga I, Siasconset, Mass.

But there was one important difference: the two bedchambers in the Lancashire example formed a distinct wing to the Great Hall or "House-Part," while in the 'Sconset arrangement they were integral parts of the original structure.

Closer to the 'Sconset model was the Welsh "hall-and-parlor" house, represented by the plan and section of a stone abode in Pembrokeshire, Wales (p. 83), where two double or wainscot beds were placed in the same relative position in the building as the fishermen's bunks or cots in the Siasconset example. A wainscot bed, by the way, is a four-poster boarded on three sides to keep out drafts — for after all, a Welsh habitation had no central heating.

It appears to have been the custom in the fifteenth century in Wales to divide the one-room dwelling into two parts by means of a *furniture* wall, exactly the way in which we in the second half of the twentieth century partition off the living area from the dining room or kitchen by means of built-in furniture dividers. The furniture separating those spaces saves the cost of a partition. In Wales the usual method was to place the furniture — the dresser and shelves in particular — to serve as a barrier between the living and the sleeping quarters. Where there were separate beds and certain members of the family wished privacy, the partitioning was formed by the back or long sides of a box bed, or by a chest of drawers, or by a curtain. A good example may be seen in the *Llainfadyn House* (1762) at the Welsh National Folk Museum, Cardiff.

From this furniture-wall arrangement the Welshman next developed the hall-and-bower scheme with an actual partition between Great Room and bedchamber by means of a screen of straw or of laths and reeds, a curtain or a boarded partition, as the diagrams show (pp. 83, 84).

This kind of vertical board screening was also called the "palis," and practically every early Siasconset whale house had one. On the other hand, there is no evidence to indicate that 'Sconseters sometimes did *not* use cloth or reeds or furniture-walls instead of wooden planks for their partitioning. In fact, one Nantucket dwelling is recorded as having had down through the late nineteenth century a series of hooks across a beam in the sitting room, from which fasteners hung either a partition of thin boards in sections or a heavy leather curtain, thereby converting half the cottage space into sleeping quarters.[6]

It is interesting that in England the cottage type of wooden screen or parclose was not very high and at some places resembled cow-stall partitions.

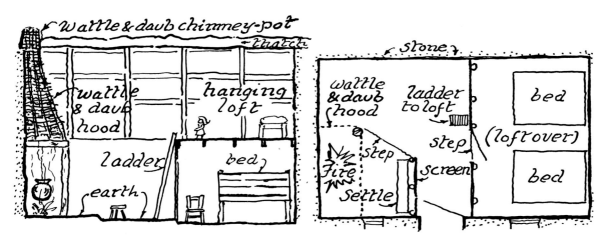

Longitudinal Section & Floor Plan of Typical Cottage, Pembrokeshire, Wales

4 – Appearance of the Hanging-Loft

In the Welsh house the feature of most significance was the *baulk* or boarded piece of garret, which covered only the space over the twin beds, leaving the Great Room open to the rafters (p. 83). Actually, as far as origins are concerned, the Welsh baulk was thought to be derived from the gallery located at the end of the English medieval hall. But in Wales it does seem to have had a cruder begin-ing: the baulk floor was at first made by placing boards across the tops of the box or wainscot beds.

At any rate this small piece of garret, the baulk — really amounting to a half- or partial-loft — was called the *crogloft*, meaning the "hanging-loft," from the Welsh word *crogi*, "to hang."

The usual way of reaching the Welsh hanging-loft was by a removable ladder; but sometimes when there was no ladder, you scrambled up on chairbacks.

Almost every early 'Sconset whale house was at first a crogloft habitation. Its Hall or Great Room was open to the rafters, as we have already seen, and there was the dark, triangular space of the baulk, the hanging-loft, over the twin staterooms.

Where the Welsh ladder was sometimes off-center of the Great Room or cov-ered the doorway to the bedchamber (p. 88), the 'Sconset arrangement was to place the ladder between the doors to the twin staterooms. If the ladder interfered with circulation in and out of these doorways, the cottager could arrange to push up his ladder over the baulk floor or pull it up in nautical fashion to the rafters by means of a rope.

One traveler through Wales in 1797 told how at a country inn he was assigned a "state room," which was a crogloft located at the very brink of a stepladder —

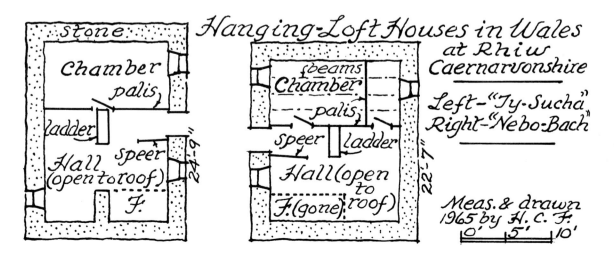

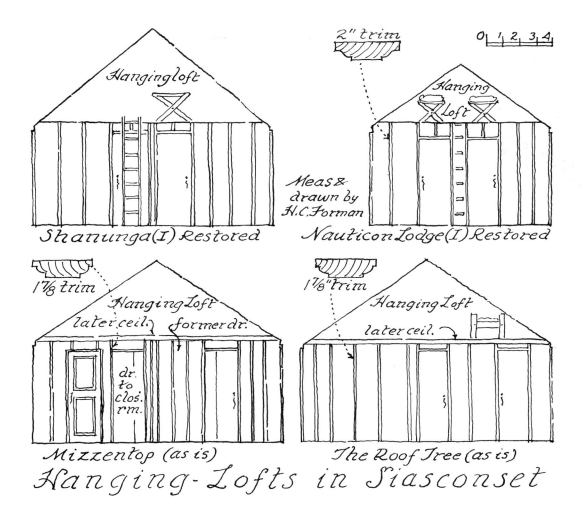

Hanging-Lofts in Siasconset

Shanunga (I) Restored

Nauticon Lodge (I) Restored

Mizzentop (as is)

The Roof Tree (as is)

Meas & drawn by H.C. Forman

with much danger of falling off the little "gallery" onto the Great Hall floor. He noted that when he went to sleep, his head came very close to bumping the roof.

Some think that the hanging-loft floor was put over the bedchambers to keep roosting chickens from dirtying the beds, but at 'Sconset that theory may be discounted, because the space of the baulk was used by two men of the boat's crew.

In Wales the hanging-loft was customarily dark, windowless and almost airless — what air there was coming from the Great Hall. Sometimes a glass tile inserted in the clay tile roof admitted a faint light; occasionally there was used a small skylight which could not be opened. There appear to have been no windows in the gable over the hanging-loft. For that matter, probably the little lie-on-your-stomach window in the south gable of the typical early 'Sconset cottage was a later insertion, placed there years after the original house was built.

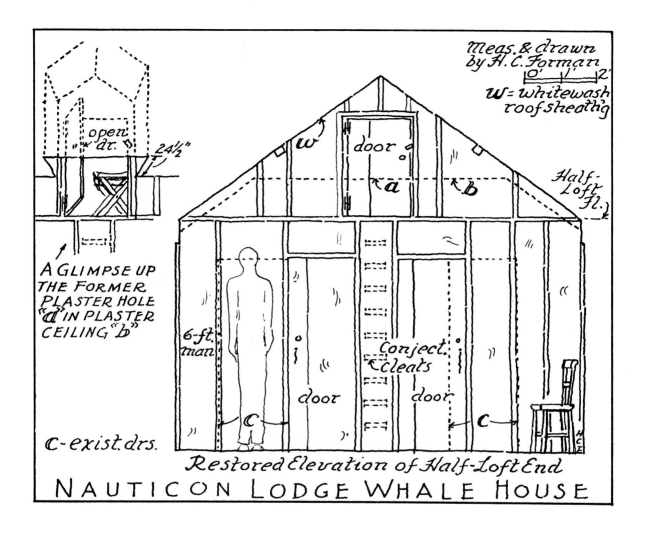

A GLIMPSE UP
THE FORMER
PLASTER HOLE
"a" IN PLASTER
CEILING "b"

C - exist. drs.

Restored Elevation of Half-Loft End

NAUTICON LODGE WHALE HOUSE

5 – Baulk Development in Nantucket and Wales

What makes the Siasconset whale house of particular interest is that it usually followed somewhat the same course of development in its hanging-loft as occurred in Wales; and a few technical expressions are necessary in describing the comparisons.

First, at *Nauticon Lodge*, 'Sconset, as far as this writer has been able to ascertain, a board partition (pp. 85, 86) for privacy was *later* erected upon the hanging-loft to close it off from the Great Room. A low door was placed in the center of this new partition to seal off completely the sleeping space.

Underhill well delineated this scheme, as follows: "A floor was laid over the two bedrooms by which a cramped attic three and four feet high was created, with a little door opening into it from the main apartment. It was reached by cleats nailed on the partition underneath [or by ladder]."

In the same way the closing off of the hanging-loft was also what happened in some Welsh dwellings (p. 88), as in Caernarvonshire. When the family was too poor to build boards to shut off the baulk, they hung up a screen of calico or other cloth.

Another arrangement in 'Sconset obtained at *Columbia Cottage* (p. 87), a building which according to a tentative study by this writer was found to have had its hanging-loft boarded up *at the same time* that the twin staterooms below were

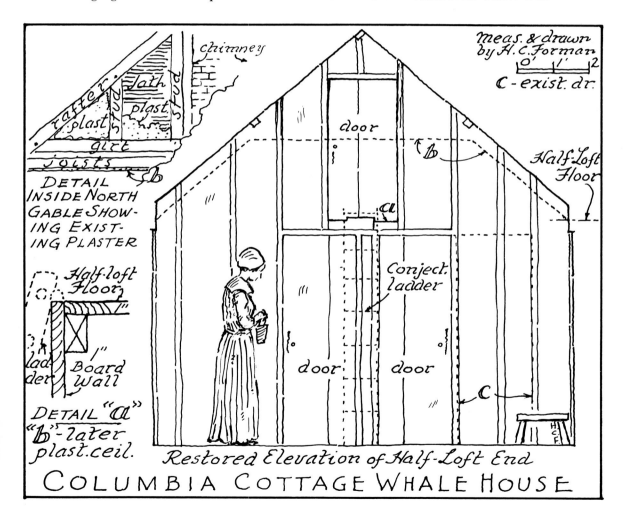

Restored Elevation of Half-Loft End
COLUMBIA COTTAGE WHALE HOUSE

Hanging Loft

1ˢᵗ Stage "Nebo-Bach"

narrow boards

4'-6" dr.

ladder on hooks

5'-9" dr.

2ⁿᵈ Stage "Tan-y-Capel"

Hanging-Loft Houses in Wales at Rhiw, Caernarvonshire. Meas. & dr. H.C.F. '65.

built. In other words, it appeared that the baulk was never open to the Great Hall, and therefore missed the customary first stage of development, the open hanging balcony.

It may seem strange, but *Nauticon Lodge* and *Columbia Cottage* formed the exception rather than the rule in Siasconset. *For the customary development of the baulk was to make it a full loft over the whole house.* It seems that in our very early investigation of the 'Sconset fisherman's cottages we were puzzled at finding in *Shanunga* that the floor over the Great Room was three inches higher than that over the staterooms — the discrepancy in floor level being situated exactly over the board partition below. Of course the carpenter had needed thicker joists for spanning the Great Hall than for the smaller staterooms. Some structures have a full loft absolutely level, that is, as level as the crudities of the village construction allow; and there is usually the telltale division in the garret floor to indicate that the Great Room was once open to the Rafters in true medieval fashion. In some places a new flooring of the attic has obliterated the division.

For all that, it was also the custom in Wales to turn the baulk into a full garret after a number of years, thereby making a lengthy sleeping space for the whole family. In that case the access ladder led up through a hole punched in the Great Hall ceiling. The complete loft over a house was well known in Pembrokeshire and western Carnarvonshire.

In early Nantucket you can not get away very far from the Old Country, where changes in medieval construction were generally followed later, particularly in Siasconset.

To simplify this somewhat parallel development of the crogloft or baulk in Wales and 'Sconset, we have made the following diagram, using examples from the latter place:

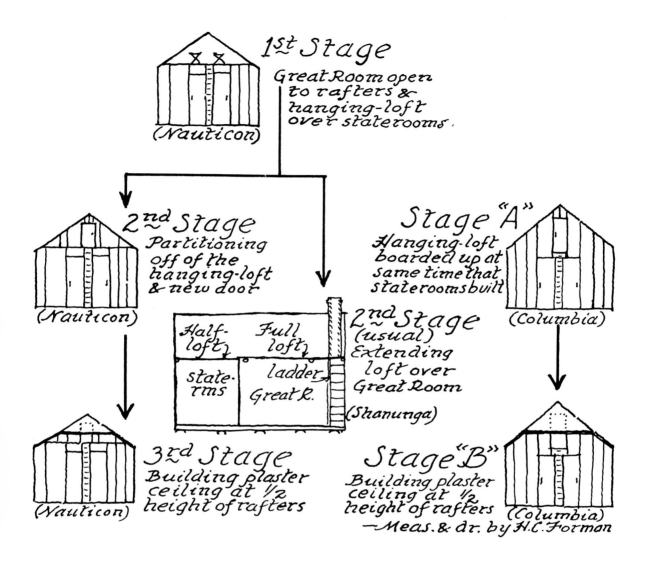

1st Stage
Great Room open to rafters & hanging-loft over staterooms.
(Nauticon)

2nd Stage
Partitioning off of the hanging-loft & new door
(Nauticon)

Stage "A"
Hanging-loft boarded up at same time that staterooms built
(Columbia)

2nd Stage (usual)
Extending loft over Great Room
(Shanunga)

Half-loft | Full loft
state-rms | ladder, Great R.

3rd Stage
Building plaster ceiling at ½ height of rafters
(Nauticon)

Stage "B"
Building plaster ceiling at ½ height of rafters
(Columbia)

—Meas. & dr. by H.C. Forman

Note that *Columbia Cottage* in its Stage A and Stage B seems to have developed like *Nauticon Lodge* in its 2nd and 3rd stages.

If the reader should think that the original 'Sconset habitation was crowded with six men in it, how packed was the Welsh home! A cottage in Raglan, Monmouthshire, had a very good Great Hall, ten feet by twelve in size, with a small scullery at the back. The bedchamber was about two feet lower than the Hall and in area only *four* feet by *ten* feet, over which was a small hanging-loft. Eight persons slept in this tiny nidification: three children under the roof, and three more, with their parents, in the closetlike stateroom.

6 – Croglofts in England and Scotland

The kingdom of Wales had no monopoly on baulks, for the other countries in Great Britain also had them. In England the invention of the hanging-loft over the inner chamber or bower appears to have been Anglo-Saxon, which means that the feature was 1500 years old.

The Saxon house, made up of a Hall open to the rafters, had at first an inner chamber partitioned off from the Hall. Then a partial garret, called by the Saxons a "bōlke" (balk or baulk), was constructed over the inner room. Although this upper "chaamer," as it was called, was not five feet high, it must have been a comfortable sleeping space for a person wishing to get away from the refuse, muddy straw and dirty messes on the earth floor of the Great Hall. The baulk floor was reached by a "stee" or ladder.

In the northern counties of England, like Yorkshire, and in Scotland, the customary cottage of medieval style was a hall-and-bower dwelling of two rooms, an open-roofed kitchen — which in fact formed the Hall — and an inner bed-chamber, which might be ceiled over in order to provide storage in the loft — the baulk. Such buildings were called "but" and "ben" houses, where the "but" was the kitchen and the "ben" the chamber.[7]

In Lancashire in northwest England the hanging-loft today has a complete partition wall and is called the "scaffo'd." The door in this wall through which hay is thrown is called the "scaffo'd hole," and that is also where the corn harvest goes.

7 – The Progenitors of the 'Sconset Dwellings

This, then, is the conclusion. The ancestors of the Siasconset whale huts go back in time fifteen centuries to the homes of the Anglo-Saxons. More particularly those examples in Siasconset descend immediately from domestic medieval types of buildings in the northern shires of England, in Scotland, in Ireland *and above all in Wales, where the arrangement and development come closest to the 'Sconset models.*

It is interesting that when the English gave up using the central hearths in Britain, they extended their loft floors right across the whole house, therewith causing themselves a lot of trouble, by blocking off the upstairs chamber or chambers, access to which had been by stepladder reaching from the Great Hall. Yet that is exactly what happened to *most* of the 'Sconset whale houses. The stepladder had to be moved over against the chimney at the opposite end of the cottage from the hanging-loft, which thereupon became a whole loft. In England the ladder or "stee" was often fastened by hooks to a hole in the upstairs chamber floor.

8 – A Maryland Comparison

A Free State variation of the Welsh cottage with twin staterooms separated by board partitions was discovered in 1961 very much by accident by this writer. The brick slave quarters at the *Ripley Plantation* probably dates from about 1793 and has a floor plan astonishingly similar to that of the 'Sconset whale house in the first stage or phase of its development. The smaller of the two batten doors to the staterooms was for the children of the family. The floor is of earth in the Great Room while there is a step up to the plank floor of the staterooms. The chimney is at the other end of the cottage, as at Siasconset. There is no baulk or hanging-loft; in fact the plaster ceiling is halfway up the height of the rafters, as exemplified in the ceilings over the Great Rooms of *Nauticon Lodge* and *Columbia Cottage*, 'Sconset examples already discussed.

In the following chapter we come across an interesting Virginia comparison.

An old picture of the *Betsy Cary House,* now *Shanunga,* shows the smaller section be-lieved to have been built around 1682. The cottage originally had bevel-edge siding and wooden chimney.

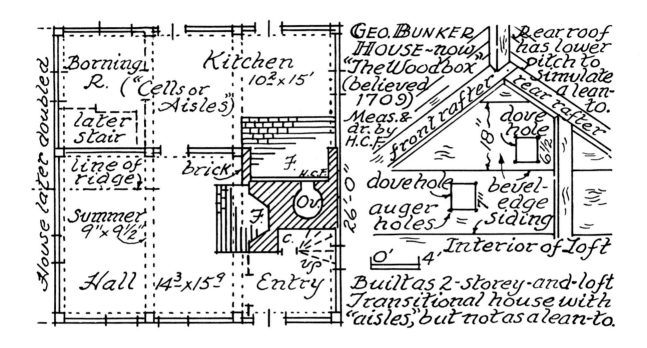

Borning R. ("Cells or Aisles")

House later doubled

later stair

line of ridge)

Summer 9"x 9½"

Hall 14³x15⁹

Kitchen 10²x15'

brick

F.

F. H.C.F.

Ov.

c.

up

Entry

GEO. BUNKER HOUSE~now "The Woodbox (believed 1709) Meas. & dr. by H.C.F.

26'-0"

Rear roof has lower pitch to simulate a lean-to.

front rafter

rear rafter

18"

dove hole 6½

dove hole auger holes

7"

bevel-edge siding

Interior of Loft

0' 4

Built as 2-storey-and-loft Transitional house with "aisles," but not as a lean-to.

VIII

More About the Whale Houses

1 – Marshy Floors

As WE CONTINUE to examine the early structures in Siasconset, the more medieval they are found to be. A good many of the homes are reported to have originally had earthen floors, the wooden ones having been incorporated later. In fact Underhill believed that all the ancient dwellings were without a wood floor, a statement which is perhaps not accurate.

At the same time the usual medieval dwelling in both England and Wales had a dirt floor, covered with rushes or green grass, upon which meals were eaten. Within the memory of men now living, certain old domiciles at Bwlch Mawr in Caernarvonshire, Wales, would have dry ferns and rushes strewn upon the floor, upon which the "table" would be set with wood platters, broth, meat, milk and cheese. The threshold, of course, was the threshing floor, where clay and rushes and grass were all chopped together by passing feet — animal and human.

2 – Cooking Porches

Other parts of the Siasconset lodging were as medieval as the baulk and the clay floor. Underhill recorded that the village cooking was frequently performed out of doors over wood fires in camp style, and that pot, kettle, skillet and spider sufficed for utensils. The iron pot was suspended over the fire by a sapling supported by forked sticks. "Their food," declared the intrepid Underhill, "was cooked as only men can cook, and as women would hate themselves for cooking it."

95

It is possible that many of the original whale houses had no fireplaces — all cooking being done under the open sky to the tune of the sea breezes. Likewise, in England of the Middle Ages down to the fifteenth century cooking was done either in the open air or in light timber sheds or shelters, something like the carports of today.

There again, the early 'Sconseter, in construction a medievalist to the roots of his hair, did the same thing. As indicated, he sometimes cooked outside; other times he prepared meals in a little shanty of inclined boards, or in a porch open to the weather, or in a shed kitchen usually tacked onto the north gable-end of his house. Colloquially the shed kitchen, with its roof of one pitch, was on Nantucket called a "porch" — because it actually was an open porch enclosed by boards. Such light shanty additions formed "outshots" or "outshuts," which in England are any excrescences from the main body of a building. In Britain the kitchen outshut of a medieval dwelling was known as the pantry or buttery (p. 82), which, since the twelfth century and before, formed a lean-to shed usually attached to the gable-end of the Great Hall. That was the very 'Sconset scheme.

Gaines Farm Quarters, Hanover Co., Va.

COMPARATIVE VIRGINIA AND NANTUCKET "I"-HOUSES Restoration drawing by Author

Shanunga (Phase IIa) Siasconset, Mass.

Meas. & dr. H. C. Forman · 1957.

3 – The "T"-House and a Virginian Comparison

When the village whaleman extended his little twin staterooms outward in order to make larger sleeping accommodations, he built what were "warts" to Nantucketers, but small "outshuts" to Britishers in the Old Country. Notice how the Englishman in the Lancashire cottage already described (p. 82) added a tiny bedchamber to one side of his Great Hall.

As Underhill has correctly explained, the projections on the 'Sconset cottage *at first* occurred only on the two staterooms — making a roof reaching downward front and rear to within three or four feet of the ground. For this development we have coined the words "T"-house or "T"-plan, which marked the second phase in the building of a whale homestead. Of interest is the comparison (p. 98) of the 'Sconset "T"-house, represented by *Shanunga II,* with the *Gaines Farm Quarters* in Virginia. In each building the outshuts are on the long sides of the house, not at the gable-end; but in the Virginia example the fireplace is between the state-rooms, not at the other end of the house as it is in the Siasconset domicile.

4 – Welsh Chimneys

Turning our attention to the north end of the early 'Sconset dwelling, we find that the original method of heating the interior was by board chimneys, some of which were in place as late as 1820 — definitely of the style known as "Hangover Medieval." Now the wood chimney belonged to the Middle Ages. By the year 1400 most homes in England, if they had chimneys, used wooden ones. They were especially common in the late 1300s and comprised little more than great hoods or canopies of wattle-and-daub or lath-and-plaster, either hanging over the fire or supported by the second-story floor. Usually the stack was made of wood or clay-and-straw or even a barrel with the bottom knocked out.[1]

Both English and Americans spoke of such wooden country chimneys as being "Welsh." In St. Mary's City, the first capital of Maryland, for instance, the inhabitants were ordered in 1685 to have all their Welsh chimneys lathed, filled, daubed and plastered. The landscape of the English colonies in America during the seventeenth century was one of wooden chimneys, and Nantucket Island formed no exception. In our sectional diagram of a Welsh homestead (p. 83) there has been shown a typical basketwork Welsh chimney.

The discovery of the traces of a former wood chimney in 1955 in one of the best preserved Siasconset whale houses, *Shanunga,* seems to prove the tradition of

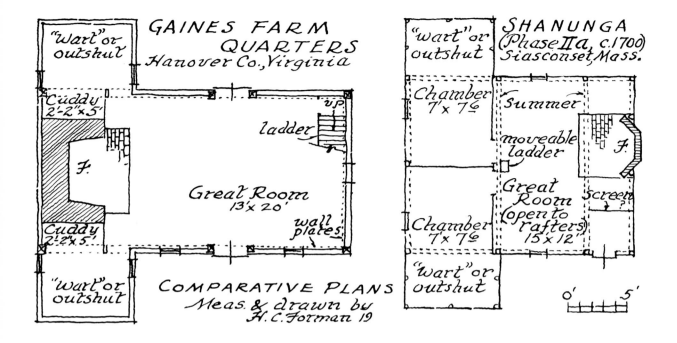

GAINES FARM QUARTERS
Hanover Co., Virginia

"wart" or outshut

Cuddy 2'-2"x5'

F.

Cuddy 2'-2"x5'

"wart" or outshut

ladder

up

Great Room 13'x20'

wall plates

COMPARATIVE PLANS
Meas. & drawn by
H.C. Forman 19

SHANUNGA
(Phase II a, c.1700)
Siasconset, Mass.

"wart" or outshut

Chamber 7'x7½'

Chamber 7'x7½'

"wart" or outshut

Summer

moveable ladder

F.

Great Room (open to rafters) 15'x12'

screen

0'   5'

such chimneys there. As related more fully in a later chapter about that particular dwelling, the original fireplace appears to have been wooden with a lath-and-plaster backing called a "reredoes," but without jambs, breasts, hood, throat or flue to channel the smoke upward to the boarded stack hole in the roof (p. 100). The hearth evidently was dirt. The smoke would rise lazily, heavily sooting the open rafters of the Great Room as well as the treetrunk posts and siding boards of the gable-end.

When a brick fireplace was later inserted in the gable-end wall, the smoke still meandered upward without benefit of smoke chamber or flue, finding its way out through the hole in the roof. Underhill reported that "brick chimneys replaced those of boards in the early nineteenth century," indicating that it was not until that late date that the cottages obtained flues.[2]

It is possible that some other early examples like *Auld Lang Syne* (p. 127) and *Nauticon Lodge* (p. 144), both in 'Sconset, had the complete wooden works: place for fire, reredoes, hood to collect smoke, flue and stack on the roof. One reason why there may have been wooden hoods in the village is that the first cross or tie-beam in the Great Room of a whale house was usually only three-and-a-quarter feet out from the chimney gable-end wall—just far enough out conveniently to support a hood — whereas the other tie-beams were placed seven or more feet apart. At *Nauticon*, as will be shown in a later chapter, there was a faint echo of the medieval principle of louvre vents which the English once used for bonfires in the middle of their Great Halls.

5 – Traces of A Speer

The smoked-up interior of the north end of *Shanunga* revealed a vertical edge of soot ("s.l.", p. 100), running from floor to chimney girt and located just forty inches inward from the front doorway. This blackened edge on the wood siding boards may indicate the former existence of a "speer" or "spur," that is, a protecting screen against the gusts of wind which were wont to come in the Great Room and blow out the fire on the hearth. Such evidence is indeed slender; but the speer was used in the Anglo-Saxon dwelling, and was common in the English and the Welsh house, as shown on the plan on page 82. It was used in Wales even as late as the nineteenth century. In short, it made a kind of covered inner porch, which later developed into the typical New England vestibule. On the inside of the speer, opposite the fire, was usually a wooden bench where you could sit and warm yourself. Above the bench some shelves for holding dishes and kitchen utensils were built.

NAUTICON LODGE AS A "T"

The way Phase II looked with Early "Wart" Additions. Restor. H.C. Forman

Unusual horizontal board-and-batten wall (right) on *Mizzentop* boathouse, Front Street, 'Sconset. At left, chimney and rain barrel of *House of Lords. Platt Photo from Collection of Clara Wilson.*

SHANUNGA
SIASCONSET
Phase IIa (c. 1700?)
Restoration Drawings
by H. C. Forman

· CROSS · SECTION ·
THRU WOOD CHIMNEY
"s.l."= soot line; dots = soot

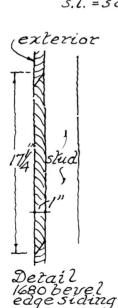

Detail
1680 bevel
edge siding

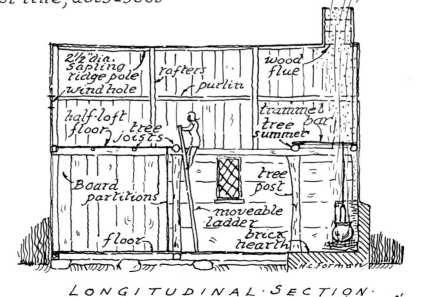

LONGITUDINAL · SECTION ·
THRU WOOD CHIMNEY

6 – Whale-House Roofs and Walls

As far as research has disclosed, Siasconset roofs were of six varieties, as shown on the diagram. The simplest and crudest was the running of wide boards side by side up and down the roof across the purlins — which were the horizontal members between rafters. Naturally the rain came through the cracks between the boards, so much so that such roofs were used on outshuts, sheds, enclosed porches, fish houses and other outhouses, where water was no problem. Until recent times the fish shanties in Codfish Park below 'Sconset Bank had a few plain board roofs through which water came in as through a sieve.

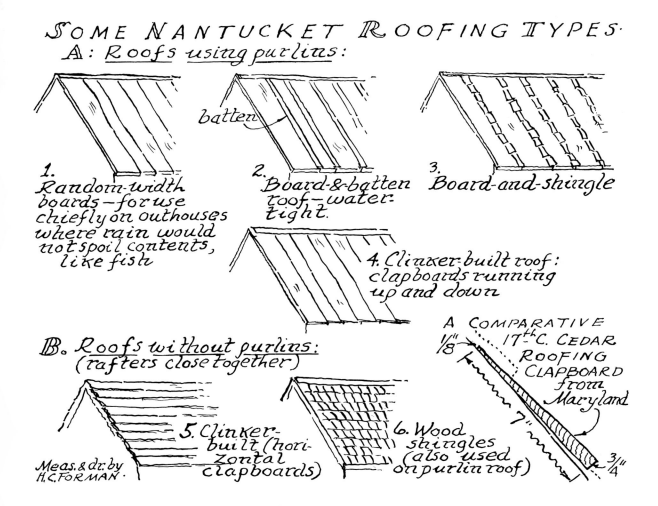

SOME NANTUCKET ROOFING TYPES.

A: Roofs using purlins:

batten

1. Random-width boards — for use chiefly on outhouses where rain would not spoil contents, like fish

2. Board-&-batten roof — water-tight.

3. Board-and-shingle

4. Clinker-built roof: clapboards running up and down

B. Roofs without purlins: (rafters close together)

5. Clinker-built (horizontal clapboards)

6. Wood shingles (also used on purlin roof)

A COMPARATIVE 17th C. CEDAR ROOFING CLAPBOARD from Maryland

1/8"   7"   3/4"

Meas. & dr. by H.C. FORMAN.

Another old view of Siasconset, showing Codfish Park, below the Bank. Here are two drays — barrel-carts — a dory, a water-pump with raised platform for filling barrels and a fish house with **up-and-down board roof**.

The diagram shows two methods of covering the cracks between the boards: by batten strips and by shingles. Both forms of roofing are generally unfamiliar to us today. When the boards were overlapped in *either* a vertical *or* a horizontal direction, they were "clinker-built," that is, clapboarded. In short, clinker-built means having the external planks of a ship, built so that the edge of one plank overlaps the edge of another, thus helping to push down the waves. Clapboards are usually split, feather-edge boards with thick butts made of oak and lapped. But other clapboards are regular boards without the feather-edging. None of either variety has been found on any early 'Sconset roof; nevertheless, there are descriptions of such in that settlement. Clapboarded roofs were common to medieval England and have been found *in situ* on early roofs in Maryland, like *Cedar Park*, and in Virginia, like the *Adam Thoroughgood House* and the *Brush-Everard House*. They were also used in New England, as for instance at William Rix's dwelling of 1640 in Boston.

Because almost all the early 'Sconset roofs appear to have had purlins, it is probable that most of the clinker variety had up-and-down roofing boards which overlapped each other. Within the memory of men now living on Nantucket Island there once stood a one-story cottage on the shore of Sesachacha pond at Quidnet which had an up-and-down clinker roof. When there were no purlins, and the rafters were set close together, then horizontal clapboards were employed.

Underhill reported that when the early 'Sconset structures were made more comfortable in the early nineteenth century, the "old clinker-built roofs were taken off, and replaced [with the boards] side by side," so that wood shingles could be nailed down.

While the usual medieval roof in America was steep, that in Siasconset was flattish. The very early Nantucket Town roof, as represented by the *Jethro Coffin House,* approximated an angle of fifty-two degrees to the horizon; that of early Virginia, fifty-four degrees; and that of 'Sconset only thirty-five degrees. When all is said and done, the fisherfolk on the east side of Nantucket Island were a canny lot: they needed a roof ridge only five feet above the baulk floor — sometimes less — thereby making just enough room for a man to crawl to his camp cot in a horizontal manner. The headroom was low, the roof pitch was small and the roof was economical to build, thus saving shillings.

As for outside wall covering, the standard early method in the village of Siasconset was bevel-edged siding boards, one inch thick and usually varying in width from twelve inches to twenty-four, nailed across the posts and studs, as detailed on page 100. The boards fit tightly together, and inside and outside their surfaces are flush. That was another type of building material widely used in the England of the Middle Ages, and very prevalent in this country, as at the *Loomis House,* Windsor, Connecticut, or in the *Slicer-Shiplap House* (c. 1723) in Annapolis, Maryland.

Sometimes when the wind is terrific in 'Sconset and makes the very buildings sway and bulge, the Islanders must have calked the joints of their bevel-edged boards by means of clay, clam mortar and plaster, or some such material — although actual traces of such have not been found. Wood shingles on walls for their protective qualities appear not to have been added to the exterior siding until after 1800 — although it is of course possible that in a very few buildings shingles were used before then.

Vertical and horizontal clapboards — the clinkers which we have already noted for roofs — were also used on walls. These must have been fairly wide boards, because the very narrow horizontal clapboards seen today in the village and in old photographs of buildings there date from after 1850 and are Victorian. No signs of vertical-clapboard, or even board-and-batten, exterior walls have been found, but early 'Sconseters must have used them, since they were common medieval methods of construction. In another of his little works, *The Credible Chronicles*, Underhill described the villagers' "rough boards nailed to uprights and rafters, one overlapping the other [i.e., clapboards] or battened to prevent, as far as might be, the rain driving through."

We do know that there was one example of wall construction in 'Sconset where horizontal boards had their joints covered by batten strips — a kind of horizontal board-and-batten — perhaps a unique example known in this country. Such a covering was to be seen (p. 100) in the nineteenth century on the boathouse of the *Mizzentop*, 'Sconset, the remains of which stand today across the Front Street from the whale dwelling.

7 – Finishing the Inside of the Whale House

Directly connected with the subject of vertical boards for walls is what was known in medieval England as "wainscoting," a kind of woodworking which did not become general until the 1500s. King Henry III in 1223 had the wainscoting of the Royal Great Chamber painted green, and the boards were set vertically and tongued and grooved for warmth and privacy. In Sussex, England, at a house of the late fifteenth century in Church Square, Rye, is an early type of oak wainscot made of tongued-and-grooved clapboards, overlapping on the front, but flush at the back. Another interior type comprised boards and battens, running vertically from floor to ceiling — the battens of course sealing the cracks. *That* was the usual medieval or hangover-medieval paneling or screening found in early Siasconset. The British called it "muntin-and-plank" work.

Sometimes the 'Sconset battens are plain; others have their edges molded with quarter-rounds or cyma curves (p. 85). Occasionally there are no battens at all, but tongued and grooved boards with beaded edges, usually of nineteenth-century date.

Lathing and plastering seems not to have made their appearance in 'Sconset until the very late eighteenth century — although Underhill preferred to think the time was the first quarter of the nineteenth. He told of the change in his way:

"A startling innovation was made by a well-to-do fisherman that aroused the jealous criticism of all his neighbors. He actually caused the interior of his dwelling to be plastered! For years he was the subject of animadversion, and it did not cease until the last family was able to indulge in the same extravagance. And such plastering! Neither laths, nor lath lumber were easily procured on the island. But 'Sconset ingenuity was equal to the emergency. Bark was peeled from cedar logs, spread out flat, split in strips in portions of its lengths, placed on the studs and furrings, stretched apart and nailed fast; and then the mortar [plaster] was pressed by the plasterer's trowel into the interstices; and when it hardened, it was firmly held in place."

Bark strips (p. 229) were one way of doing it, but Underhill failed to mention the very roughly-split oak laths on several whale-house walls, as at *Auld Lang Syne* (p. 128), which was common.

8 – Doors, Claddings, Wind-Holes and Sash

The usual door in Siasconset was like the wainscoting, that is, of boards, usually one plank or two planks wide, held by battens on the back. Since in the early days people were smaller and the village architecture was on a minor scale, the doors averaged only *six* feet high and *two* feet wide. Some were even five inches shorter than six feet: witness the five-foot-seven-inch high stateroom doors at *Nauticon* (p. 86). Compare these dimensions with the average outside door today: seven feet by three. When two-panel doors are found in the village, they apparently are to be dated from the first half of the eighteenth century.

The outside 'Sconset door generally extended down a few inches below the sill in order to keep out driving rain. It always opened out, because the villagers figured that the building would be more difficult to blow down with the door opening out than with the door hung inward in the usual manner.

The door hardware of the early period is of the common medieval types: wrought-iron H-, H-L-, strap- and T-hinges; at the same time when the owner could not afford expensive iron, which was scarce, he used wooden hinges and wood gudgeons, which are pins or pintles (p. 106), as at *The Maples*.

The customary method of fastening a front door was by a wooden latch on the outside which fitted into a wooden catch on the jamb (p. 210). As Underhill has well described the arrangement, a cod line was fastened to the latch and passed through a gimlet hole in the door above the latch, and a knot was made on the inside end of the string to prevent it from slipping through the hole. These string ends have been drawn on the stateroom doors in the drawings on page 87. When a caller knocked, the latch was lifted from the inside by pulling the string. No one has ever informed us how you got out of the cottage if the string jammed or your enemy cut it — then the latch could not be lifted from inside.

When the early 'Sconseter could not afford wooden doors, he used curtains, which were called "claddings" in Britain of the Middle Ages. For a stoop he sometimes placed on the ground a hatch which had floated ashore from a vessel.

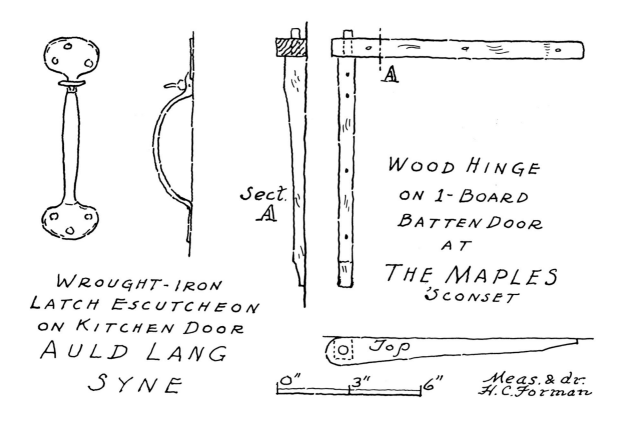

WROUGHT-IRON
LATCH ESCUTCHEON
ON KITCHEN DOOR
AULD LANG
SYNE

Sect.
A

WOOD HINGE
ON 1-BOARD
BATTEN DOOR
AT
THE MAPLES
'SCONSET

Top

0"   3"   6"

Meas. & dr.
H. C. Forman

As for wrecks, Underhill pointed out that many an old 'Sconset door and sash had come from ill-fated ships which hit the dangerous shoals known as Bass Rip and Old Man's Rock.

Interior doors had not only wooden latches, but frequently wrought-iron thumb-latches, like those in *Auld Lang Syne*. Closet doors usually had buttons — small wood catches turning on a nail or screw (p. 201). How puzzling of Underhill to mention buttons which held exterior doors opening out, and not to explain how the owner turned the button from inside.

At first, Siasconset windows must have been very simple, and we can cite those of medieval England as a guide to what was used. For one thing there must have been plenty of "wind-eyes" or "wind-holes," used more in the hanging-loft or baulk, to give a bit of light and ventilation. Such holes probably had oiled paper, linen, canvas or other transparent material across them which were removable.

When the holes were large, the material was probably stretched across a protective wooden lattice made of either wickerwood or fine rifts of oak, in a checkerboard pattern.

One English writer of 1519 told of paper or linen cloth stretched across the lozenges — diamond wood strips — which made "fenestrals," small transparent openings. Fenestrals are framed blinds of cloth, canvas, paper or linen.

One must not forget that "leaves" or shutters of boards were very common and could be arranged to open in or out. And they could be used with or without fenestrals. Old photographs of the village indicate that many buildings had board shutters with the battens on the outside, and that blocks of wood with hooks were fastened to secure them (p. 180).

Casement windows were a further development in Old England. In the thirteenth century a rare, glazed window, probably a casement, was ordered for the Queen's wardrobe at Westminster, so that the chamber would not be as windy as before. In the time of the Anglo-Saxons, and even before then, the better dwell-

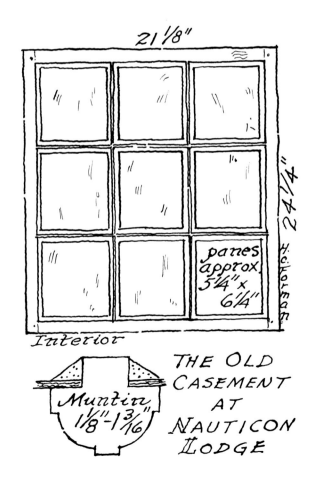

ings are reputed to have had for their casement windows panels of horn fixed in wooden calmes or bars. Wooden calmes, not lead, were probably used in early 'Sconset, and perhaps there was horn as well. But it seems logical to assume that there were few, if any, wrought-iron casements with leaded glass and fancily-designed iron latches, such as those found in medieval work in Virginia and England. The village was too poor and plain.

From evidence found today, the early village window on the first floor, like that at *Heart's Ease* (p. 206), averaged only fourteen to sixteen inches wide — barely enough room for your shoulders. Probably many openings in the community at first had wood casements, which were later reconverted into "guillotine" sliding sash, of medieval vintage. The guillotine could, of course, drop suddenly on wrist or neck, followed by surprised body pain. At any rate, the narrow width of the opening allowed for a sash of a *width* of either two six-by-eight-inch panes or two seven-by-nine-inch panes. What the proportion of casements to guillotine sash was in early Siasconset is not known, but a guess is that more than half the openings had wood casements with square or diamond glass held in place by calmes or muntins of wood. The small wood casement, less than two feet wide, with nine odd-sized bubble-glass panes, in place at *Nauticon* (p. 107), is a good illustration. It is a type of casement probably used in the first quarter of the eighteenth century; seventeenth-century casements were usually narrower.

It is interesting that in the Squam excavations (1938-41) on Nantucket there were reputed to have been found three fragments of quarrels or diamond panes.

Underhill stated that many old windows in 'Sconset were brought from Town. "It mattered not," said he, "that no two were alike in size and shape. It was enough that they admitted the light and kept the ungentle zephyrs at a respectful distance."

9 – A Rare Village Chimney

The most interesting of the brick chimneys which exist at 'Sconset has until this writing passed without notice. Although dating from about 1800 and of the Hangover Medieval Style, the two-storied chimney at *Sans Souci* on Broadway represents the persistence of an early kind of "freestanding" stack into later times. The stack (p. 187) is actually an incipient — not a fully developed — freestanding or offset chimney. It stands a little bit free of the wooden gable as a protection against fire. Such a feature is believed to have been used in medieval English architecture because of the overhang of thatch along the rake of the gable. No one wanted to have dry thatch touching the chimney stack, which at times could

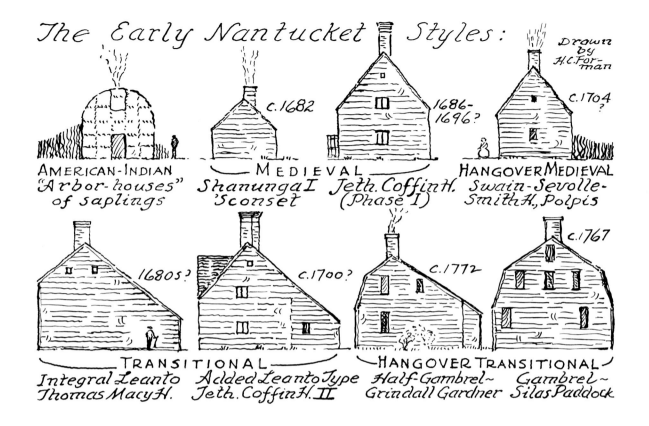

The Early Nantucket Styles:

Drawn by H.C. Forman

c.1682

1686-1696?

c.1704?

AMERICAN-INDIAN
"Arbor-houses"
of saplings

MEDIEVAL
ShanungaI
'Sconset

Jeth. Coffin H.
(Phase I)

HANGOVER MEDIEVAL
Swain-Sevolle-
Smith H., Polpis

1680s?

c.1700?

c.1772

c.1767

TRANSITIONAL
Integral Leanto
Thomas Macy H.

Added Leanto Type
Jeth. Coffin H. II

HANGOVER TRANSITIONAL
Half-Gambrel~
Grindall Gardner

Gambrel~
Silas Paddock

get hot. In Maryland and Virginia the freestanding chimney was a common form for 200 years and more, and in England for much longer than that.

Speaking of the persistence of the Medieval Style in Siasconset, we conclude with a short digest of the two chief styles of architecture found there: first, the Medieval, represented by *Shanunga* (I) and *Auld Lang Syne* (I), which lasted from the establishment of the whaling station about 1676 to about 1700 — some twenty-four years. Second, the Hangover Medieval, represented by the *George C. Gardner House* (p. 150), *Dexioma* (p. 159) and most of the other buildings of the old village, which flourished from about 1700 through the time of Edward F. Underhill's Pochick Street development of the 1880s in 'Sconset. For, of course, Underhill enthusiastically tried to imitate the early whaling habitations. His cottages represent as much a persistence of the style of the Middle Ages on these shores as does the *George C. Gardner House* of the mid-1700s and *Castle Bandbox* of 1814, also in 'Sconset.

OUTLINE OF THE NANTUCKET ARCHITECTURAL STYLES

EARLY:

1. American Indian: No known examples.
2. Medieval (c.1660 – c.1700):
       Examples: Shanunga (Phase I), 'Sconset.
                  Jethro Coffin House (I), Town.
3. Jacobean: Shown in details, like curved door heads.
4. Transitional (c.1680 –c.1730):
       Examples: Thomas Macy House, Tattle Court.
                  Jethro Coffin House (II), c.1700.
                  Elihu Coleman House, 1722.
                  Major Josiah Coffin House, 1724.
5. Hangover Medieval (c.1700 – c.1890):
       Examples: Old North Vestry, c.1730, Town.
                  Swain-Sevolle-Smith House (Phase I), Polpis.
                  George C. Gardner House, 'Sconset.
6. Hangover Transitional (from 1730):
       Examples: Svargaloka, 'Sconset.
                  Silas Paddock House, c.1767, Town.

LATE:

7. Georgian (c.1720 – c.1790):
       Examples: Maria Mitchell House, 1790, Town.
                  Job Macy House, 1750s, Town.
8. Federal or Early Republican (from c.1790):
    a) Hangover Georgian ("Post-Colonial"):
       Examples: 33 Milk Street, 1820, Town.
                  4 New Dollar Lane, 1809, Town.
    b) Classical Revival:
       Examples: Three Bricks, 1838, Town.
                  Athenaeum, 1847, Town.
9. Gothic Revival (c.1820 – c.1900) :
       Example: First Congregational Church, 1833.
10. Victorian Gothic (c.1865 – c.1900) :
       Examples: The Nantucket Hotel (destr.), Brant Point.
                  Underhill's Ever-Green Park, 1882, 'Sconset.

IX

The Two Oldest Known Buildings on Nantucket

1 – The Chief Discovery at Shanunga

BEFORE WE COME to survey Nantucket's only whaling village still standing, it seems meet to scrutinize two buildings in that settlement which are so significant to our story that they will form a guide to our understanding of most of the others. Both of them are *baulk* or *crogloft* dwellings and both stand on Broadway, 'Sconset; they are the oldest structures known to still stand on the Island.[1] We have mentioned them before: they are *Shanunga* and *Auld Lang Syne*. The former was also known as *Betsy Cary House* or *Saint's Rest;* the latter as the *Captain Henry Coleman House.*

In 1888 Underhill stated that the smaller portion of *Shanunga* was "near 200 years old and was brought from Sesachacha." On the other hand Hussey in his brochure[2] of 1912 claimed that the early section was then about 230 years old, an age which would point to around 1682 for its building date — the time when William Penn laid out the great city of Philadelphia. From our own studies of the early portion of the house we believe that the date c. 1682, is substantially correct; if it errs, it is on the side of being too late. Underhill also mentioned that the interior of the early part had been little changed, except to put on lath, plaster and paper, and that its rude beginnings can be seen in the exposed joists overhead.

Our discoveries at *Shanunga* in the summer of 1955 lend color to this account, and we here record a gist of them. The dwelling was then occupied by tenants who for a while condescended to allow the writer into the rooms to take measurements.

111

After studying the framed measured drawings of the house made in 1945 for the Historic American Buildings Survey, the writer found them to be so full of errors and omissions that it was decided to remeasure the whole place. The governmental sheets had missed, it seems, the most significant aspect of the building.

At all events the building contractor who was the tenant had gotten the owner's permission to make some interior alterations, and at the time of this author's visit was in the process of uncovering the framing of the fireplace end of the oldest portion of the domicile. Accidentally, but fortunately, the *footings* of an early brick fireplace were at that time exposed to view and were measured, as shown in our diagram of what we call the Phase II fireplace, page 113. Furthermore, the original treetrunk posts, splayed at top and bottom, were also uncovered along the fireplace wall, and together with the chimney girt above them had been roughly plastered over to keep the wood from burning. In fact over these framing members were soot marks from a thousand fires. Even the bevel-edged siding boards for a wide distance around the site of this fireplace were heavily blackened.

On this first visit the writer gained the loft of the early section and found still extant upon the old siding boards above the site of the fireplace a large area of soot, one inch thick — indisputable evidence of a wooden chimney. Rare as hen's teeth are wooden chimneys in the United States; consequently the one at *Sha-nunga* formed an important discovery.

The next day the writer, back again to complete his studies, found that the tenant and his family made long-continued excuses against an entry into the house. One of the children who brought out clothes to hang on the line let slip the reason: the author was *persona non grata* because unwittingly the previous day he had caused dirt to fall through cracks in the loft floor upon the clean white beds below. In truth the floor had swayed and bellied down when walked upon, and the filth had sifted through the ceiling boards. After intercession by the caretaker of *Sha-nunga*, the writer was permitted in the house for twenty minutes, while the tenants watched through open doorways the work of measuring.

Meanwhile the tenant contractor had been busy during the previous night. Without the slightest suspicion of what he had laid bare, he had covered up the fireplace wall with compo-boards in a hack job. The coincidence of the visit of a specialist and a contractor's uncovering of original source material about the fireplace might not have occurred again in three hundred years. But we had found the golden apple, and we did not let it go.

The brick (Phase II) fireplace — the footings of which were measured at that time — once projected through the north gable-end wall of the original structure *so that the inner face of the fireplace lined up with the bevel-edged siding boards*

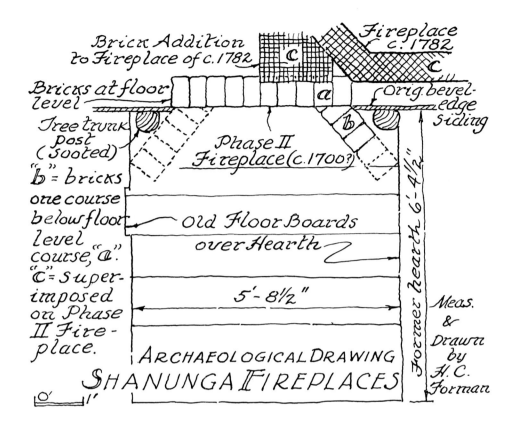

Brick Addition
to Fireplace of c. 1782

Fireplace
c. 1782

Bricks at floor
level

Tree trunk
post
(sooted)
"b" = bricks
one course
below floor
level
course "a".
"C" = super-
imposed
on Phase
II Fire-
place.

Phase II
Fireplace (c. 1700?)

Orig. bevel-
edge
siding

Old Floor Boards
over Hearth

5'- 8½"

Former hearth 6'- 4½"

Meas.
&
Drawn
by
H. C.
Forman

ARCHAEOLOGICAL DRAWING
SHANUNGA II FIREPLACES

0'   1'

both above and beside it. The sectional diagram on page 100 will help the reader to visualize this arrangement. There was no brick flue. The smoke rose freely without a channel from the hearth to the stack on the roof.

The fact that this brick fireplace once snugly fitted between treetrunk posts (p. 116) *which were wholly sooted all the way from the floor level to the chimney girt* proved that the fireplace was a later insertion in the wall — a technical point of the highest importance. What kind of fireplace must have been there before the brick one? A wooden one, without jambs — else how would the lower part of the treetrunk posts have been heavily sooted? The wooden fireplace may have been the common type of medieval lath-and-plaster backing, known as the rere-does, for fire prevention purposes.[3]

The *Betsy Cary House,* 'Sconset, when used as a post office, in August 1887. The "Shanunga" sign hangs from John Beard's cottage at the left. Captain Baxter is reading a letter in front of his land craft, the *Swiftsure. Baldwin Cooledge photo.* BELOW: *Tuckernook,* another whale house.

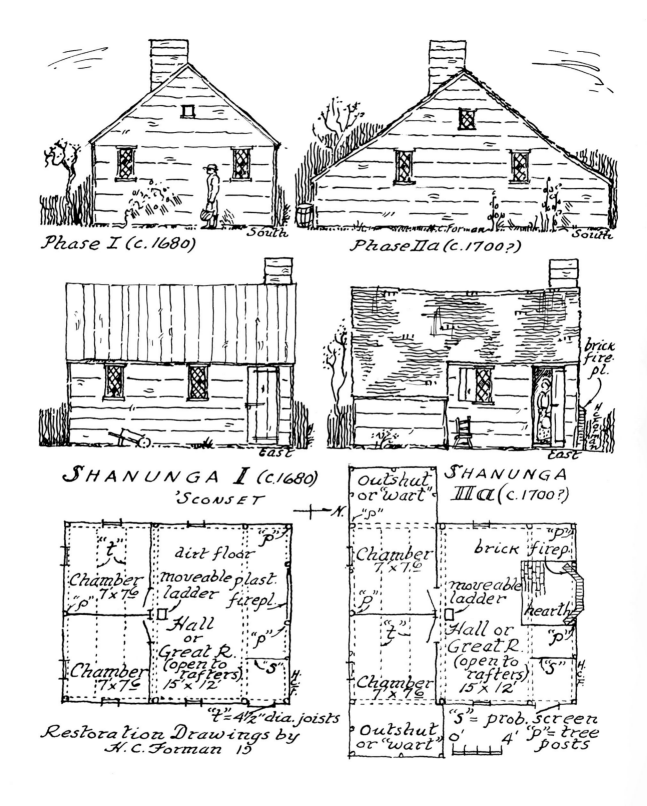

Phase I (c. 1680)

Phase IIa (c. 1700?)

SHANUNGA I (c. 1680)
'Sconset

SHANUNGA IIa (c. 1700?)

Restoration Drawings by
H. C. Forman 19

2 – Shanunga: The First House

Having outlined the archaeological discovery, we are now ready for the four evolving stages of *Shanunga* — steps shown briefly in our *Evolution Chart* on page 130. For the purpose of our restoration drawings we have shown the original Shanunga, Phase I (p. 116), comprising a Hall or Great Room, in size twelve feet by fifteen and open to the rafters, as well as a hanging-loft, reached by a moveable stepladder or by cleats, over two staterooms, each seven feet square. These twin chambers are separated from each other and from the Great Room by vertical board partitions. The interior construction of the cottage was entirely exposed to view; there were no plaster walls.

As has been mentioned before, on the right-hand side of the fireplace, at a distance of forty inches from the front doorway, the writer found that soot marks upon the bevel-edged siding ended in a straight, vertical line, indicating that there might have been some kind of a screen wall there to protect the fire on the hearth. There are three girders or tie-beams across the Great Room which have been shown dotted on our plan (p. 116). The first of these was the chimney girt, plastered over to keep it from burning. Then some forty inches out into the room was a summer beam; a second summer spanned the room just in front of the board partition and formed the edge of the baulk flooring.

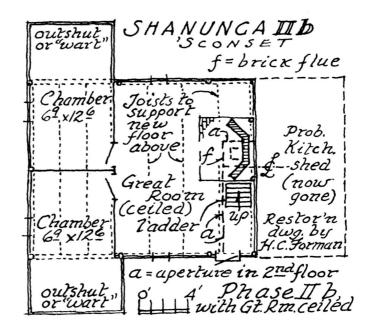

The six downstairs windows may have originally been wood casements with waxed paper over cross sticks or with wood calmes and glass. Accordingly the drawings have been made to show the simplest kind of casement. In the hanging-loft there was probably some kind of wind-hole for ventilation.

The roof construction was of trees and saplings. Wall plates some five-and-a-half or six inches in diameter were set up to carry the rafters, which were probably five inches in diameter. The sheathing formed probably up-and-down clinkers, as described in the last chapter.

Shanunga I formed the most elementary of whale houses; but its space was designed carefully to fulfill its function.

3 – Making a Full-Loft Cottage

Phase IIa — we have had to divide the second stage into two parts — saw the twin staterooms becoming too small for the occupants and the consequent building of warts or outshuts to make them larger, thus making a T-plan house (page 116). At that time, possibly about 1700, a wood floor downstairs was probably put in, and the Phase II brick fireplace already described was erected. From the evidence of the filler boards in the old boards of the Great Room floor the brick hearth projected out six feet into the room. In other words the fires were large and built not too close against the fireback — as they were earlier in the wooden fireplace. As indicated before, there was no flue to this fireplace, and the smoke rose up along the boards of the sooted gable-end.

It is curious that the outshut on the Broadway side was built slightly broader than the one on the Pump Square — perhaps the result of an early idiosyncrasy.

The next stage, Phase IIb, may have taken place soon after 1700. The occupants got rid of the hanging-loft by extending the floor the full length of the Great Room. Note that the floorboards over this room run lengthwise, instead of crosswise as over the staterooms, and are three inches higher. Evidence of a large hole[4] for a brick flue, rising from a new brick fireplace entirely within the building, may still be seen in the garret floor. Also the ladder was moved over against the chimney (p. 117).

The third stage, Phase III, brought the addition of a tall kitchen wing on the north side. Underhill thought that the highest portion of *Shanunga* was built about a hundred years before he wrote, 1888, thus indicating a time in the 1780s. The kitchen itself was capacious enough (p. 122) — twelve feet by twenty-three. Its fireplace backed up against the foundation of the old Phase II fireplace (p. 113) and even covered over part of it. In the two small bedchambers above the kitchen is a vertical board partition with large twig coat hooks (p. 136). With

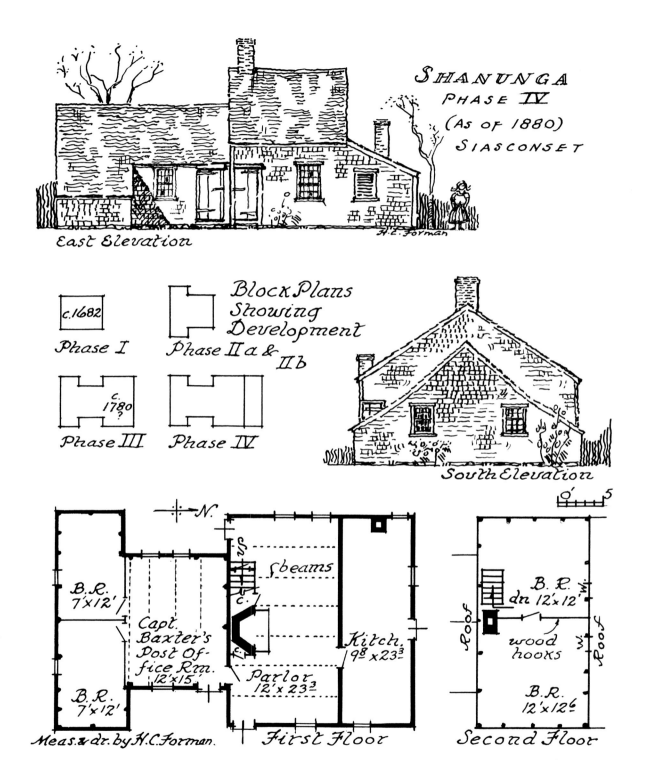

East Elevation

H.C. Forman

SHANUNGA
PHASE IV
(AS OF 1880)
SIASCONSET

Block Plans
Showing
Development

c.1682

Phase I

Phase IIa & IIb

c. 1780?

Phase III

Phase IV

South Elevation

N.

0' 5

B.R. 7'x12'

Capt. Baxter's Post Office Rm. 12'x15'

beams

c.

Kitch. 9⁸ x 23³

Parlor 12'x 23³

B.R. 7'x12'

Meas. & dr. by H.C. Forman.

First Floor

dn B.R. 12'x12'

Roof

wood hooks

Roof

B.R. 12'x12⁶

Second Floor

the scarcity of metal on Nantucket even as late as the 1780s, it was natural for the Islander to make his coathangers from the nearest tree.

It was possibly during this third phase that the downstairs floor of the "T"-house was painted in rug patterns of wavy parallel or fishnet lines of black on a gray field (p. 121).

The final development came in Phase IV, after 1800 or thereabouts, with a further addition to the north measuring seven and a half feet wide. This became the nineteenth-century kitchen lean-to. The earlier kitchen of the 1780s was then evidently paneled completely around with vertical boards and changed into a parlor. After that series of changes very little was done to Shanunga in the last 150 years.

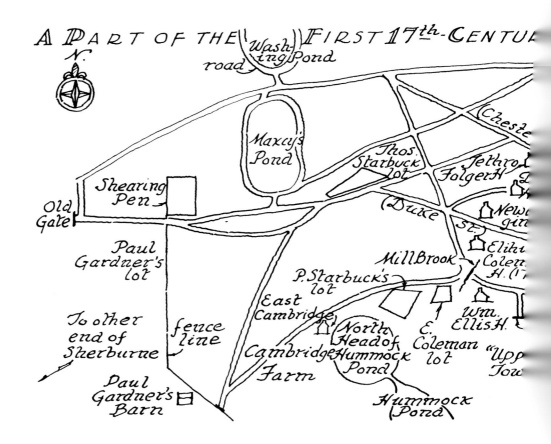

4 – Later History of Shanunga

Mr. Brown's governmental drawings include what he called a former early privy, actually a recent necessary house, located in the southeast corner of the yard and now destroyed. What did stand in that particular location was, according to Underhill, a little barn (p. 120) with its gable-end facing Pump Square. It was probably all that was "left of a house once owned by an old man named John Beard." As revealed by early photographs, the Beard hut stood there as late as 1911.

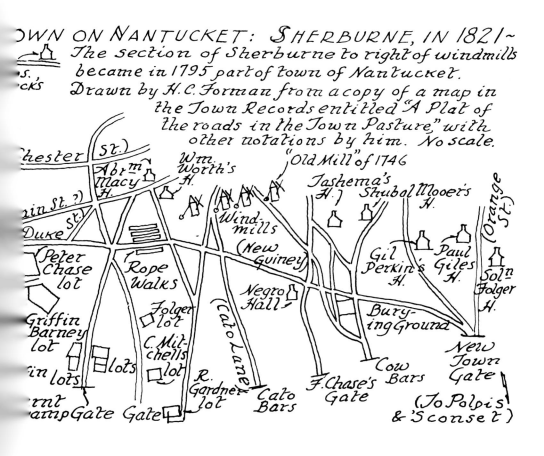

OWN ON NANTUCKET: SHERBURNE, IN 1821~

The section of Sherburne to right of windmills became in 1795 part of town of Nantucket. Drawn by H. C. Forman from a copy of a map in the Town Records entitled "A Plat of the roads in the Town Pasture," with other notations by him. No scale.

A man by the name of Uriah Swain owned *Shanunga*, probably about 1800. Our own researches have disclosed that in 1835 the owner was "B.C." — that Mistress Betsy Cary who gave the name to the house and who kept tavern there, as already described. Captain William Baxter became Mrs. Cary's son-in-law and for years brought the mail over to Siasconset from Town. Although Underhill's account gives the story as happening in the late nineteenth century, it could have happened in the late seventeenth as well, and therefore is worth repeating. "In the corner of the room where the business of the post office is carried on [evidently the original Great Room] is an ancient clock that has marked the hours for four or five generations. Mrs. [Betsy] Cary, the mother of Mrs. Baxter, for years used the building for a public house. For years before 1873 when the post office was established, it was used for the distribution of the mail matter brought from town by Capt. Baxter, who as he came over the hill on Main Street, tooted his fish horn; and the event of the day was the gathering of the people at the [post-office] window to await their mail matter, and for each letter or paper received, one whole cent went into the coffers of the grasping old mariner! And yet there are those who boldly assert that he did not get rich!"

The good Captain Baxter liked to toot his horn for the photographer (p. 123), or read the weekly paper in front of his eighteenth-century wooden lady figurehead, salvaged, it is thought, from the ship *Shanunga* which went ashore in 1852 at Tom Nevers Head. The quarter board from that wreck gave a brand-new name to the old Betsy Cary tavern.[5]

Painted Rug Patterns on Shanunga Floors

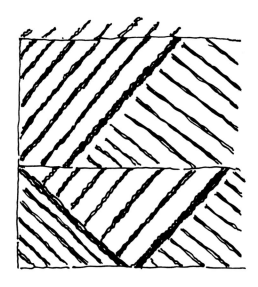

The parlor in the 1780 portion of the *Betsy Cary House*, or *Shanunga*, has some vertical board walls but the mantel is modern. *Photo, author.* BELOW: Hot 'taters and coffee on the kitchen hearth of *George C. Gardner House*, 'Sconset. *Wyer Photo.*

In front of the *Betsy Cary House*, Captain Baxter shows villagers how he blew his horn when he drove with mail over 'Sconset hill. BELOW: Baxter relaxes beside his ship's figurehead. Note Dickens-like boy at left.

"And Baby makes ten." *Auld Lang Syne,* 'Sconset, as it looked in 1880-82. This whaling cottage is the oldest known building on the Island. BELOW: View of 'Sconset from across South Gulley. *Baldwin Cooledge Photo (after 1887).*

5 – Introducing Auld Lang Syne

The other oldest known building on the Island is the *Captain Henry Coleman House,* generally called *Auld Lang Syne,* on Broadway, only two doors south of *Shanunga.* Because much of the original interior woodwork has disappeared from *Auld Lang Syne, Shanunga* forms the more valuable source material for a study like this one.

According to Underhill *Auld Lang Syne* (p. 124) is "without doubt the oldest house on the [Siasconset] Bank." Like *Shanunga* it was erected on its present site, and "is as it has appeared as far back as human memory can go, except that, within, it was at sometime lathed and plastered." Further, he went on to state: "It was first owned by Michael Coffin, who employed several Indians to fish for him during the season, while he remained ashore to do the cooking. . . . Its rough and ragged shingles, and depressions in the roof tell of its antiquity. In its battered front door are three worn out key holes. Within are large fireplaces leading to a heavy chimney. The house is claimed to have been built in 1675, and before a building had been erected on the site of the Town. In 1814, it was owned by Jonathan Upham" — thus rambled Underhill.[6]

6 – Like Shanunga Except for the Porch and Child's Closet

Auld Lang Syne went in its first two phases of development much like *Shanunga,* as may be seen in the Evolution Chart (p. 130). But the original rectangular hut was a foot shorter in length and a foot longer in width than *Shanunga,* and the staterooms a bit smaller. The ridgepole at *Auld Lang Syne* is only thirteen and a half feet from the ground.

Our isometric drawings (p. 127) show how the floor plan of the whale house was arranged in Phases I and IIa. There was probably a Phase IIb, as with *Shanunga,* where the hanging-loft became a full loft and the stepladder was moved over next to a new, brick, inside chimney. If anyone has any doubts that the Great Room was lofted over with beams and sawn boards, let that person crawl up to the garret and examine the division in the floorboards exactly at the edge of the hanging-loft.

Sometime in the very early nineteenth century, or even possibly in the 1790s, the roof of *Auld Lang Syne* was extended northward to make a kitchen addition some eleven and a half feet long, forming Phase III (p. 129). Back-to-back fire-

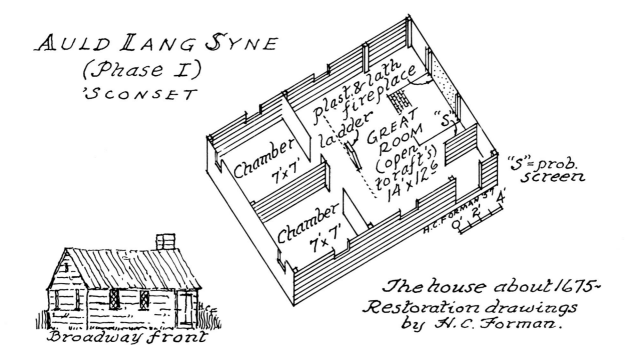

AULD LANG SYNE
(Phase I)
'SCONSET

Chamber 7'x7'

plast. & lath fireplace

ladder

GREAT ROOM (open to rafters) 14' x 12.6'

"S"

Chamber 7'x7'

H.C. FORMAN 37   0' 2' 4'

"S" = prob. screen

Broadway front

The house about 1675~
Restoration drawings
by H. C. Forman.

places were constructed, and the front doorway was moved a little further north-ward in order to come *en face* with the new ladder and new chimney.[7] Although at present open to the rafters, the kitchen was formerly lofted over; also the kitchen fireplace trim, rafters and wall plates, and much of the woodwork, except the two doors (p. 129) flanking the fireplace, are not original.

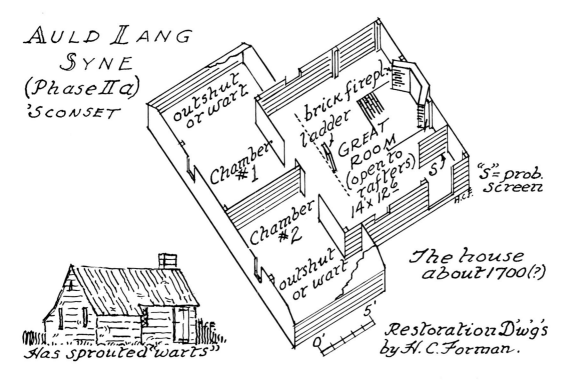

AULD LANG SYNE
(Phase IIa)
'SCONSET

outshut or wart

Chamber #1

brick firepl.

ladder

GREAT ROOM (open to rafters) 14' x 12.6'

"S"

Chamber #2

outshut or wart

H.C.F.

"S" = prob. screen

Has sprouted "warts"

The house about 1700(?)

0'   5'

Restoration Dwg's
by H. C. Forman.

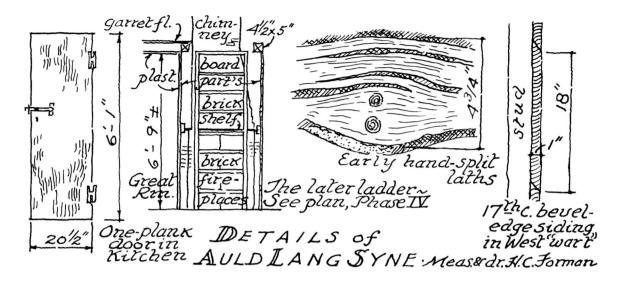

garret fl. · chimney 4½"x5"

plast.

board part's

brick shelf

brick fire-places

6'-9"

Great Rm.

The later ladder ~ See plan, Phase IV

6'-1"

20½"

One-plank door in Kitchen

Early hand-split laths

4¾

stud

18"

1"

17ᵗʰ c. bevel-edge siding in West "wart"

DETAILS of AULD LANG SYNE ·Meas.& dr. H.C. Forman

It was probably during Phase III that what we have called a Child's Closet Room was inserted. It formed a tiny three-foot-wide stateroom taken off of one of the twin staterooms, as may be seen in the floor plan on page 129. It is interesting that in a very few other whale cottages in Siasconset the same development occurred. In that period, too, the house was lathed and plastered — the laths (p. 128) being very irregular cuttings from pine boughs, and the wall plates were encased with beaded boards (p. 229) to give a dressier appearance.

Soon after 1890 a wart was added to the rear of the dwelling, forming the final development, Phase IV (p. 129). During the intervening years somebody sawed off at the ceiling level some of the vertical board partitions of Staterooms 2 and 3, in order to make a large Great Room. It is a great pity that *Auld Lang Syne*, the oldest structure known on Nantucket Island, has lost irretrievably much of its original framework and millwork.

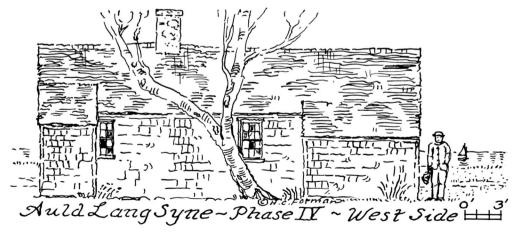

Auld Lang Syne ~ Phase IV ~ West Side   0' 3'

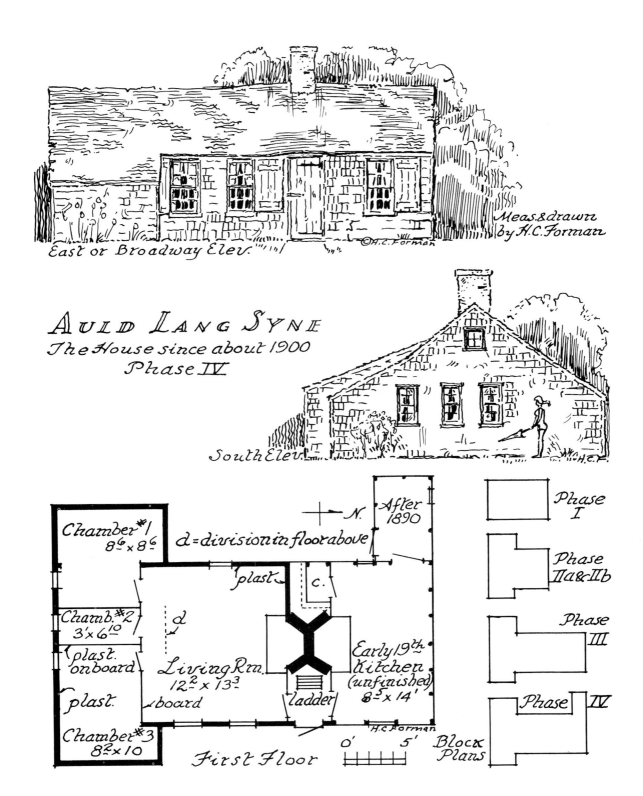

East or Broadway Elev.

Meas.&drawn
by H.C.Forman

©H.C.Forman

AULD LANG SYNE
The House since about 1900
Phase IV

South Elev.

H.C.F.

Chamber #1
8⁶ × 8⁶

d = division in floor above

After 1890

N.

plast.

c.

Chamb. #2
3' × 6¹⁰

d

plast.
on board

Living Rm.
12² × 13³

Early 19th
Kitchen
(unfinished)
8⁵ × 14'

plast.

board

ladder

Chamber #3
8² × 10

First Floor

H.C.Forman

0'   5'

Block
Plans

Phase
I

Phase
IIa & IIb

Phase
III

Phase IV

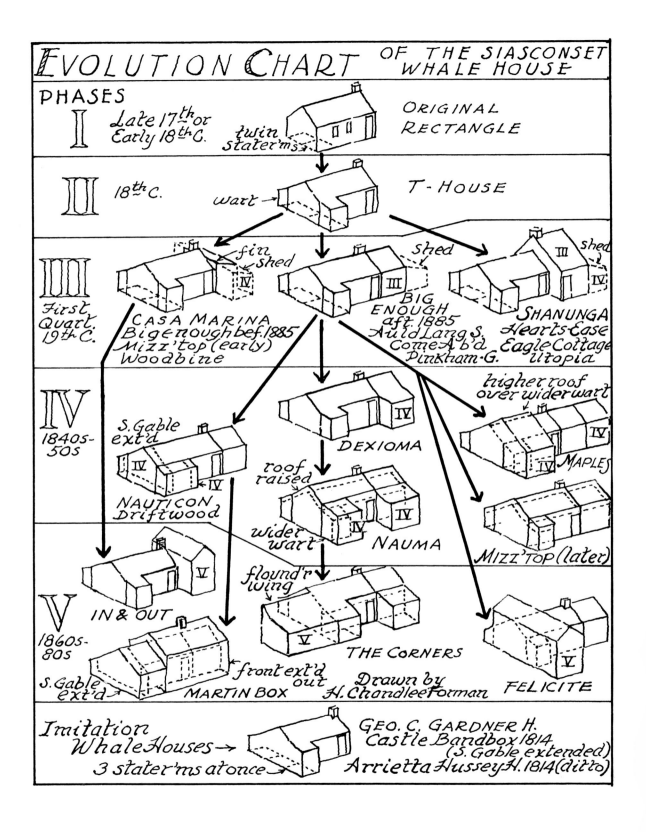

EVOLUTION CHART OF THE SIASCONSET WHALE HOUSE

PHASES

I Late 17th or Early 18th C. twin state'rms. ORIGINAL RECTANGLE

II 18th C. wart → T-HOUSE

III First Quart. 19th C. fin shed
CASA MARINA
Big enough bef. 1885
Mizz'top (early)
Woodbine

shed
BIG ENOUGH aft. 1885
Auld Lang S.
Come A.b'd
Pinkham·G.

shed
SHANUNGA
Hearts Ease
Eagle Cottage
Utopia

IV 1840s-50s
S. Gable ext'd
NAUTICON Driftwood

DEXIOMA

roof raised
wider wart
NAUMA

higher roof over wider wart
MAPLES

MIZZ'TOP (later)

V 1860s-80s
IN & OUT

S. Gable ext'd
front ext'd out
MARTIN BOX

flound'r wing
THE CORNERS

Drawn by H. Chandlee Forman

FELICITE

Imitation Whale Houses →
3 state'rms at once →

GEO. C. GARDNER H.
Castle Bandbox 1814
(S. Gable extended)
Arrietta Hussey H. 1814 (ditto)

X

Whale Houses and Lean-Tos on Lower Broadway: Svargaloka to Nauticon

1 – A Chart to Trace Development

THE FOREGOING CHAPTER has described the evolution of the two earliest structures known to be standing on Nantucket Island — whale houses which have not been changed very much by alterations and "so-called improvements." The remaining whale cottages in Siasconset for the most part have suffered many changes which in turn have greatly affected their appearance. Besides, it would be repetitive and tedious to describe at length each building in detail; therefore in order to save words we have classified all the ways in which the 'Sconset whale habitations developed, in an Evolution Chart (p. 130), a diagram which is the result of eleven years of research on early Nantucket buildings.

Structures in Siasconset which do not fit the whale-house category, such as our next example, below, have been given a full description in the text.

The surprising thing about the early village is that the buildings were so much alike, especially in their first stages of development. In a simple community like 'Sconset nonconformity was evidently frowned upon, so that nearly every home developed somewhat around the same plan. There were few exceptions to the standard. Nonetheless, our first abode to be described is very much the exception — a fact due largely to the place from which the cottage was transported. It is not a whale house at all.

131

Lower Broadway, 'Sconset, in the 1880s, showing, at left, the George C. Gardners in front of their cottage — an imitation whale house. Beyond are *High Tide* (Phase III) and *Casa Marina*. BELOW: A good view of *High Tide* (Phase IV) with the zigzag fence, of the same time.

2 – Svargaloka, Catslide Paradise

The village plan (p. 40) shows that the first property on Broadway north of the South Gulley Bridge, built before 1881, is a lot owned in 1834 by George Myrick on which he had a domicile — probably the same homestead described by Under-hill[1] as having been brought from Sesachacha early in the nineteeth century and later removed from Siasconset. At any rate nobody knows anything about the shape and appearance of the Myrick lair, so that our drawing of it for the re-construction of the 'Sconset Street (p. 72) had to be conjectural — one of the rare instances of such on those drawings.

At present an eighteenth-century farmhouse, *Svargaloka*, stands on the Myrick lot. It belonged to Charles C. Folger, and was brought by Elijah H. Alley before 1877 from Hawthorn Lane near Town to Siasconset. There was nothing unusual about that removal, for probably more than half of all early Nantucket buildings have been peripatetic. The above date, 1877, is, by the way, the year in which Miss Eva Channing, a student of Sanskrit, who named her cottage *Svargaloka*, "Land of Paradise," made a drawing of Broadway from an upper north window of the house (p. 155).[2]

The immediate cause of the removal of this farmhouse to 'Sconset has a good deal of human interest. We tell this story because it reveals a kind of colonial Nantucket party about which little seems to be known. A cornhusking gathering

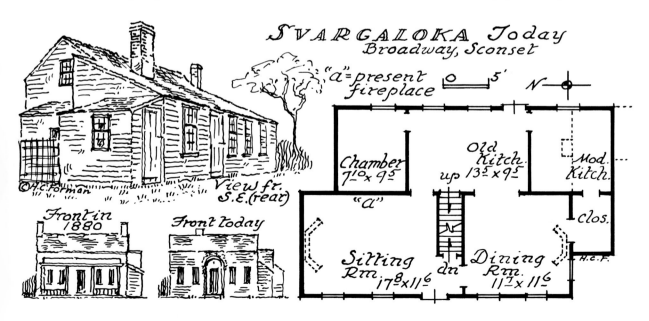

was held one night at Levi Coffin's farm back of Siasconset where all the young people of the neighborhood were having an extremely good time. In those days one of the games was to find the red ear of corn during the husking — the winning couple gaining the privilege of exchanging kisses in private. At this party the finders of the red ear went outside the house to osculate and were not too occupied with each other, it is said, to notice smoke rising from a point eight miles away, toward Town. It developed that the "bound boy" who lived on the Charles C. Folger farmhouse — later called *Svargaloka* — had been angry at not having been invited to the cornhusking celebration at Levi Coffin's and had set fire to a barn on the Folger farm. The barn unfortunately was full of cattle and freshly packed with corn. Soon after the fire Elijah Alley moved the Folger dwelling to 'Sconset; rebuilt, it became known as "Land of Paradise." Years afterward, the cellar hole of the Folger home was still to be seen along Hawthorn Lane.

As indicated *Svargaloka* does not fit the usual 'Sconset floor plan (p. 133). On the Broadway front are two sizeable rooms, a sitting room and a front bedchamber, the sizes of which are given on the drawing. At the rear are "cells" or "aisles" — rooms which make the dwelling a lean-to with a catslide roof, dropping low to the ground on the ocean side. The cell rooms run about eight-and-a-half feet square and comprise back bedchamber, dining room and kitchen. This last room projects outward from the south end of the house as a half-gable, somewhat in the same manner as that on *The Corners*, in the same village. Then, too, there are a couple of little warts or outshuts against this half-gable, making a very picturesque composition.

Close by the south gable-end of the place stood, in the 1890s, a small barn with a gable-end facing the street and with double-doors beside a single door (pp. 72, 124). At the rear of the barn was a necessary house with protective latticework and on the south side, at a point where the Bridge commenced across the South Gulley, were extensive fish racks.

When Broadway became more important than other village streets, all the cottages which fronted on Front Street and backed on Broadway had their front doors changed around to the Broadway side — that is, with the exception of *Svargaloka*, which was not one of the early 'Sconset buildings.

3 – Whale House Woodbine, Now Moved

Next north once upon a time stood a tiny cottage known as *The Woodbine* (p. 72), a quaint bower brought about 1820 from Sesachacha and rebuilt on Siasconset Bank in a manner so that it was set endwise to Broadway. Poor Owen

Parker is thought to have brought the habitation in pieces to 'Sconset, but to have pretended that he did not know how to put it back together again. The consequence was that certain inhabitants of kindly dispositions assisted in its rebuilding. In 1884 the lodging was moved to another location in the village — to the corner of Hill Street and McKinley Avenue, where it was grossly changed and given the name of *Thornycroft*.[3]

By means of a study of an old photograph (p. 115) and of what today remains of *The Woodbine*, forming part of the house on Hill Street, this writer has been able to make a rough restoration drawing (p. 72) which shows a whale dwelling with tiny twin staterooms. As illustrated in the Evolution Chart (p. 130), a kitchen or "porch" shed was added to the Broadway end of the house. The half-gable projections, called "fins" by this author, gave the place its character.

4 – How Bigenough's Kitchen Changed Shape

Close by *The Woodbine* on the north side once stood another whale domicile which shows in a few faded old photographs (pp. 115, 137). Unfortunately the tiny quarters by the name of *Bigenough* has been largely destroyed by turning it into a garage for the Victorian monstrosity, the *Big Sunflower*. Home of Abijah Swain and later of Henry Paddack, the earlier name of *Bigenough* was *Tuckernook*.[4] At first the kitchen was a low shed; then, after 1885, the shed disappeared and the main roof of the house was extended northward to cover a new kitchen addition. Both these additions are shown on the Evolution Chart (p. 130).

No one knows how many 'Sconset whale houses first had a shed kitchen, then later a kitchen covered by the main roof extended northward, but there must have been many examples. At any rate our restoration of the Broadway street (p. 72) shows the cottage with the *shed* kitchen "porch."

5 – Red-Ochred Sanford House and Two Others

At the lower end of Broadway, immediately opposite *Svargaloka*, is the small cottage of Captain John C. Morris, which originally was a very old barn. Next north of it once stood a small domicile which we have labeled the "Unknown House," because no one seems to know whose it was. At any rate the reader may inspect a drawing of it (p. 72).

On the southwest corner of Broadway and Main Street — the road which goes toward Town — was once situated the *Frederick C. Sanford House* (pp. 136, 137).

It was on that site as early as 1814 and formed the home of Peter Myrick, later (1835) becoming the property of James Macy. Underhill is authority for the statement that Captain Edward Joy believed the house was clinker-built and painted over with red ochre. At all events old photographs show it to be around 1860 a story-and-a-half cottage, having reached the early-nineteenth-century phase with porch shed on the east or Broadway side and a large wart on the south or rear. One photograph, taken soon after 1884 at the corner of Main Street and Broadway, shows an empty field surrounded by a picket fence where once stood the *Sanford House*.[5]

6 – Casa Marina Where Saucers Were Notched

There is a wider interval than the usual fourteen-foot roadway between what is left of the *Bigenough* building and the next abode northward, *Casa Marina,* in order to allow for the traffic from Main Street as it wound eastward to the Bluff.

Casa Marina itself is a whale house which has been much changed (pp. 137, 138). Underhill wrote of its former picturesque appearance and of its "strict" 'Sconset type to be seen. He claimed that it was standing in its present location in 1814 and was owned by John Russell, but our own investigations[6] revealed that it perhaps should not be included in the view of the restored Broadway street (p. 71). "Aunt" Sarah Coleman was another owner of *Casa Marina,* and she was reputed to be very pernickity about her furniture and knick-knacks. She marked her plates, cups and saucers by filing notches on their edges.

Rear of the Frederick C. Sanford House (gone)

Unknown H. (gone)

An old photograph showing where Broadway crosses Main Street in 'Sconset. Fence of *Sanford House* in foreground; *Casa Marina* beyond. BELOW: Lower Main Street in 1860s, showing *Sanford House* in center. *A. J. Freeman Photo.*

A view of *Casa Marina,* 'Sconset, probably in the 1880s, before it was greatly altered. Beyond is *Bigenough,* after the kitchen shed "porch" had been removed.

Our restoration drawings of the homestead are based on old photographs and on measurements of the existing structure (pp. 71, 139). The development is shown on the Evolution Chart, where it may be seen that the building evolved like *Bigenough* and *The Woodbine.* Note, too, the whole south gable-end was extended outward to give more space to the twin staterooms.

In spite of the stripping of almost all the old woodwork, there still remains a couple of two-panel doors of the eighteenth century. A post with bracketed top, marked "p" on the floor plan (p. 139), has been covered by plaster. In Underhill's time there was a perpendicular ladder in the Great Room which led up to the little five-foot-high hanging-loft which Mrs. Almy, the postmistress, many a time in her girlhood days climbed to sleep in an old-fashioned cot bed.

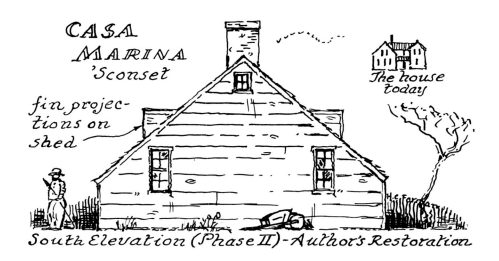

CASA MARINA 'Sconset

fin projections on shed

South Elevation (Phase II) - Author's Restoration

The house today

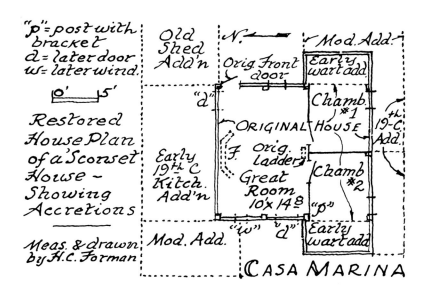

"p" = post with bracket
d = later door
w = later wind.

0'   5'

Restored House Plan of a 'Sconset House - Showing Accretions

Meas. & drawn by H.C. Forman

Old Shed Add'n

N.

Orig. Front door

"d"

ORIGINAL

Early 19th C Kitch. Add'n

F

Orig. Ladder

Great Room 10' x 14⁸

Mod. Add.

"w"   "d"

Mod. Add.

Early wart add.

Chamb. *1

HOUSE

Chamb. *2

"p"

Early wart add.

19th C. Add.

CASA MARINA

An interesting though spotted view, made from a glass plate, showing the *Lucretia M. Folger House,* left, before its Greek Revival dressing. BELOW: *Casa Marina,* with *High Tide* beyond it.

The old *High Tide,* 'Sconset, was removed from this earthly scene about 1900. This view shows its fourth or final phase, embellished by Harrison Gardner's Norman-Chevron fence.

7 – The Ebbing of High Tide

A Victorian dwelling stands today on the site of *High Tide,* one house north of *Casa Marina,* and was brought there about 1900 from Ever-Green Park, an Underhill development once located at the beginning of the North Bluff, 'Sconset.

High Tide was, it appears, not much better than a chameleon, because it frequently changed its aspect. Although not a trace of the old building remains, the writer has pieced together bit by bit the four main phases of development of the domicile (p. 143). Its development, by the way, does not fit any of the categories in our Evolutionary Chart (p. 130), so it is necessary to give a description. The first step, Phase I, possibly dating from the very end of the seventeenth century, comprised a little Great Room, twelve feet by fourteen in size, open to the rafters, with twin staterooms and hanging-loft or baulk. In the early eighteenth century *High Tide* became a "T"-house in the usual way. From then on the habitation developed uniquely. In Phase III (p. 71) it was considerably altered and enlarged, the roof tree having been lengthened to the northward to include a sizeable kitchen addition, which in Phase IV (p. 141) was made greater in depth and higher than the little "T"-house of Phase II. These changes are well illustrated in the photographs of the 1860s (pp. 137, 140).

Even Underhill took note that within nine years — that is, between 1879 and 1888 — *High Tide* was twice enlarged, and according to him each enlargement has made it even more 'Sconsety in appearance than before. Perhaps by this time the reader can guess what " 'Sconsety" means.

In Phase V a dining room, and beyond it a new kitchen, were added on the ocean side of the old Great Room, then called the Parlor. In the dining room itself a ladder was suspended from the ceiling by a rope in nautical fashion, so that you could gain access to the loft. Under the floor was a cold cellar reached by a trap door. Further, the roof of this oldest portion of the cottage became higher than the roof of the wing to the north.[7]

It has not been learned exactly when *High Tide* was destroyed, but it was probably between 1893 and 1900 when the owners decided that the antiquated relic should be moved elsewhere in the village. It was not foreseen that when the ancient pile was loaded upon a wagon, the structure would fall down like a pack of cards. 'Sconset buildings easily went up and more easily came down.

The lower end of Broadway, in the 1880s, with *Svargaloka* in the distance.

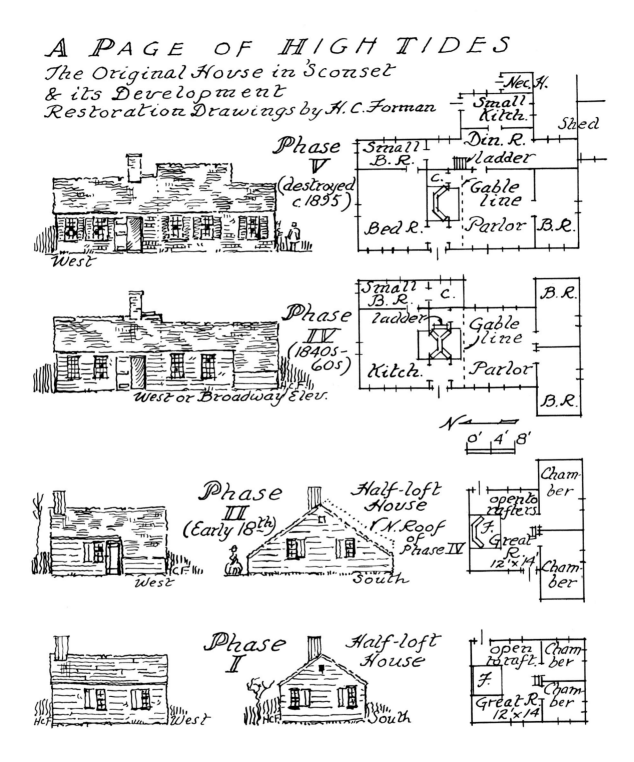

A PAGE OF HIGH TIDES
The Original House in 'Sconset
& its Development
Restoration Drawings by H. C. Forman

Phase V (destroyed c. 1895)

West

Nec. H.
Small Kitch.
Din. R.
Shed
Small B. R.
ladder
C.
Gable line
Bed R.
Parlor
B. R.

Phase IV (1840s–60s)

West or Broadway Elev.

Small B. R.
C.
B. R.
ladder
Gable line
Kitch.
Parlor
B. R.

N
0' 4' 8'

Phase III (Early 18th)

Half-loft House
N. Roof of Phase IV

West
South

Chamber
open to rafters
F.
Great R. 12'x14'
Chamber

Phase I

Half-loft House

West
South

open to raft.
Chamber
F.
Great R. 12'x14'
Chamber

"19th c. Stable   *East or Broadway Elev.*

0'   4'

Nauticon Lodge Today
Measured & drawn by H. C. Forman

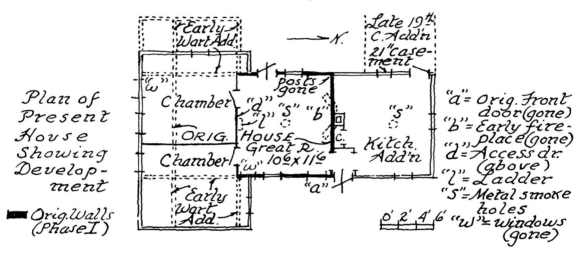

Plan of
Present
House
Showing
Develop-
ment

■ Orig. Walls
(Phase I)

"Early
Wart Add."

→ N.

Late 19th
C. Add'n

21" case-
ment

"w"

Chamber   "d" "s" "b"

posts
gone

"s"

ORIG.   HOUSE
"l"

Chamber   Great R.
"w"   10⁶ x 11⁶

c.

Kitch.
Add'n

"a"

"Early
Wart
Add."

"a" = Orig. Front
door (gone)
"b" = Early fire-
place (gone)
"d" = Access dr.
(above)
"l" = Ladder
"s" = Metal smoke
holes
"w" = windows
(gone)

0' 2' 4' 6'

The South
Gable Re-
stored

Exist'g

Showing Phase II ~
with Early "Wart"
Additions

Hanging-Loft
Section

Whitewash'd
Sheath'g

Metal
louvre
"s"

plast. ceil.

Ladder

8 – A Folger House Which Canted

Across Broadway from *High Tide* stands a white clapboarded dwelling, recently known as the *Lucretia M. Folger House* (p. 146), which had its beginning in an old cottage belonging to Peter Chase. The roof is surmounted by a walk, but it was not always thus: it originally was a very plain, shingled edifice, with a cat-slide roof, now gone, and no walk. In the native tongue adapted by Underhill in his account, the house "canted over to the westward," that is, toward Centre Street. In the 1860s there were seventeen courses of black dilapidated shingles on the front (p. 140), and only eleven on the back. The place has been changed around so much that it did not seem worthwhile to make a floor plan of it. It was a lean-to with central chimney, never a whale house (p. 72). The village plan (p. 40) shows that Peter Chase's lot was part of the No. 1 Sheep Common and lay where "His House Stands."

9 – Unusual Louvres and Loft at Nauticon

The next homestead to the north is *Nauticon Lodge,* already mentioned in a former chapter in connection with the development of its hanging-loft, shown on the diagrams on pages 85 and 86. As has been described, the triangular space above the hanging-loft was boarded in for privacy from the Great Room, and a small door inserted. When the plaster ceiling to the Great Room was put in at a height of halfway up the rafters, a kind of plaster box ("a" on page 86) was built in the ceiling so that the little door could continue to open outward — the only example of such a contraption in the village.[9]

Nauticon was probably built in the very early eighteenth century, though there is the possibility that it is very late seventeenth century. Today it has a sign on it reading "1734," whereas Underhill in his day noted a sign with "1735" and volunteered the information that Captain Edward Joy thought that the building was much older. Among the owners of the property were Obed Coffin, his son-in-law Jonathan Colesworthy, and Josiah Sheffield, who was found by this writer to have had in 1835 as the "contents of this Piece, a House."[10]

How *Nauticon* expanded through four phases is shown both on the Evolution Chart and on the floor plan (p. 144). It is very interesting that the early wart additions to the twin staterooms were extended a little to the northward, while the staterooms themselves were projected outward to the south.

A good, clear picture, taken in the 1880s, looking north on Broadway, 'Sconset, showing at left the *Lucretia M. Folger House* in Greek Revival dress, with *Nauticon* beyond. On near right, *Casa Marina. Wyer Photo.*

One of the significant discoveries occurred at *Nauticon* with the finding of metal louvres with chains to open shutters for the purpose of letting out smoke. The louvres are in the center of the ceilings of the Great Room, now the Parlor, and of the Kitchen, and above them in the roof there used to be further louvres which have now disappeared. Marked "s" on the floor plan, they date from the nineteenth century and may even be Victorian. Nevertheless they are symbolic in that they approximate the nearest thing on Nantucket and perhaps in New England to the *English medieval* louvre, where the smoke rose lazily from a central bonfire to a louvre or vent hole in the roof. At this cottage is perhaps a faint echo of a medieval feature once common to the great halls of Great Britain.

It was at *Nauticon* that a nine-pane casement was found (p. 107); in fact the original windows may have been all casements and wind-holes. But in the restoration drawings (pp. 72, 99, 144) they have been shown as narrow guillotine sash of eight panes, like those illustrated in early photographs of the south gable (pp. 45, 162). As for the floor plan, the board partition between the staterooms was probably on center and there was no middle window in the gable-end.

That the earliest part of *Nauticon* dates from around 1700 is indicated by the small scale of the structure — the Great Room being scarcely large enough to contain a small family seated; and by the small doors to the staterooms, only five feet and seven inches high — scarcely enough for our modern American teenagers to pass through without stooping. The exterior plank doors themselves are only a couple of feet wide and lack three to four inches of being six feet high — not sufficiently ample for many American men.

Sheffield Lane (p. 40) is the narrow and short space of grass between *Nauticon* and a cottage fully discussed in the last chapter, *Auld Lang Syne*. It is also interesting that along with his lot and house, Josiah Sheffield held a tiny piece of ground to the southward, separated from it by a one-rod-wide street which no longer exists and which is now blocked by the *Nauticon* stable or barn.

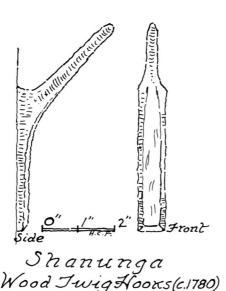

Side

Front

Shanunga
Wood Twig Hooks (c.1780)

Whale Houses on Middle Broadway: Gardner House to Martin Box

1 – First Imitation Whale House

So many of the early Siasconset buildings were built alike and developed along similar lines that it may seem monotonous to the reader to take note of or describe each one. But for the record it seems worthwhile to be pernickity, as the Islanders would say, about each structure.

An example belonging to the Hangover Medieval Style of architecture is the *George C. Gardner House* (p. 150), located on the east side of Broadway just north of the site of the old *High Tide*. A sign with the date, "1751," is presently affixed to the Gardner House, but that year is the vaguest guess. It is said that the sign-painter knew how to make only ones, fives and sevens. Be that as it may, Underhill believed that the homestead was erected by Prince Gardner, and that "it stood there in 1814." The architecture of the house is such that it may have been built in the second quarter of the eighteenth century. Inasmuch as Prince Gardner did not take a wife, Anna Swain, until 1792, it does not appear that he constructed the dwelling.[1]

Like almost all the early cottages on the east side of Broadway the abode faced not that street, but Front Street. But the place did not follow the developmental pattern of the usual lodging in the village, that is, commencing with a rectangle for floor plan. It seems to have at first been built as a "T," if evidence of the positions of the great diagonal braces of the wood framework is any criterion (see plan inked solidly black, p. 152). The whole frame of the "T"-house appears to have been

149

mortised, tenoned and pegged together — one piece. The place, too, is more capacious than the usual whale cottage, the Great Room being nearly eleven feet by seventeen in size. Further, that room seems never to have been open to the rafters, because an elaborate beam-and-girder system was constructed in order to make a large loft chamber above it. Also these beams have eighteenth-century beading upon them. And lastly the arrangement of the three staterooms on the first floor — all of equal size to the very inch — and the neat, balanced manner of placing the doors and windows in these chambers indicate strongly that the "T"-dwelling was all of a piece.

The *George C. Gardner House,* Broadway, seems to have been built originally as a "T" and formed an imitation whaling house. It is more capacious than the usual 'Sconset dwelling. *Photo, Hamar.*

THE GEORGE C. GARDNER HOUSE
'Sconset 0'——5' East or OceanSide

In other words, at the time the *George C. Gardner House* was started, it copied not the simple, early, rectangular whale huts, but those which had already sprouted warts on the staterooms — "T"-homesteads. As the engraved copper plate of 1791 proves, the majority of the 'Sconset structures of that time were "T"s. In short, the *Gardner House* is actually an imitation whale house, and has been represented as such on the Evolution Chart (p. 130).

The steep staircase beside the chimney, with a door at the next-to-bottom step, is wedged into a tiny entry facing the former front door. The lower steps are set slantways, turning toward the door to the Great Room and away from the kitchen door — a very good indication that when the steps were built, there was no kitchen "porch" addition.

Of special interest is the Wyer photograph (p. 156) of the kitchen with Joe Clapp on the left and George C. Gardner on the right. Although the scene was made in 1882, these men sit with old-fashioned clay pipes before the fire as generations of 'Sconseters had done before them — as far back as a century before the American Revolution. Wyer entitled his original view, "Sailing Old Voyages Over."

2 – To Headache House and Dexioma

North of the *Gardner House* and on the same lot once stood a long, narrow dwelling with gable-ends facing Broadway and Front Street. This was called *Headache House*, because of its incurably smoky chimney, and was owned at one time by Jonathan Chase (p. 155). Also once the hut was doubled in length, the

·NORTH·   ·WEST·

·SOUTH·

THE GEORGE C. GARDNER HOUSE
'SCONSET
In the Late 19ᵗʰ Century

■ Original House

☐ Additions

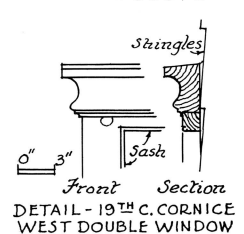

Shingles

Sash

0" 3"

Front   Section

DETAIL—19ᵀʰ C. CORNICE
WEST DOUBLE WINDOW

Meas. & drawn by
H. C. Forman '55

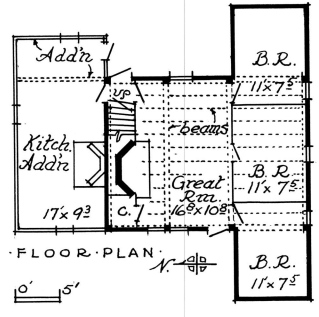

Add'n

up

Kitch.
Add'n

17'x 9³

beams

B.R.
11'x 7⁵

Great
Rm.
16⁸x 10⁸

C.

B.R.
11'x 7⁵

B.R.
11'x 7⁵

·FLOOR·PLAN·   N

0' 5'

newer half extending toward Broadway. A blank gable-end faced Front Street, and the other end is shown only conjecturally in our restoration of the Broadway thoroughfare (p. 71). The smoky chimney stood near the Front Street gable just north of the roof ridge. In the long south elevation there was only one small window.[2]

One of the most perfect gems of all the 'Sconset whale houses is *Dexioma*, from the Greek, $\triangle E \equiv I\Omega MA$, meaning Welcome. The place was formerly known as the *Captain George Wilber House* and in 1814 was owned by Stephen Hussey. From its architecture the building evidently dates from the first half of the eighteenth century. When Captain Wilber was making some alterations, he found behind a diagonal beam four copper cents of the dates 1800, 1801, 1802 and 1803, as well as an old Spanish coin with the pillars of Hercules, worth six-and-one-quarter cents and current in the early nineteenth century.[3]

The south portion of *Dexioma* is the original cabin, which comprised a small Great Hall and twin staterooms — a phase which is still preserved in the present cottage (pp. 71, 159). Our Evolution Chart (p. 130) shows how the abode developed, even the kitchen extension to the northward sprouting side warts in the 1840s or '50s. The front kitchen wart, that is, the outshut on the *old* front facing Front Street, contains a narrow bedchamber and a small pantry with trap door in the floor covering a circular storage bin of cobblestone, shown in the diagram on page 158. At what period the kitchen became a bedroom is not known, but it possesses four built-in drawers next to the fireplace. The Boat House, just east of the house, once had double doors, and is of interest as having a mast and tree-studs.

3 – Snug Harbor, an "L"-Whale House

Insofar as we have been able to survey the next building to the north by the name of *Snug Harbor*, the present structure had its beginning in the usual rectangle, but did not develop the habitual two warts on the twin staterooms. Evidently the fisherfolk forgot to put a little outshut on the rear or Broadway side, so that the place was an "L." Then, too, the partition separating the staterooms may early have been placed off-center of the house, as it remains today (p. 160). The west stateroom is characterized by diagonal corner braces set, not between corner posts and sill as customary, but between corner posts and wall plates. Perhaps the salty joiners thought that they were working on shipboard.

Snug Harbor is known to have belonged to Seth Folger and later to John H. Shaw.[4] The view of the restoration of Broadway (p. 71) also shows the cottage, but its development is not shown on the Evolution Chart because of its lopsidedness.

Paneling (restored) in an Imitation
Whale House : The George Gardner H.

4 – Traces of Quaint Rose Cottage

Between *Auld Lang Syne* and *Shanunga* stands today a Victorian edifice, *General Quarters* or *Barnaby Lodge*, which occupies the site of a little tumble-down structure by the name of *Rose Cottage,* removed in 1881 by Captain Charles H. Rule. This cottage (pp. 72, 155) was squatty and is said to have contained only four rooms; further, it had been twice removed from the edge of the Bank, being so small a structure that the change of site was easily effected by rolling it on spars.

Each year it was occupied in the summertime and in the fishing season. In 1814 it served as the home of Benjamin Paddack. One cannot give credence to the tradition that it once was an Indian wigwam, because the person starting that story had no idea what was a wigwam.

No one seems to have known what happened to *Rose Cottage* after it was torn down. This writer very much by accident learned of the existence of the remains of the housing on Morey Lane in 'Sconset and found there that it had become a combination pink "sandwich" of Victorian and Twentieth-Century work. Only the overall size of the house, eighteen by twenty-eight feet, remained to contribute anything to the restoration drawing (p. 72). Everything else had been changed: even the floor heights had been increased. What a pity that a building which was thought by Underhill to have been probably older than *Auld Lang Syne* (c. 1675) should have suffered such outrageous improvements.[5]

5 — What Man Hath Wrought at Liberty Hall and Mizzentop

On Broadway, opposite to the house known as *Shanunga* and to the abbreviated street called Mitchell, stands a dwelling which in olden time was named *London Tower*, but which in recent years goes by the appellation of *Liberty Hall*. Although this habitation had its origins in a fisherman's whale shanty, such as has been shown in our restoration of the Broadway street (p. 71), Underhill admitted that the place had been extended by a second-story wart, extensive changes had been made within and without and the fisherman's cottage is no longer to be seen.[6] What a minimization! Even though the overall size of the dwelling — twenty-seven-and-a-half by twenty-and-a-half feet — is still there, not a piece of original woodwork inside or out is visible. All the windows, the front door and the narrow clapboards are of nineteenth-century vintage.

A little of the early house may be seen in the three chronological photographs of about 1885 through 1890 (p. 162).

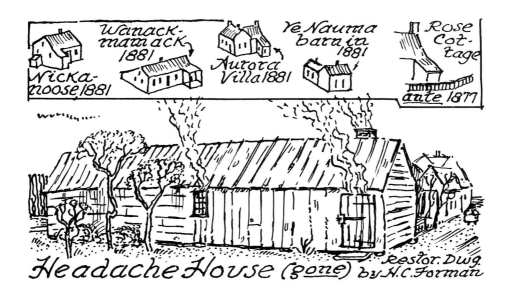

Headache House (gone)   Restor. Dwg. by H.C. Forman

Retired sea captains Joe Clapp, left, and George Gardner in the *Gardner House* kitchen, 1882. *Wyer Photo*.

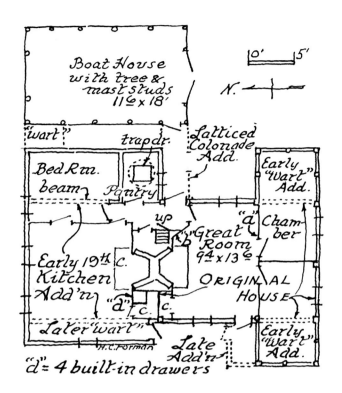

Boat House
with tree &
mast studs
11⁶ x 18'

0'   5'

N.

"wart"   trapdr.   Latticed
Colonade
Add.

Bed Rm.
beam   Early
"Wart"
Add.

Pantry

up   "a"   Chamber

Early 19th c.   "b" "Great
Kitchen   Room
Add'n   94x13⁶

"a" c.   c.   ORIGINAL
HOUSE

Later "wart"
H.C.Forman   Early
Late   "Wart"
"d"= 4 built-in drawers   Add'n   Add.

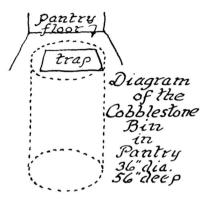

Pantry
floor

trap

Diagram
of the
Cobblestone
Bin
in
Pantry
36" dia.
56" deep

DEXIOMA
Today
in Siasconset
Original House
Early 18th Century

Measured & Drawn
by H.C. Forman

Present South Elev.
(Boat H. doors restored)

Present
West Elev.
(without 19th c.
vestibule)

1½" VERT. BATTEN
ON PARTITION
DETAILS   "b"

2¼" DOOR TRIM

"a"

Dexioma, the *Captain George Wilber House,* 'Sconset, was built in the first half of the 18th century. *Photo, author.* BELOW, RIGHT: *Dexioma* before 1920. LEFT: *Sans Souci* in very late 19th century.

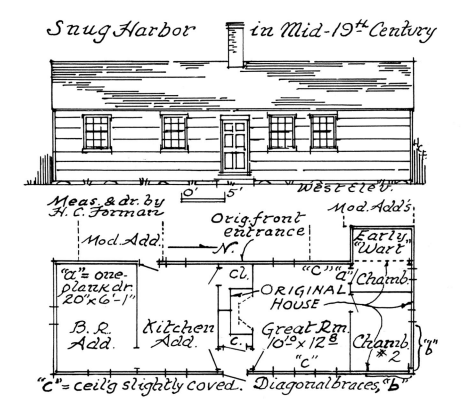

Snug Harbor in Mid-19th Century

West Elev.

Meas. & dr. by H. C. Forman

Orig. front entrance — N.

Mod. Add's.

Mod. Add.

Early "Wart"

"a" = one-plank dr. 20"x6'-1"

cl.

"C" "a" Chamb.

ORIGINAL HOUSE

B. R. Add.

Kitchen Add.

C.

Great Rm. 10'-0" x 12'-8"

Chamb. #2

"b"

"C"

"C" = ceil'g slightly coved. Diagonal braces, "b"

Next north on Broadway is the *Mizzentop* (pp. 70, 164), obviously named for either the mizzen-topmast staysail, or the mizzen-topgallant staysail, of a full-rigged ship. The place was occupied in 1814 by Captain Edward Joy's father when he was building *Castle Bandbox* on Shell Street, and in 1834 by one "G.B.U." — evidently George Bupton, whose "House Lot" it was. In 1865 *Mizzentop* was purchased by Joseph Mitchell, who, according to Underhill, modernized it before 1879.

The Evolution Chart (p. 130) illustrates the homestead with a kitchen shed "porch" on the north end in the first quarter of the nineteenth century, and then later with the "porch" changed into a wing covered by the extended main roof of the building, as was done at *Bigenough*. The eaves were also raised twenty-two inches to make more headroom in the loft, and a gable was put on the roof facing Broadway. These are but a few of the changes which overtook the old captains' homestead.[7]

Small Net Anchor from Nantucket

H.C.F.

length 12½"

The Great Room paneling (p. 85) is of interest in having a two-panel door for the left-hand stateroom and board doors for the other two chambers. Originally, of course, the doors must have been of the same design to match each other. As at *Auld Lang Syne* there is a small child's closet room taken off one of the twin staterooms probably at the time the house became a "T." The child's sleeping space is only three feet wide.

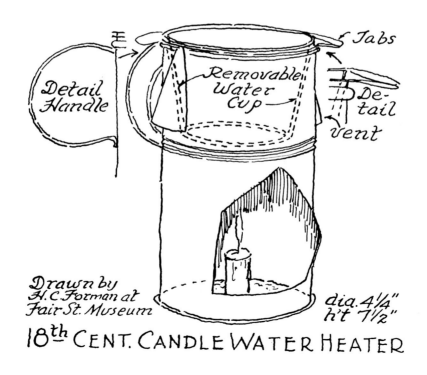

Detail Handle

Removable Water Cup

Tabs

Detail vent

Drawn by H.C. Forman at Fair St. Museum

dia. 4¼" h't 7½"

18ᵗʰ CENT. CANDLE WATER HEATER

Upper Broadway, 'Sconset (view No. 1), probably about 1885. At right is ancient whaling house *Liberty Hall,* dressed in narrow clapboards and crenellated "attic." On left is *Shanunga* and, beyond it, *The Maples.*

View No. 2 of Upper Broadway, probably in 1887, with a glimpse of the *Mizzentop,* beyond *Liberty Hall.* There is a new lamp post, and a new bust on *The Maples. Cooledge Photo.* BELOW: The same (view No. 3), probably about 1890.

6 – Lords of the Tall Tale

The House of Lords (p. 163) is the next cottage beyond the *Mizzentop,* and was built, it is said, by Gershom Drew — date unknown. Underhill claimed it was a typical Siasconset house of the larger size, then was sold by Captain Brown Gardner, whereupon it became enlarged so that it had no longer any resemblance to a quaint fisherman's abode. It had been purchased by Captain Gardner after his return from California some time in the 1850s for twenty-five dollars and four quintals or hundredweight of codfish. One would like to be able to purchase today an original colonial whale house for twenty-five dollars and some fish thrown in for the bargain. But that *was* 'Sconset.

In the *House of Lords* the fishermen for years met at night during the fishing season to swap lies about their experiences on shipboard. They were, in short, lords of the tall tale and fish story.

Our restoration drawings (p. 70) show the lodging to have been in the nineteenth century a short structure squeezed in between two cottages, but deep through to Front Street. Because of the wide gable-ends the ridge was forced high in the sky. One entered the Parlor from Broadway, and there were two windows to the left of the front door. There was a Parlor fireplace, still in position, with a little closet beside it, under a steep staircase. The garret today carries much of its old floorboards.

West or Broadway Elev.

THE HOUSE OF LORDS 'Sconset

The house in the 1840s & 50s Restorat'n dw'g by H. C. Forman

The house today

Kitch.? Prob. early front door

Parlor 9½ x 16½ Prob. early firepl. Prob. line of early front

Early "wart add." Mod. Add.

Chamber #1

Chamber #2

up Early "wart add."

BLOCK PLAN

N. 0' 5'

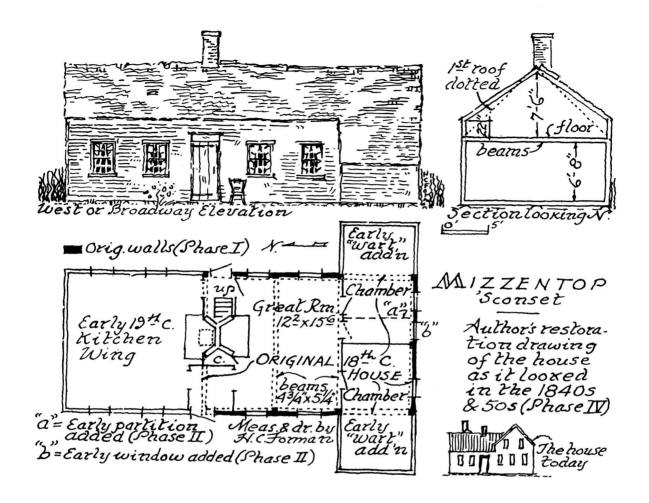

West or Broadway Elevation

Section looking N.

1st roof dotted

floor beams

Orig. walls (Phase I)

N.

Early 19th C. Kitchen Wing

up

Great Rm. 12²×15⁹

ORIGINAL 18th C. HOUSE

beams 4¾×5¼

Early "wart" add'n

Chamber "a"

"b"

Chamber

Early "wart" add'n

"a" = Early partition added (Phase II)
"b" = Early window added (Phase II)

Meas. & dr. by H. C. Forman

MIZZENTOP 'Sconset

Author's restoration drawing of the house as it looked in the 1840s & 50s (Phase IV)

The house today

On the south was a small wing which projected out from the Broadway front about a foot and a half — scarcely the typical wart of four feet in depth.

How the *House of Lords* appeared in the eighteenth century may be figured out, although it has been omitted from the Evolution Chart. The original rectangle probably measured twenty feet long by seventeen wide, including twin staterooms each seven feet by eight. The chimney probably stood at the north end, as was customary, and the front doorway was on Front Street. In the late eighteenth century warts were tacked onto the staterooms, and early in the following century the main front of the house was moved slightly outward. In modern times towers, patio, balcony and other "improvements" have changed the aspect of the ancient habitation. The sign, by the way, which is on the outside of the edifice, gives the date "1753" and may be approximately correct.

7 – Two Whaling Huts of Unusual Shape

Across Broadway from the *Mizzentop* is the *Eliza Mitchell House,* now called *The Maples,* in 1814 the home of Latham Gardner. Underhill made a mistake in designating the highest portion of the domicile as probably being the oldest. The development is shown on the Evolution Chart (p. 130), illustrating how this Siasconset whale building evolved uniquely and came to have the form in which we find it today. The front wart was enlarged to make a separate stateroom in itself and the roof was raised *only over it* to make a larger sleeping space upstairs. *The Maples* is also to be noted as having some wooden hinges (p. 106), often used when iron was scarce and dear.[8]

Another exceptionally-designed whale cottage stands next to the north, a place with the birdlike name of *The Martin Box.* Our drawings of it (pp. 73, 166) show how it looked when "Aunt" Ruth Folger laid eyes on it the first time. She was so startled by its low and lengthy proportion that she cried out that "it was a parfect rope walk." What a rope walk looked like may be seen from the drawing on page 27.

By the time Underhill made his few notes about the *Martin Box* in 1888, the dwelling had been almost unrecognizably changed, and he was wrong again in stating that the structure best illustrates the gradual growth of the fisherman's cottage. As far as its *post*-1800 growth is concerned, it was not at all typical, as the Evolution Chart reveals. The original Great Room, it seems, was only nine feet by twelve and a half in size (p. 166), and the twin staterooms were each only four and a half feet wide. The small scale and the elongated quality of the cottage were characteristic of the early building. By the 1860s-80s the place seems to have pushed out in all directions, horizontally as well as upward, as the drawings clearly show. The old Boat House addition (p. 170) also helped the picturesqueness of the ensemble.[9]

The Martin Box had one of the lowest roof-trees in the entire village. And how the seafaring folk in front of that whale cottage looked, as their ancestors had looked all through the colonial period of Nantucket (p. 171)! The old stereoptican view is a very revealing scene.

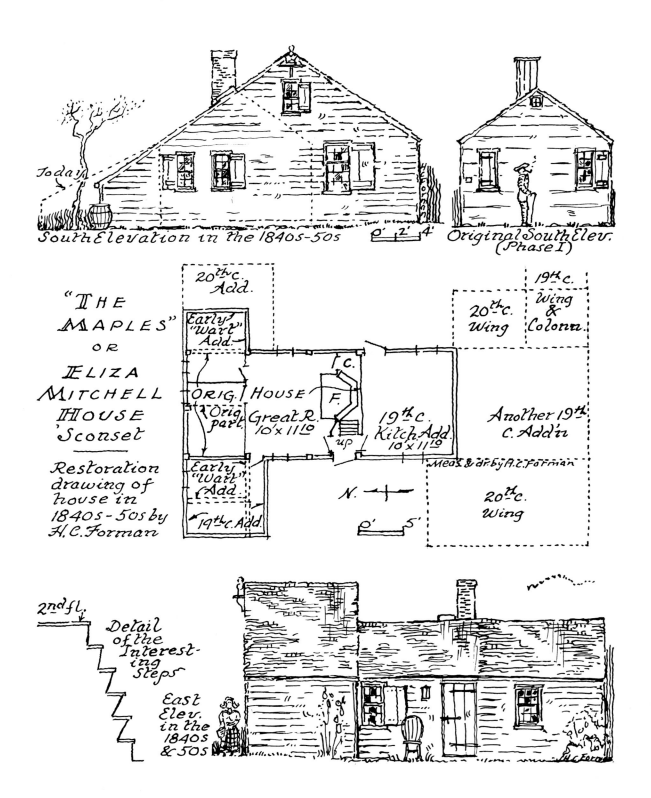

Today

South Elevation in the 1840s-50s

0' 2' 4'

Original South Elev.
(Phase I)

"THE
MAPLES"
OR
ELIZA
MITCHELL
HOUSE
'Sconset

Restoration
drawing of
house in
1840s-50s by
H. C. Forman

20ᵗʰ c.
Add.

Early
"Wart"
Add.

ORIG. HOUSE
Orig.
part.
Great R.
10' x 11'⁰

Early
"Wart"
Add.

19ᵗʰ c. Add.

T. C.

F.

up

19ᵗʰ c.
Kitch Add.
10' x 11'⁰

Meas. & dr. by A. C. Forman

N. ←┼→

0' 5'

19ᵗʰ c.

20ᵗʰ c.
Wing

Wing
&
Colonn.

Another 19ᵗʰ
C. Add'n

20ᵗʰ c.
Wing

2ⁿᵈ fl.

Detail
of the
Interest-
ing
Steps

East
Elev.
in the
1840s
& 50s

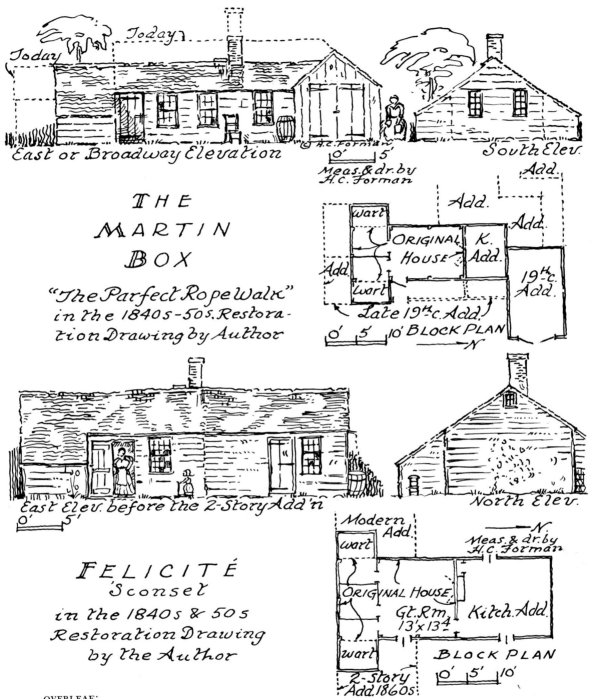

East or Broadway Elevation   © H.C. Forman   South Elev.

Today   Today

0'   5'
Meas. & dr. by
H.C. Forman

THE
MARTIN
BOX

"The Parfect Rope Walk"
in the 1840s–50s. Restoration Drawing by Author

Add.
Add.
wart
ORIGINAL
HOUSE
K.
Add.
Add.
Add.
19th c.
Add.
wart
Late 19th c. Add.
0'   5'   10'   BLOCK PLAN
N

East Elev. before the 2-Story Add'n

0'   5'

North Elev.

FELICITÉ
'Sconset

in the 1840s & 50s
Restoration Drawing
by the Author

Modern
Add.
wart
ORIGINAL HOUSE
Gt. Rm.
13' x 13'
Kitch. Add.
wart
2-Story
Add. 1860s
BLOCK PLAN
0'   5'   10'

Meas. & dr. by
H.C. Forman
N

OVERLEAF:

The Maples, formerly the *Eliza Mitchell House,* 'Sconset, was a whale house of the early 18th century. The unusual shape resulted when the original staterooms were widened, lengthened and heightened. *Photo, author.*

The stereoptican view of *The Martin Box* shows darker shingles on the boat-house wing, marking the former double doors. BELOW: *Nonantum* in 1880 with Broadway-front Greek "attic" board.

ABOVE: An 1872 view of *The Martin Box*, showing roofs with the lines of shingles bent in the old English tradition of thatch. BELOW: A view of *In and Out*, formerly *Sunnyside*, with its picturesque kitchen "porch."

Visitors to the *Gardner House* kitchen in the 1880s: Mrs. Julia Macy Urann and Billy Bowen. Old salt Billy is also shown below, spying from the walk of the *Folger House*. For generations, Nantucketers scanned the sea like this.

Upper Broadway Whale Cottages

1 – Franklin Folger's Two-Room Hut

THERE ARE ABOUT a dozen more buildings on Broadway to survey, and then we have done with what may perhaps be called America's most picturesque street.

Just north of the *House of Lords* is a much-changed bungalow called *Nonantum*, once the home of a hermit. It has been said that the name means "Welcome." Be that as it may, Underhill declared that the place was constructed by Barzillai Folger and in 1814 was owned by him. "It was always called 'Barzilla's' house."

This last statement by Underhill is difficult to believe, because our own research has disclosed that in 1835 this property belonged to Benjamin Franklin Folger, that it comprised his "House lot" in 'Sconset, and that said Folger was one of three village hermits. Folger's home comprised only two small rooms, surrounded by a high fence, and was so thoroughly secure from the world that the place might have been called "No-man-tum-in."[1]

This writer has pretty well identified the two early rooms in the present edifice, which has been greatly changed. The floor plan (p. 174) shows the Great Room or Parlor, with a wide brick fireplace, and the early-nineteenth-century kitchen addition to the north. The twin staterooms have entirely disappeared and were probably not even there in the hermit's time. An old photograph (p. 175) shows a long, low abode facing Broadway — a house without a wart, but nonetheless with a Greek attic board at the eaves. The restoration of the street (p. 70) shows how the cottage looked at an earlier period.

173

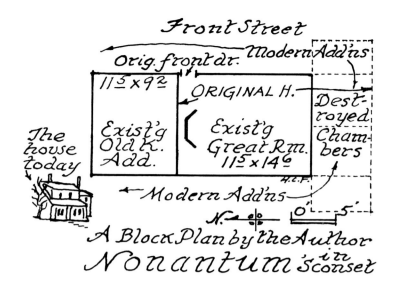

A Block Plan by the Author
Nonantum in 'Sconset

2 – A Doll Tea House

At *Columbia Cottage* (pp. 69, 174, 176), the next domicile to the north, the hanging loft or baulk was found to be boarded up at the same time that state-rooms were built — the paneling at the end of the Great Room appearing to be one piece, as has been discussed in an earlier chapter. Now known as the *Willow Harp, Columbia* was built in the early eighteenth century, according to an old letter belonging to a recent owner of the property. Among the early possessors of the cottage was Benjamin Bunker, whose mother when a widow kept a "Tea-house" there, in spite of the diminutive size of the premises for such a purpose. Bunker's son, George, when a small boy, ran errands and did chores at *Columbia*.[2]

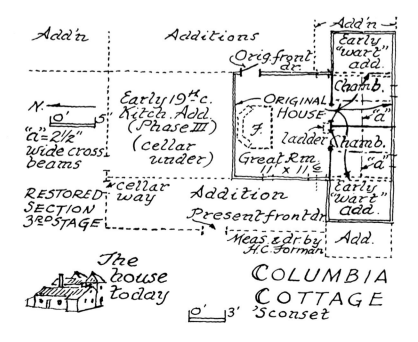

COLUMBIA COTTAGE 'Sconset

Eagle Cot.   Pinkham-Gardner   Nonantum Mizzentop   Geo.C.Gardner
              Columbia Cot.   H.of Lords   Liberty Hall

ABOVE: Looking south on Broadway, 'Sconset, in the 1860s, showing cottages as identified by author. Note type of medieval vertical-board palisaded fence commonly used. BELOW: 'Sconset from the south — oldest known photograph of the village (1860s).

Hack H. Anchorage   Val.Aldrich H.   Broadway   Cash's Fish
                               John C.Morris H.   Market   Beach

This home developed normally through rectangle to "T"-house, then in the early nineteenth century the Great Room roof, open to smoke and soot, had special treatment. It was plastered, it seems, all the way up the chimney gable to the ridge, as shown in the detail on page 87. The up-and-down roof sheathing or clinkers were also probably whitewashed, as they were at *Nauticon Lodge* — illustrated by "w" on page 86 — so that they would match the plaster gable and the plaster walls of the Great Room. Then later a plaster ceiling was built halfway up the roof rafters, thereby cutting the baulk door way down to half size. It all sounds very complicated, but the drawings should explain everything about this unusual house.

Old photographs (p. 175) show an outside entranceway to the cellar under the kitchen which had a low door and pent roof. Since the early nineteenth century this abode has suffered tremendous changes, including two square towers on the Ocean side.[3]

A little known view of Pump Square, 'Sconset, as it appeared about 1884. At left is *The Corners,* with its "flounder" wing.

umbia Cottage has a new stepladder to the hanging-loft. *Photo, author.*

The Pinkham-Gardner House, 'Sconset (destroyed) Front Street side.

3 – Quaint Whale House Sold for Fish

The modern bungalow to the north of *Columbia Cottage* stands on the site of the picturesque *Pinkham-Gardner House* (p. 69), destroyed about 1910. There is a story about the two owners of this property, Eben Gardner and Tristram Pinkham, who before 1814 held it jointly. Eben so prospered that he wanted a house to himself and therefore proposed to Tristram to name a price at which he would buy or sell. The suggestion came so suddenly that Tristram asked until Saturday to make up his mind. Came Saturday, and Tristram said that he thought that his share in the premises was fairly worth a quintal and a half (150 pounds) of fish. At that price the dwelling was sold.[4]

How the *Pinkham-Gardner House* developed is shown on the Evolution Chart (p. 130). It had twin staterooms, each said to be six by eight feet in size, and a hanging-loft reached by cleats nailed to the partition. One wonders how many whale cottages had cleats before they had removable ladders. Old photographs (p. 175) as well as an early watercolor by J. B. Reid, upon which our drawings are based (pp. 69, 180), reveal that the place was of the usual 'Sconset type, except that there was no door on the Broadway façade. In other words, for generations the owners were too conservative to change the front door around to the Broadway side, as became fashionable after 1800. Besides the wart additions to the staterooms, there was a low shed of plain boards to the north of the kitchen, and the battened door of the shed could not have been over five feet high.

Underhill noted that in his time the place was very old and had probably been changed less inside and out than any of the old houses on Siasconset Bank. The pity is that such a perfect specimen of the Medieval Style of architecture should have been permitted to disintegrate.

4 – Was Eagle Cottage Drawn by the Wilmington Artist?

Like many others in this particular area, the *Eagle Cottage,* next house to the
northward, has been greatly changed. A sign on it gives the date "1787," but the
date has not been checked for accuracy. How the place developed — very much
like *Shanunga* — is shown on the Evolution Chart (p. 130), and how it looked
along Broadway is shown in our street restoration (p. 69). Also, how it sprouted
warts and outshuts all over may be seen on the floor plan (p. 179).

One of the interesting features of *Eagle Cottage* is the narrow and almost
dangerous stepladder beside the chimney, giving access to the second floor — the
full loft put over the Great Room, and the bedroom over the kitchen. The ladder
is only ten-and-a-half inches wide and gives a good idea how narrow were the
early Siasconset ladders. This one, of course, is in the later position. The first one
served the baulk.

The handsome brick fireplace conforms to the 'Sconset type, having an opening four feet and eight inches wide, yet measuring at the back only twenty-six
inches — a wide-splayed fireplace to throw out the heat. The hearth is large, pro-
jecting out into the Great Room some thirty-two inches, and the bricks in the head
of the fireplace are supported by an iron band.

The wash drawing of 1838 by Benjamin Ferris of Wilmington, Delaware, has
been tentatively identified by this writer as *Eagle Cottage* (p. 180).[5]

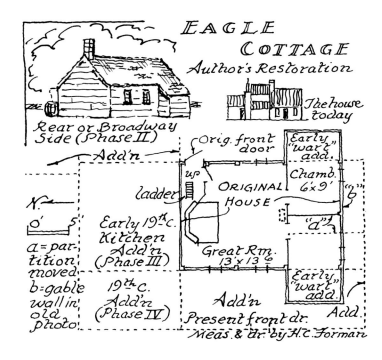

ABOVE: "A House in Siasconset on the Island of Nantucket," wash drawings made Aug. 27, 1838, by Benjamin Ferris — tentatively identified by author as *Eagle Cottage*. BELOW: Upper Broadway in the 1860s, showing (left) the only known view of early *Nauma*.

5 – Only a Stable, but a Unique Design

The next building to the north was entirely different from anything in Sia-sconset and perhaps in New England. It was *Elisha Clark's Stable* or *Barn,* now vastly changed (pp. 68, 181). By this Clark it was brought from the village of Sesachacha, and after his ownership had passed, one Cromwell Barney added the second floor on the south end, thus giving the structure its quaint aspect.[6]

Unfortunately there is nothing left of this barn but the framework, and the old wooden tower on the south end has been changed into a Victorian monstrosity.

6 – Driftwood's Builder Had an Easy Time of It

On the other side of Broadway from this cluster of structures which we have been describing is a group worthy of mention. There is old *Driftwood,* formerly *Clifton Cottage* (pp. 74, 182), which is opposite to *Nonantum.* This house *Drift-wood* was built about 1818, according to Underhill, by George Folger — about whose son Philip Folger there is an odd story. It appears that Philip was sent by his father to oversee the construction of the premises, but said that "he knew nothing about the business, and hence had an easy time."[7]

Elisha Clark's Stable in 'Sconset
Formerly one of the quaintest buildings in the United States and now entirely changed. Restoration drawing by H.C. Forman.

Like *Nonantum* this cottage has been changed from its plain rectangular shape to what seems like scrambled eggs. That is pretty stiff criticism, but tells the story. The Great Room was fourteen by eleven and three-quarters feet in size, and each of the twin chambers was only five feet by seven. After this came a whole series of pushings-up and swellings-outward, as may be seen in the floor plan and the sketch of the place today. According to the Evolution Chart (p. 130), *Driftwood* maintained for a while the developmental path followed by *Nauticon Lodge*.

It is difficult to state which early 'Sconset dwelling changed the most; at least *Driftwood* nearly takes the prize for "improvements." Besides, if it was actually built about 1818, could it have been a whale house? We have classified it as such and believe that it may have been constructed earlier (p. 74).

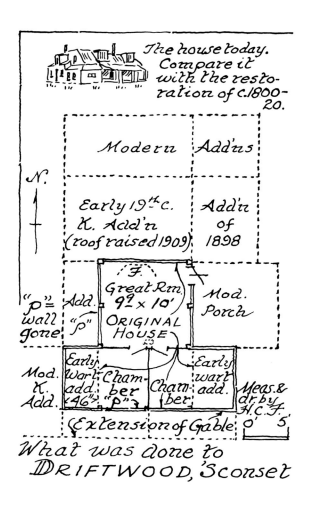

The house today. Compare it with the restoration of c.1800–20.

What was done to DRIFTWOOD, 'Sconset

7 – Nonquit and French for Happiness

Next to the northward of *Driftwood* are two cottages, the first known by the name of *Come Aboard,* formerly *Nonquit.* Owned in 1814 by Obed Mitchell, *Come Aboard,* now almost wholly changed, had a development (p. 130) which followed *Pinkham-Gardner House* and the early *Bigenough.* Our two restoration drawings show how the place looked in Phases II and III (pp. 74, 184). Some of the old studs, posts, joists and rafters in this structure still preserve some of their rounded tree-shapes.[8]

The other cottage, a whale house known as *Felicité,* French for Happiness, is reputed to have been ancient in 1814, about which time it was owned by one John Emmett.

The developmental scheme of *Felicité* is illustrated on the Evolution Chart and the measured floor plan (pp. 130, 167), but does not show that the state-room wart on the Broadway side was enlarged in Phase IV, as a transitional step to the post-Civil-War (c. 1868) two-storied gable-end wing (p. 183). Such gables were a mark of Victorianism, a weak reflection of the Gothic, and comprised a fad:

Described as very old in 1814, *Felicité,* 'Sconset, at first had a Great Room only 13 feet square. Two-story wing dates from about 1868.

we have already noted one of about 1865 on the *Mizzentop*. At all events this great Victorian addition swallowed up both staterooms and their warts, as well as half the old Great Room. Some of the wall plates in the Great Room still remain exposed and indicate that the whole original framework of the whale house was visible. To be noted also is the little closet room for a child incorporated in between the twin staterooms.[9]

A third little structure stands to the north of *Felicité*, and is two stories high, with gable-end which was set back a distance from Broadway (p. 75). An early print shows the place to have been a high one-story cottage with vertical boards facing Broadway; and on the south, two doorways adjacent to each other, with windows flanking.[10] There was a mast on the Broadway gable. The place is now called *None Too Big*, and was supposed to have been brought from Sankaty Light; at the same time it was never a whale house. But it is reputed to have had an unusual type of exterior wall construction: plaster and lath on both sides of the studding and posts.[11]

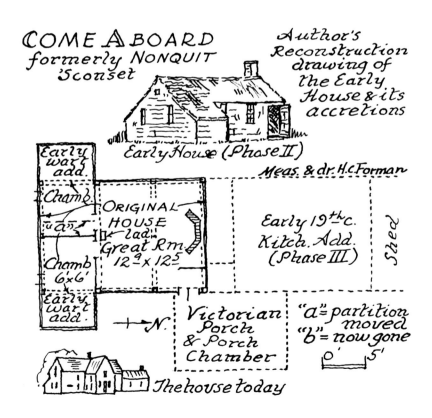

COME ABOARD
formerly NONQUIT
'Sconset

Author's Reconstruction drawing of the Early House & its accretions

Early House (Phase II)

Meas. & dr. H. C. Forman

Early wart add.

Chamb. "a"

ORIGINAL HOUSE lad. Great Rm. 12⁹ x 12⁵

Early 19ᵗʰc. Kitch. Add. (Phase III)

Shed

Chamb 6'x6'

Early wart add.

—N.

Victorian Porch & Porch Chamber

"a"=partition moved
"b"= now gone
0'   5'

The house today

8 – And Finally, Without a Care

The last dwelling (p. 159) on the west side of Broadway seems to have been, according to Underhill, a jumbled-up concoction of parts of buildings taken from Town, Madaket and a ship. This is *Sans Souci,* or "Without a Care." Its singular history indicates that it was "originally erected in Trader's Lane in Town, and was part of a duck or twine factory. The kitchen was a boat house belonging to Mr. Brown, Mrs. Belcher's grandfather. The bricks in the chimney were in the British ship, *Queen,* when she came ashore on the island. A portion of the house was taken to Madequet and thence to 'Sconset. It was moved here ['Sconset] in 1814. It was the first house on the [Siasconset] Bank to have its height increased by a second story. In 1879 it had 13 windows, no two of which were alike."[12]

This cottage was not shown on the Evolution Chart because it was not certain that it was ever a whale house — surely the "singular" history of it does not subscribe to that theory. Nevertheless the original hut (p. 187) was a rectangle with Great Room eleven feet by fifteen in size and with twin staterooms and board partitions of the usual whale-house variety. The outside siding was of bevel-edged boards, like those on *Auld Lang Syne, Shanunga,* and others. If it is true that the Phase I structure came from Town, then Town possessed a whale house — a really skeptical conclusion.

It seems safe to assume that from the original one-story-and-loft rectangle, *Sans Souci* never sprang the customary early warts on the front and rear, and never became a "T"-house in the natural course of events. Instead, as the drawings show (pp. 186, 187), the dwelling shot up to a full second story — the first such in the village, according to Underhill — and thus we have Phase II. The upstairs corner posts, wall plates and beveled-edge siding match those downstairs. The twin staterooms appear not to have sprouted a small wart until the late nineteenth century, and then it was not on the side of the domicile, but on the south end. Other outshuts were added at that time, and later.[13]

The roof used to have a trap door through which buckets of water could be hoisted onto the roof when ablaze, or a wife could look for her husband's boat at sea. As late as 1910 wood gutters ran to a spout on the north wall of the boat-house kitchen and emptied into a capacious hogshead. The door near where that barrel stood is only five feet and nine inches tall — scarcely big enough for today's teenagers.

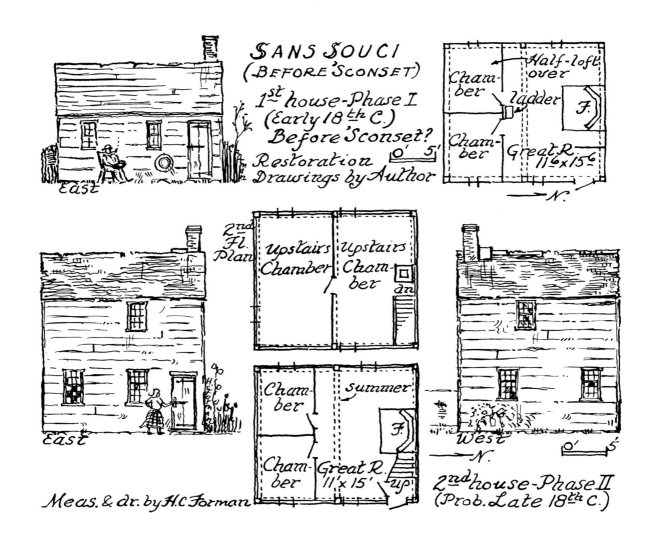

SANS SOUCI
(BEFORE 'SCONSET)

1st house—Phase I
(Early 18th C.)
Before 'Sconset?
Restoration
Drawings by Author   0' 5'

Chamber · Half-loft over
Chamber · ladder · F.
Great R. 11'6 x 15'6
N.

East

2nd Fl. Plan

Upstairs Chamber · Upstairs Chamber · an

Chamber · summer
Chamber · Great R. 11' x 15' · F. · up

East

West
N.

2nd house—Phase II
(Prob. Late 18th C.)

Meas. & dr. by H.C.Forman

West El.   ©H.C.Forman   0' 5'   North

SANS SOUCI ~ Phase III ~ Early 19th C. ~ Author's Restoration ~

East El.
SANS SOUCI ~ Phase IV ~ Late 19th C. ~ Meas. & drawn by H. C. Forman
North El.

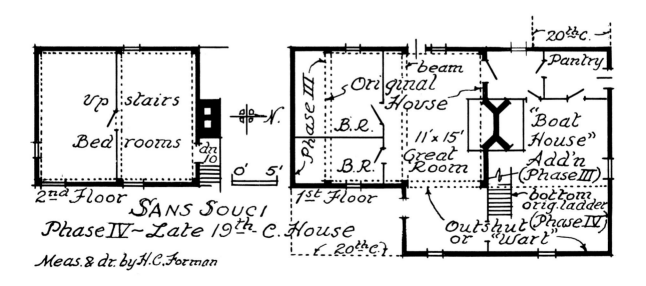

Up stairs
Bed rooms
dn 10

N.

0'   5'

2nd Floor
SANS SOUCI
Phase IV ~ Late 19th C. House

Meas. & dr. by H. C. Forman

Phase III
beam
Original House
B.R.
11' x 15'
Great Room
B.R.
1st Floor
(20th C.)

20th C.
Pantry
"Boat House" Add'n (Phase III)
bottom orig. ladder (Phase IV)
Outshut or "Warl"

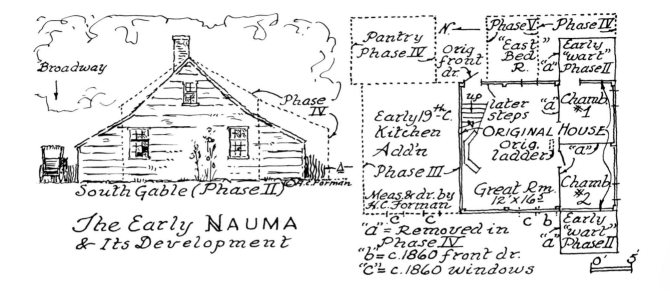

Broadway

Phase IV

South Gable (Phase II)

The Early NAUMA
& Its Development

Pantry
Phase IV

Orig.
front
dr.

N.

Phase V.

Phase IV

"East"
Bed.
R.

"a"

Early
"wart"
Phase II

Early 19th C.
Kitchen
Add'n
Phase III

up

later
steps

ORIGINAL

Orig.
ladder

"a"

"a"

Chamb
#1

HOUSE

"a"

Meas.& dr. by
H.C.Forman

Great Rm.
12' x 16.5'

c

c

"a" = Removed in
Phase IV
"b" = c.1860 front dr.
"C" = c.1860 windows

Chamb
#2

c

b

Early
"wart"
Phase II

"a"

0'   5'

9 – Nauma Floated on a Raft

Where Broadway at its northern end begins to turn toward Sankaty Road stands *Nauma* (pp. 190, 191), an Indian name meaning Sandy Point — now Great Point, Nantucket. It was brought from Sesachacha village by Reuben Joy, a cousin of Captain Edward Joy's father. Now since Sesachacha was in existence as early as the 1670s, it is possible that parts of the house date from the seventeenth century — but not probable. The place is by no means 1676 in date. The Great Room, for instance, is larger than the usual room of this kind in the village, and like the *Mizzentop's* Great Room, is early eighteenth century.[14]

The whale cottage was floated on a raft by Reuben Joy along the shore to 'Sconset, where the sections were unloaded and rebuilt on the Bank edge.[15]

The Evolution Chart and the floor plans (pp. 68, 188, 189, 192) show how *Nauma* changed like a chameleon. One of the interesting features was how the small stateroom wart on the front or Ocean side developed into a small East bedchamber, which turned into a larger East bedroom, as may be followed on the drawings. We are pretty certain about the swelling out of the front wart, because today there is a division in the floor boards in the East bedroom which shows exactly how much the wart was enlarged.[16]

In the case of *Nauma* perhaps this writer may jot down some of his reminiscences about the house, at least to the extent of throwing light on how it felt to live in the early days at 'Sconset. As a child he always thought that it was unusual to have a window between the Parlor (Great Room) and that same East bedroom, where he slept. Through the cracks of the curtains in this inside window he could watch the older members of the family and their friends enjoying themselves around the brightly lit oil lamp. That handsome oil lamp with brass figures upon its base had a bent base and could not stand vertically. The floor of the room, too, sloped at crazy angles because the boulders on which the house rested had sunk down in the ground at the corners. And because of the floor, at least six inches out of level, the Parlor table slanted. By turning the lamp around so that its tilt equalized the slope of the floor, one could get the lamp to stand up almost straight and be pronounced safe. Sometimes a child in getting up suddenly from the table would accidentally pull the table cloth and jerk the lamp, but then that was just living at *Nauma.*

One night the cottage did experience a small fire: a curtain blown by the wind was ignited by a candle upstairs. The flames burned both curtains and netting — for in those days there were no metal screens — and blackened the ceiling.

So dyed in the wool were we at Nauma that almost every article of furniture which we used in the habitation had been there for a hundred years or more, not counting our occupancy of forty-one years.

One of the beds at *Nauma* was a rope bed, the ropes passing through the heavy wood frame of the bed to make a square pattern. The straw mattress would creak when you turned in your sleep. How difficult it is for our grandchildren,

NAUMA, 'Sconset, in the 1850s-60s
Author's reconstruction drawing of Phase IV

The south gable-end of *Nauma* about 1915, before the roof "blew off" and modern dormers were built. BELOW: *Nauma* today, from the Broadway side. *Photo, author.*

ABOVE: Two views of *Nauma*, 'Sconset, in 1910, showing Broadway façade with Greek "attic" boards and the ocean side with porch, representing Phase V. RIGHT: The hand-split oak laths at *Nauma*, under glass panel.

South Elev. ©H.C.Forman   North Elev.

East or Ocean Elev.

Restoration Drawing
by H. C. Forman

NAUMA
in 1880
(Phase IV)
Siasconset

a = Phase V
b = late 19th c. front
c = china closet
j = beaded beams
r = range location
t = trap door

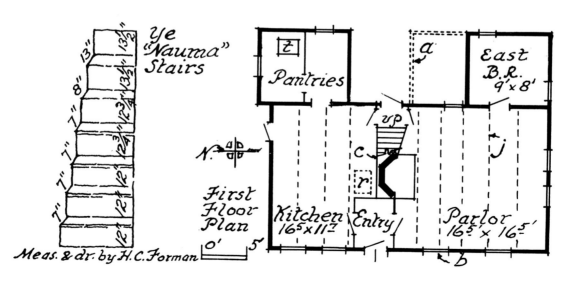

Ye "Nauma" Stairs

13"   13½"
8"   12¾" 13½"
7"   12¾" 13½"
7"   12½" 12¾"
7"   12¼" 12½"
7"   12" 12¼"
    12" 12¼"

Meas. & dr. by H.C.Forman

N.

First
Floor
Plan
0'   5'

t
Pantries

a   East
         B.R.
         9' × 8'

up

c
         j

r

Kitchen   Entry   Parlor
16⁵ × 11⁷   16⁵ × 16⁵

b

with all their luxuries, to visualize how close we were in 1910 at *Nauma* to the seventeenth-century kind of life. They shall never see us in our childhood carrying buckets of water from a village street faucet — yet we did those chores hundreds of times. Our bathtub was a daily dip in the Atlantic, rain or shine.

In the pantry was a trap door, "t" on the plan (p. 192), which gave access to a small root cellar with a milk shelf. It is impossible to forget the feeling of reaching down into that black hole for provisions — butter on greasy paper, eggs, bacon and the like. But that cavity was the refrigerator.

In putting a bathroom on the loft floor — the ancient necessary having been discarded — the local carpenter inadvertently sawed through what looked like an insignificant post in the chamber over the Parlor, and in the twinkling of an eye the floor dropped a whole foot. The post, it seems, held the Parlor ceiling to the roof. It is told that the carpenter, seeing the already low Parlor ceiling bellying downward and the mansion about to collapse, ran home and brought back an iron tie-rod, which he placed inside a partition in order again to connect the floor to the roof. But in spite of the tie-rod, the bedroom floor always shook violently because the small three-by-four-inch beaded beams of the nineteenth century, spaced three feet apart, were not adequate for a span of sixteen and a half feet across the Parlor.

The staircase (p. 192) has a seventeenth-century look even if it is not of that date. There are only seven steps, no two of which are the same size or shape. It is a medieval style of stair-in-a-box which hung over into the late eighteenth-century. And it was to us very dangerous. The doorway to the north bedchamber was partly over the top riser, so that if you stepped out the door in the dark, you might well step off onto the first floor, seven and a half feet below. But you could do that in other 'Sconset houses. Consequently at the head of the stair there was placed a movable bar and hinged board, to widen out the floor, thus serving the purpose of a gate, so that at night we might be preserved from finding ourselves a bag of broken bones on the way to the Nantucket Hospital. We used to call the stair the "escape scuttle," because there was something about it which smacked of a hatch on shipboard.[17]

10 – Athearn Theory and Bank-Edge Street Homes

At the north terminus of Broadway and facing down that thoroughfare is the *Frederick M. Pitman House*, now *The Sea Spray* (p. 191), with the date 1796 on a sign upon a wall. Another, older sign upon the building probably read "Whale Spray." According to Underhill the place was moved some time in the nineteenth century by Mr. Pitman from Guinea, the Negro section of Town. Our drawing of the rear of this house (p. 194), taken from two faded photographs, shows that that portion was one of the quaintest medieval buildings on the Island, and was obviously a whale dwelling with two stateroom warts and a kitchen "porch." In fact, the rear part probably formed the "Home" of James Athearn, which stood in 1835 on this very spot. It is a shame that all this picturesqueness has vanished before the push of modern improvements.

Along with *Nauma* there are two other buildings which stand facing the "Highway" along the edge of the Bank, a street of which the greater length has caved into the ocean. One cottage, *Nickanoose,* was brought between 1814 and 1820 from Sesachacha, by Nicholas Meader, and the other, the *Robinson House,* was carried from the same place about the same time by Nicholas' son, George Meader. Both are shown on the map of the village (p. 40), and both have been considerably changed. The two places were probably whale houses when they were brought from Sesachacha, and we do know that *Nickanoose* (p. 155) some eighty years ago had the appearance of the typical 'Sconset fisherman's shanty with a wart on the east stateroom and another one tacked on to the south gable-end at the southwest corner of the building.[18] Some of the original framework is still visible in a section of the present edifice.

Having covered Broadway, we are now ready to have a look at three other lanes in Siasconset and their whale huts.

A Medieval 'Sconset Cottage
Showing the rear section, now destroyed, of the Fred M. Pitman House.
Drawn by the Author from two old faded photographs.

XIII

Lanes Through the Old Pump Square

1 – Centre Street as Far as the Pump

THE EARLY 'SCONSETER, it seems, was never done building. He lay awake nights and invented reasons for construction work. In order to get to sleep he counted not sheep but houses. Life to him without a new shanty or structure to erect was an empty waste without a purpose. That is the reason why it is said that every native-born villager now has to his credit at least six buildings. The only trouble appears to be that if that rapid pace of adding wings, knobs, warts, excrescences, outhouses and outshuts is continued, all remaining portions of original 'Sconset will disappear forever. Too much has already gone.

The three highways, Centre Street, Shell Street and New Street (village plan, p. 40), which abut or run through the old Pump Square, are not as early in date as the three streets, including Broadway, which parallel the Bank, if the copper engraving of 1791 may be believed. As for the Square itself, it was not until 1776 that the Siasconset Well was put down upon that irregular patch of mud.[1] Centre and Shell streets crossed that open space in a north and south direction, while New Street began at the Square and extended westward across the moors in the direction of Town.

The first early whale house stood on the open plot with grass, flowers and trees, situated on the left at the beginning of Centre Street. There stood as late as 1834 the *George C. Chase House,* no longer extant. In 1881 there was on the same

195

Bird's-eye view of the Pump Square, 'Sconset, about 1881. Note codfish drying rack or "flake" in *Nauticon* yard. Curved shingle courses on *Nauticon* roof are in thatch tradition. *Wyer Photo.*

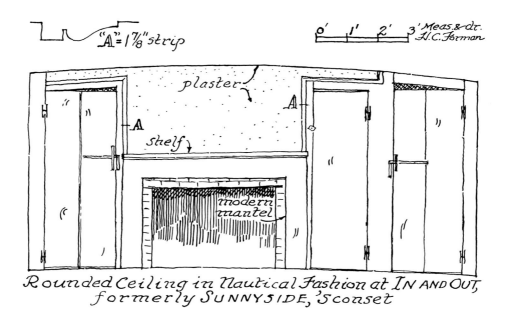

"A"=1⅞"strip

0'   1'   2'   3' Meas.&dr.
                  H.C.Forman

Rounded Ceiling in Nautical Fashion at IN AND OUT, formerly SUNNYSIDE, 'Sconset

location a small and elongated barn belonging to a Mrs. Cathcart which was believed by Captain Edward Joy to be part of an ancient house owned by Obed Coffin.[2]

The next property to the north holds another imitation whale dwelling, which has three names: the *Arietta Hussey House, Cathcart House* or *Takitezie* (pp. 200, 211). An imposing cottage with high warts, this dwelling was erected and owned in 1814 by James Josiah Coffin. In this writer's opinion the place was built as a "T"-house, like the *George C. Gardner House* on Broadway, and has been designated on the Evolution Chart (p. 130) as an imitation whale hut. The twin staterooms were designed to have warts from the very first year, 1814, and then later a tiny child's closet about three feet wide was taken off the west stateroom, as shown on the plan (p. 207). In a subsequent era all three bedchambers were projected southward five feet, as the divisions in the old floor boards prove. The Great Room, it seems, was never open to the rafters, but constructed with its present beaded ceiling beams. In more-recent times the premises were thoroughly Victorianized.[3]

Next to the north on Centre Street is an interesting whaling cottage by the name of *Sunnyside,* now *In and Out* (pp. 201, 204). Overlooking the Pump Square, the house was claimed by Underhill to be very old and to have belonged to William Gardner in 1814.[4] The Evolution Chart reveals that *In and Out* had in its third phase, about 1800, a kitchen "porch" shed (p. 206) which was later swollen up into a two-story wing — something like the tall addition on *Felicité,* but in reverse. One of the curiosities of the place is that when the Great Room ceiling was finally ceiled over, the workman evidently made it slightly arched (p. 198), perhaps to resemble the underside of a ship's deck. We have seen this same curvature, but not as pronounced, in certain other whale houses in the village. Also, at *In and Out* the floors sank down along the side walls. How may one account for the triangular spaces over the three doors in the fireplace side of the Great Room? Either the doors themselves sagged and filler strips were put in, or the door heads sagged on one side when the floor sank and filler strips were likewise put in the triangular spaces.

This is the way 'Sconset villagers lined up for water in generations past (view taken soon after 1884). Well on Pump Square was founded in 1776.

The Great Room or Parlor, *Arietta Hussey House,* 'Sconset, erected 1814, is marked by beaded studs, boarded dado and large overmantel panel. *Photo, author.*

When the Great Room of *In and Out,* or *Sunnyside,* was ceiled over, the workmen arched the ceiling to resemble underside of a ship's deck. *Photo, author.*

2 – A Flounder Wing and Utopia

Continuing across the Pump Square, we reach the picturesque whale abode by the name of *The Corners,* formerly *Meeresheim* (pp. 199, 204). This place has been the object of artists' efforts for generations, largely because of its split gable-end, which we have given the name of "flounder wing" — after the half-gables of Alexandria, Virginia. In 1814 *The Corners* was owned by Shubael Barnard. As may be seen in the Evolution Chart (p. 130), it developed along what may be termed the most complicated path of all the early village dwellings, going through the "T"-house, *Auld Lang Syne, Dexioma* and *Nauma* stages, until it reached its own fulfillment in the present structure with the flounder wing. One of its unique features is the brick shelf at the back of the Great Room fireplace on which pots and other receptacles were kept warm. The little entry beside the chimney (p. 204) has its walls all askew, and the stepladder rises parallel to the chimney instead of against it.[5]

The next building up the street is a whale cottage with stirring nautical words on its sign: *Don't Give Up the Ship.* Formerly it was known as the *Clark House,* the *Horace Folger House* or *Utopia* (p. 205). It is reputed to have been built on its present site and not moved from elsewhere. Built by Richard Swain, so it is said, the place was lived in by Richard's son, Richard, in 1814, and later was owned by Thomas Barney and by Mrs. Nancy Clark, the widow of Uriah Clark. Of all the Siasconset edifices this one comes closest to *Shanunga* nearby on the Pump Square. But there is a slight difference: *Utopia* has no wart on its east stateroom (plan, p. 207). It is probable that the wart was never built, and that the cottage was an "L," like *Snug Harbor* (p. 160). Even so, we have shown *Utopia* on the Evolution Chart. The Great Room, by the way, is a real cuddy — only ten-and-a-half feet by eleven-and-a-half — and its ceiling is curved like that at *In and Out,* already mentioned. The twin doors to the staterooms have wooden hinges, like those at *The Maples*; but the pintles have been removed. Unlike *Shanunga,* the place has its brick chimney in the exact spot where once stood a wooden stack.[6]

length 16¾"

Nantucket Wood Bed Screw for Rope Beds

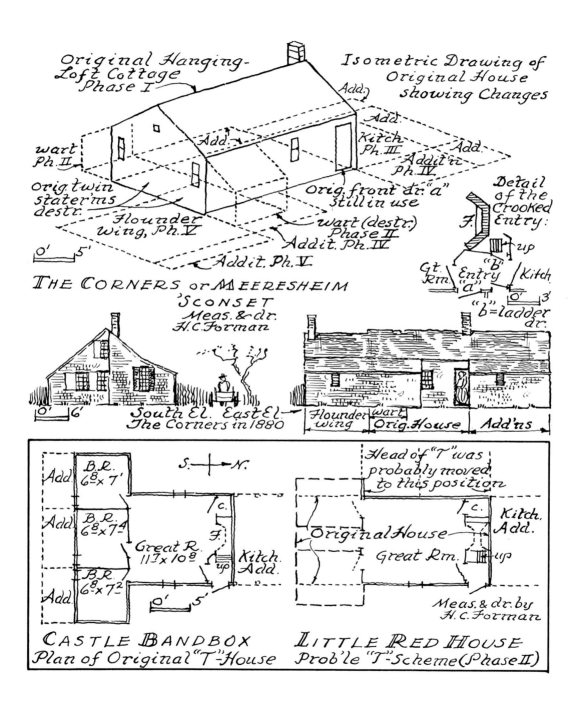

Original Hanging-
Loft Cottage
Phase I

Isometric Drawing of
Original House
showing Changes

Add.)

Add.

Kitch
Ph. III

Add.

wart
Ph. II

Add'n
Ph. IV

orig. twin
stater'ms
destr.

orig. front dr. "a"
still in use

Detail
of the
Crooked
Entry:

Flounder
Wing, Ph. V

wart (destr.)
Phase II

Addit. Ph. IV

0'   5'

Addit. Ph. V

"b"   up

Gt.
Rm.   Entry
"a"   Kitch

THE CORNERS or MEERESHEIM

"b=ladder
dr.

'SCONSET
Meas. & dr.
H.C.Forman

0'   3'

South El.   East El.
The Corners in 1880

0'   6'

Flounder
Wing   wart
Orig. House   Add'ns

Add
B.R.
6⁸ x 7'

S.   N.

Head of "T" was
probably moved
to this position

c.

Add
B.R.
6⁸ x 7⁴

F.

Original House

c.   Kitch.
Add.

Great R.
11⁷ x 10⁸

Kitch.
Add.

Great Rm.   up

Add
B.R.
6⁸ x 7²

up

0'   5'

Meas. & dr. by
H.C.Forman

CASTLE BANDBOX
Plan of Original "T"-House

LITTLE RED HOUSE
Prob'le "T"-Scheme (Phase II)

Early scene of 'Sconset's Pump Square, showing *The Corners,* or *Meerscheim,* right, and *In and Out,* left. BELOW: An old view of Pump Square from *Folger's Crow's Nest* on New Street. In foreground is *Uncle Nat's Shanty,* used as ice-cream saloon.

Utopia, the *Horace Folger House,* Centre Street, was probably an "L" whaling house. This shows the Robinson and Wilson families posing, Sept. 1884. BELOW: *Heart's Ease* and, right, the backs of *The Martin Box* and *Driftwood.*

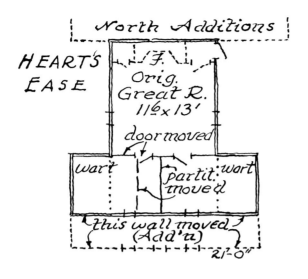

HEART'S EASE

North Additions

'F.'
Orig. Great R. 11⁶ × 13'

door moved

wart

partit. moved

wart

this wall moved (Add'n)

21'-0"

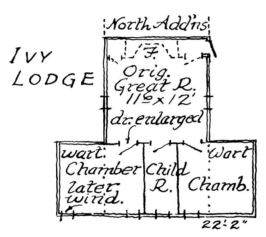

IVY LODGE

North Add'ns

'F.'
Orig. Great R. 11⁶ × 12'

dr. enlarged

wart. Chamber later wind.

Child R.

Wart Chamb.

22'-2"

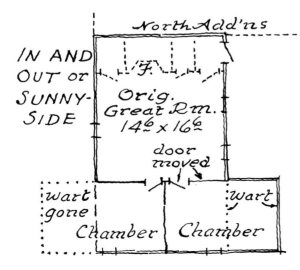

IN AND OUT or SUNNY-SIDE

North Add'ns

'F.'
Orig. Great Rm. 14⁶ × 16⁶

door moved

wart gone

Chamber

Chamber

wart

MORE WHALE HOMES: RESTORED "T"-PLANS (PHASE II) OF CENTRE ST. HOUSES, SIASCONSET
Showing Additions and Alterations

– – – – Exist'g Walls
- - - - - Additions
· · · · · · Destroyed Walls
Meas. & drawn by H. C. Forman

One of the best known of the early 'Sconset whaling houses is *Heart's Ease,* perhaps built in the very late 17th century. *Photo, author.*

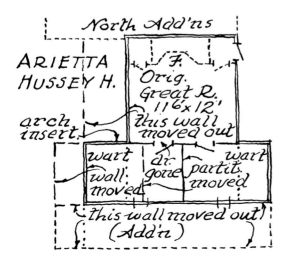

ARIETTA HUSSEY H.

North Add'ns

F.
Orig. Great R. 11'6" x 12'

arch insert.

this wall moved out

wart wall moved

dr. gone

partit. moved

wart

this wall moved out) (Add'n)

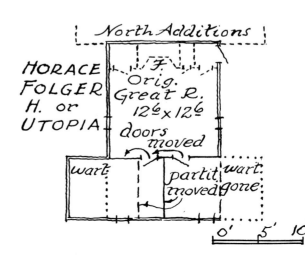

HORACE FOLGER H. or UTOPIA

North Additions

F.
Orig. Great R. 12'6" x 12'6"

doors moved

wart

partit. moved

wart gone

0'   5'   10'

3 – Roof Tree and a Wifee's Heart's-Ease

The *Irving House,* or *Roof Tree* (pp. 205, 209), is situated to the north of *Utopia,* and like it is an "L"-shaped whale house with only one wart, on the west side.[7] A drawing of the Great Room paneling with the small, one-plank doors to the staterooms is shown on page 85. The cottage is reputed to have been built by Sylvanus Coffin and was owned by him in the twenty years after 1814.

We come next to one of the most photogenic and best known of the early 'Sconset buildings: *Hearts Ease,* sometimes hyphenated into *Hearts-Ease* (pp. 205, 207). This is the honeymooner's dream of a snuggery, rose-covered on sides and roof. Owned in 1814 by Jonathan Jenkins, the place is undoubtedly much older than that.[8] About 1820 Reuben Starbuck made additions to it and employed a mason to lath and plaster the interior. The story goes that a little grandson of Sylvanus Gardner watched the plasterer at work there, and then ran home to exclaim: "Grandma, he is putting on the whole broadside of the house at once." Thereupon his grandmother, who was Gardner's wife Annie, spoke up and declared that Reuben Starbuck had had a wife, a *wifee,* and now he had got a dandy, and he supposed that he must plaster his house. The story, if nothing else, represents the Siasconset ethic that one must not pretend to be better than his neighbor. Also the reference gives a pretty good indication of the time — about 1820 — when villagers went about plastering their dwellings.

The small size of the Great Room, barely eleven feet square, the tiny staterooms, and the low ceiling, may indicate a very late seventeenth-century date for *Hearts Ease* (p. 206). The Evolution Chart (p. 130) gives an idea how the place developed — like *Shanunga* except that the whole south gable-end was extended outward four and a half feet in the early 1800s. It was probably Reuben Starbuck who added the kitchen "porch," only nine feet wide, and who hid the Great Room rafters by plaster-ceiling the room and moved the stepladder over from the baulk to the chimney.

4 – Ivy Lodge and the Home of the Walking Sankaty

Formerly the *Asa P. Jones House, Ivy Lodge,* the next cottage to the northward, is a long dwelling (pp. 209, 210), the original section on the south having been doubled in size, now making *Ivy North* and *Ivy South.* There is the possibility that the dwelling is not a whale house, but an imitation one, like the *George*

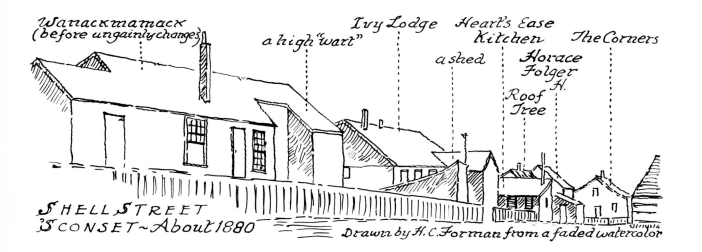

Wanackmamack
(before ungainly changes)
a high "wart"
Ivy Lodge
Heart's Ease
Kitchen
The Corners
a shed
Horace
Folger
H.
Roof
Tree

SHELL STREET
'SCONSET ~ About 1880

Drawn by H. C. Forman from a faded watercolor

C. Gardner House. The floor plan (p. 206) shows that the child's closet room does not seem to have been taken off either of the twin staterooms, but was placed in the center between them from the beginning. Of interest was the open porch off the kitchen on the Centre Street side (p. 210), a feature which indicates somewhat how the very earliest kitchen porches in Siasconset once appeared.

In 1814 *Ivy Lodge* was already old, had clinker-built siding painted with red ochre and was owned by Mathew Barney.[9]

Just beyond *Ivy Lodge* stands *Wanackmamack* or *Wanackmamack Lodge* (p. 155), named for one of the two principal Indian chiefs of Nantucket, and pronounced Wanack'-mamack'. Unfortunately the lodging has been changed greatly by successive uglifications and Victorianizations, but nonetheless there can be traced on the interior the usual "T"-house and kitchen "porch" addition — probably an imitation whale cottage. One of the high warts, that on the west stateroom, may be seen in an old, faded watercolor of the 1880s, painted by J. B. Reid, of which an ink drawing, with our own building identifications, is here included.

23½
high
32" long

A
Nantucket
Box Wagon Seat

ABOVE: *Ivy Lodge*, the *Asa P. Jones House* (1880s). The open shed, now gone, shows the kind of medieval-kitchen porch "outshut" common to the village. BELOW: Early types of Islanders at a Shearing Festival.

Shell Street, 'Sconset, 1869-70, showing the Pump in distance. At left, *Hop Cottage* and *Thomas Brock House,* destroyed whale huts; at right, *Arietta Hussey House.*

Wanackmamack appears to have been erected in 1815, or soon afterwards, by Felix Slocum Folger, and was kept as a public house or tavern for many years by Charles Elkins.[10] It was his wife, Susan E. Elkins, who was called the "Walking Sankaty," because wherever she went after dark, she always carried a lantern.

The last cottage on Centre Street is *Aurora Villa* (p. 40), which Underhill thought was brought from Sesachacha village and rebuilt in 'Sconset between 1824 and 1830 by Obed Joy. The original rectangular shape and the later "T"-form, if they ever existed, seem to be impossible to trace out today; nevertheless, the fact that the older part was brought from Sesachacha would indicate that it was a whale house.[11]

Centre Street, of the same time, showing at extreme left a portion of catslide roof of *Lucretia M. Folger House.*

5 – Some Shell Street Berths

On Shell Street, the last of the five thoroughfares to parallel approximately the line of the Bluff, there were five ancient cottages, of which the first three have disappeared.

The first, by the name of *The Anchorage* (p. 175), stood at the northeast corner of Main and Shell streets on land owned by Latham Paddack. Old photographs indicate that the cottage had a central chimney and a small ell at the rear, but no one knows where the place came from or if it was a whale house.[12]

Next northward stood a little, dark, odd-shaped house belonging once to Fred Willets Folger. It was known as *Hop Cottage,* or *Hoppe Cottage* (p. 211), and in the years immediately before its disappearance, as *Waldorf-Astoria, Jr.* Beside this murky snuggery was a tangle of sour-cherry trees embowered by hop vines, which in Middle Dutch were known as "hoppes," carrying three- or five-lobed leaves and inconspicuous flowers. In England, by the way, blackbirds and some other birds feed on spent hops, and become drunk so that they can scarcely fly. At all events the building was popularly known as the oldest one then standing in the village and was believed to antedate *Auld Lang Syne.*

From photographs it may be seen that *Hop Cottage* comprised two structures jammed together and ill-fitting — the south portion being the older, and probably

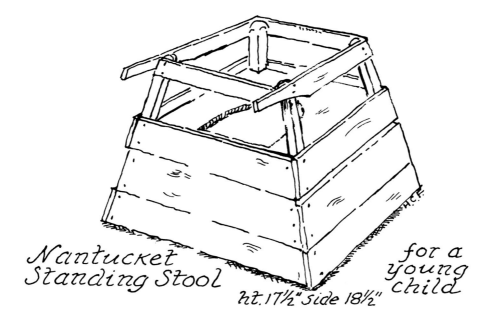

Nantucket Standing Stool *for a young child* ht. 17½" side 18½"

a whale house. The higher, north section had a kitchen shed "porch." "It was current talk among the boys in those days," related Underhill, "that Aunt Keziah Luce [owner of *Hop Cottage*], favored by the darkness of the night, would take boards from fences and elsewhere, and bring to the place to be nailed on the building the next day during construction." At least we know how some of the *Waldorf-Astoria, Jr.,* was erected, or that gossip is a dangerous thing.[13]

At the corner of New and Shell Streets, standing exactly opposite the village pump, was the *Thomas Brock House,* which had disappeared by the year 1881. It was a dwelling, probably a whaling hut, brought from the edge of the Bank to prevent it from falling into the ocean in the great gale of October, 1841. And that is all which is known about it — a mystery house (p. 211).[14]

Past the Pump Square, we find, there was a narrow alleyway in the shape of an ell on the left-hand side of Shell Street. Although a part of the lane remains, nobody knows its old name. It wound around the little old barn of *The Corners* and extended as far as *Castle Bandbox,* where it came to a dead end. *Castle Bandbox* (or *Band-Box*), shown on pp. 215, 217, and on the Evolution Chart (p. 130), is an imitation whale house, constructed in 1814 by Captain Edward Joy's father out of an old shop which stood in Mooers Lane in town.[15] Note that the three staterooms are of equal size (p. 203), exactly like the *George C. Gardner House,* an imitation whaling abode.

Underhill is the authority for the statement that there were no fences in 'Sconset before 1830 and that Captain Edward Joy put up the first fence in the village around the home of his father, *Castle Bandbox.* It appears that the fence "was done by Capt. Joy under the advice of old Stephen Coleman, because the movement of the cows on his land annoyed him. It was made of boards given him by his uncle, old Benjamin Worth, then living in Asa P. Jones' house [*Ivy Lodge*] from an old fence taken down in Plainfield. Old Sylvanus Coffin was much distressed at the innovation, because it compelled him to go perhaps seventy-five feet further to reach his lot." It is very difficult to believe that there were no fences in the village from the time of its founding about 1676 through 1830 — not quite two centuries. Englishmen loved fences in the medieval villages of England.

The last old cottage going up Shell Street is located north of the Asa P. Jones barn and nearly opposite to *Aurora Villa* and is appropriately known today as *The Little Red House* (p. 203). This was probably a whale dwelling and was purchased in Sesachacha village by George Gibbs from Solomon Folger. It was brought to 'Sconset after 1824.[16] George's brother, Samuel Gibbs, also purchased a cottage in Sesachacha about the same time, from Benjamin Folger, a brother of the above Solomon, and had it transported to 'Sconset, but Father Time has done away with it.

OVERLEAF: *Castle Bandbox,* Shell Street, 'Sconset, is an imitation whale house built in 1814 by Captain Edward Joy's father. *Photo, author.*

The Chanticleer about 1910. Left half was Uriah Bunker's

6 – Chanticleer, Hack-House and Others

New Street, shown dotted on our plan of the village (p. 42), was laid out in 1836, a year after the scheme was made, and had lots marked for individuals on both sides.[17] On the north side of New Street is *The Chanticleer*. The left-hand section of the older part of the present edifice was Charles Paddack's dwelling house, and was probably originally a whale house. It at first stood on the edge of the Bank and belonged to Uriah Bunker, then was removed to its present situation and added to by having a chaise house from Town jammed against its east or right-hand gable-end. The Paddack parlor was described by Underhill as measuring only six feet and one inch from floor to ceiling. Tall men were not permitted to dance hornpipes there, unless they entered into bond with the owner of the building to pay damages if they broke the plaster.

The Gale of 1841 must have caused a great deal of consternation in the village, especially among people living on the highway along the Bluff edge. Some structures went over, others were moved further back, even as far as *The Chanticleer*. On Elbow Lane, just off Broadway, for instance, is the *Captain Valentine Aldrich House* (pp. 124, 175), which is made up of part of two habitations, one of which was taken from the Bank edge at the time of the October gale of 1841 and belonged to Nathaniel Coffin, and the other of which was the most southerly house in Siasconset, located along Bluff edge close against the South Gulley and was owned by Eben Barnard and Stephen Coleman.[18] Although the Aldrich whaling domicile has been much changed, one little stateroom wart remains upon it.

'Sconset dray of a kind used for hauling fish or seaweed over the beach since the 17th century (Aug. 1887 photo). *Castle Bandbox* at left, *Ivy Lodge* beyond. BELOW: An old view of New Street, entitled "Any vegetation this morning?"

At this 19th-century Nantucket dance, facial expressions, gestures, dress, all hark back to the 17th century. The board platform obviously was put down for the occasion.

st of the offshore whaling at Nantucket. (Stereoptican views).

There are several other ancient structures in the village which can not be described for lack of space. One was a small den, which stood in 1814 on the site of the present post office. It was owned by Obed Coleman and his son, and was known as the *Hack-House,* because Obed himself ran a hack. At one time the shanty, which of course may have been part of a whale hut, was possessed by "Uncle" Reuben Ramsdell, who evidently inherited such poor ears that one time he knew nothing about the roof blowing off until he noticed the stars above him as he lay in bed. About 1872 or '74 that contraption was disjointed and transported to the west side of Morey's Lane in the village where it became famous as Billy Bowen's hideout, *Sea Shell,* now gone with the wind.

This picture of an old sea captain lying in his bunk looking up at the stars brings to mind that early Siasconset was a whaling station where the fishermen and their families squeezed themselves into their tiny staterooms and hanging-lofts for sleep. There is no other picture like that in the whole United States.

Still, 'Sconset is changing year by year, getting away further by the hour from the old medieval-styled fishing village which it used to be. This account has stressed, if nothing else, the continuous and callous changes which have taken place there over almost three centuries. This first summer resort in the American Colonies cries out for an historic zoning law rigidly enforced down to the smallest details.

Billy Bowen's "SEA SHELL" Once the "HACK HOUSE" after an old photo. H.C.F.

XIV

First Buildings in Nantucket Town

1 – Influences on Urban Architecture

IN SURVEYING the present Town of Nantucket for early buildings, we find that there are a few examples of the Medieval and Hangover Medieval Styles, as well as of two other styles, the Jacobean and the Transitional, which may be included in that broad category known as "Early" Nantucket — that is, before the Georgian.

It must be admitted that the Town is full of folksy traditions and building idiosyncrasies. For the one, there is the story about why Nantucket chimney stacks always lean southward. But of course that deviation is explained on the Island not by the workmanship, but by nature: the cold north rain causes the masonry joints on the north side of the chimney to freeze and expand. Clinkers, as we have seen, were used on some Island homes, but actually they were a boating material, where the overlap of the boards helped boats to push down the waves. Then, too, how may the six rafters in an old Centre Street abode which are spliced in the middle be explained? Nantucket rafters have no braces, and anyway, the middle of the rafter is the weakest point in such a member.

In wading into the complex subject of early Town building as a reflection of Island life, we soon learn that one of the thorny problems to be reckoned with is that many ancient town structures have been changed so much that chronology becomes difficult. Then, too, as Worth has well expressed it: "Buildings are found [in Town] in which the construction seems to antedate the period when the land could have been occupied. The only explanation is that the houses were first erected elsewhere."[1]

221

In short, in Nantucket as at 'Sconset we meet time and again with examples of the peripatetic proclivities of certain edifices. As against the desire for alterations and additions, held by those builders and joiners who could not sleep at night for scheming how they were going to change things, must be placed the attachment which Nantucketers have held for the old architectural styles — the old ways of doing things — and their reluctance to discard or cast away ancient habitations and antique customs.

Moreover the insular position of the Island and the strong tide of Quakerism in the early days did produce a lag as far as new experiments in building were concerned. We can be sure that life and construction in early Massachusetts did not keep quite abreast of the fashions of England; and in those two respects Nantucket also dragged its feet behind "the continent," the mainland of America. So powerful were the Friends on the Island that over a long period they maintained as little decoration and ornament as possible upon their buildings. Then, too, even if the Islanders were not Friends, they would be sure to vote against any new-fangled embellishments brought from off Island for their homesteads. The Quakers were taught by their religious beliefs to live and dress simply, and to use moderation in building a home. All told, they formed a stabilizing influence, and had an eclectic effect, upon Town building, until the 1810s, when whaling prosperity and worldly forces broke down the Quaker bulwarks.

But it is not wholly fair to blame the lack of progress in architectural fashions and decoration upon the Friends. There were other factors, like isolation, as has been indicated. The population in the early days included many persons born in Great Britain; and the inhabitants of England, generally speaking, loved the Gothic and were leisurely in giving it up, even after the year 1700 had passed. Further, the influence of shipbuilding upon Town construction was strong. Some of the joiners and cabinetmakers made ships as well as buildings and often embodied in their homesteads things nautical, like ship's knees, a rope handrail or a moveable ladder to a hatchway.

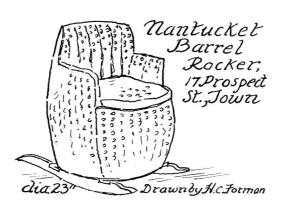

Nantucket Barrel Rocker, 17 Prospect St., Town

dia 23"   Drawn by H. C. Forman

Pencil sketch by W. M. Bartholomew (d. 1902), illustrating a Nantucket Island cottage that has fallen on hard times. Note two outshuts. BELOW: View of lower Main Street in Town in the 1890s, showing (a, b, c) three groups of row shops. False fronts were later added to a and b.

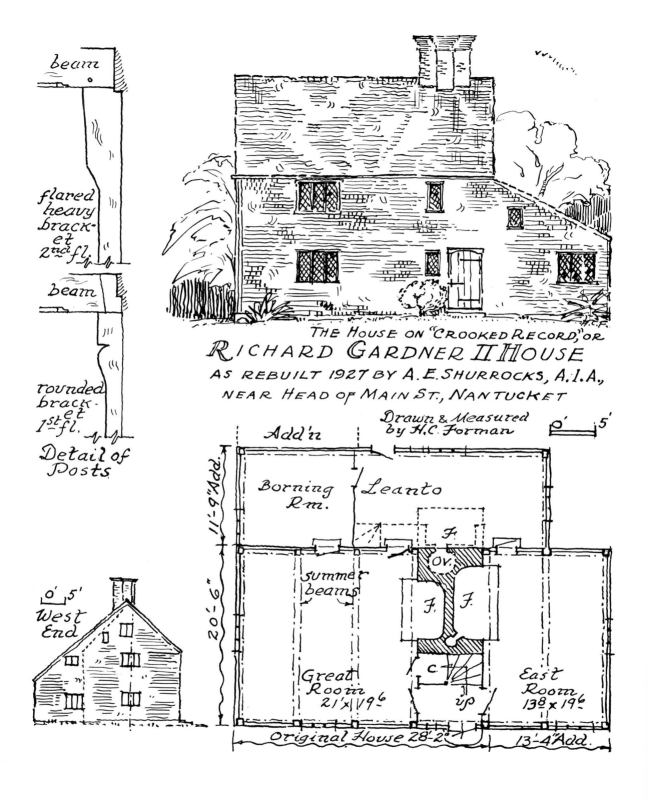

beam

flared heavy bracket 2nd fl.

beam

rounded bracket 1st fl.

Detail of Posts

THE HOUSE ON "CROOKED RECORD," OR
RICHARD GARDNER II HOUSE
AS REBUILT 1927 BY A.E. SHURROCKS, A.I.A.,
NEAR HEAD OF MAIN ST., NANTUCKET

Drawn & Measured by H.C. Forman

0'   5'

0' 5'
West End

Add'n

11'-9" Add.

20'-6"

Borning Rm.   Leanto

F.

Ov.

summer beams

F.   F.

Great Room 21' x 19'6

C.

up

East Room 13'8 x 19'6

Original House 28'-2"

13'-4" Add.

2 – The One-Room Plan

That there once existed in early Sherburne and later in Nantucket Town one-room-and-loft cottages of the style of the Middle Ages is probable, but to our knowledge at this writing none is extant. The first part of the little hideaway, without its additions and outshuts, shown in the Bartholomew sketch (p. 223), represents the type. On the other hand, we do know about examples of the one-room house, *two stories high,* such as the original *House on the "Crooked Record"* (1690s ?), at 139 Main Street, and the original *Zaccheus Macy House* (c. 1700), at the corner of Main and Gardner Streets. These lodgings follow pretty much coeval specimens of medieval style in Connecticut and elsewhere in New England. The first *Thomas Lee House* (1664), at East Lyme, Connecticut, is a good comparable example, where the floor plan was a single room on each floor, and there was a little staircase vestibule or entry beside the great gable-end chimney.[2]

In old England itself during the sixteenth and seventeenth centuries there were many farmhouses with only a single room on each floor and a chimney at the end.

3 – Saving a Homestead with Jacobean Trimmings

The first of the two Town edifices mentioned above is the *House on "Crooked Record,"* sometimes known as the *Joseph Gardner dwelling* or the *Richard Gardner II House* (p. 226). In its first stage (Phase I) it forms a good example of Medieval Style with Jacobean decoration.[3] The place is believed to have been constructed by Richard Gardner II, who married in 1674 and was father of Joseph Gardner.

This habitation in the years immediately preceding 1927 was a dilapidated carriage-house and store about 500 feet from its present location upon a large tract of land, the "Crooked Record," so-called because of its irregular shape. A sliding barn door had been installed in the south wall of the former Great Room, or Hall. Also, the brick chimney some nine feet square had been removed; but on the chimney girts, which are the beams against the chimney, mortar marks still remained.

Our plate (p. 224) shows the domicile, with later additions, redrawn from the blueprints of 1927 made by Mr. Alfred Shurrocks, A.I.A.

One of the important discoveries before the removal of the building to Main Street was the front door head having an elliptical curve, here illustrated standing

LEFT: Front of *House on "Crooked Record"* as rebuilt in 1927 by Shurrocks. RIGHT: Typical open-well stair of the Transition at *Captain Richard Gardner House* (*c.* 1724), with squat balusters and newels on a closed stringer. *Photos, author.*

LEFT: Part of East Room as restored in *House on "Crooked Record,"* Nantucket, in 1927. *Photo, author.* RIGHT: *House on "Crooked Record"* when it was used as a carriage house. Note original Jacobean door head on floor at right.

on end in an old photograph (p. 226) of the Great Room. Restored in the present house, such a door head is a feature of the Jacobean Style of England, the style of 1603-25 named for James I. The *Jethro Coffin House* (p. 230) on Nantucket is said to have once had a curved front door head,[4] but no original sources, like the Shurrock's blueprints, have been found to corroborate this. One of the finest examples of Jacobean door heads in this country was the cupid's bow over the enclosed porch doorway at old *Bond Castle* in Maryland.

In the *House on the "Crooked Record"* is another design of Jacobean inspiration. While the upstairs corner posts are the usual medieval brackets — heavy, tapered or flared, known locally as "gunstocks," and derived from tree trunks, as we have already seen at *Shanunga* (p. 100) — the downstairs posts (p. 224) possess the infrequently found *rounded* brackets with shoulders, something like the *echini* and *abaci* of archaic Greek capitals. Actually such rounded brackets are Jacobean folk capitals, the most ornate one in this country being perhaps at *Christ's Cross* in Virginia.[5]

The Jacobean was marked in England by Flemish features, such as curvilinear lines in masonry gables, wood door heads, stairs, capitals and the like. On Nantucket the style shows in sparse details, forming a trimming or dressing upon the Medieval Style.

The framing of the *House on "Crooked Record"* has been considered the most elaborate on the Island. For one thing the Great Room has not the usual single summer beam, but a pair of them, running parallel to the fireplace wall (p. 181A). Each beam and girt has chamfered edges and lamb's tongues. On the right side of the great fireplace, with its recessed and curved back and its herringbone brick panel, is a small door opening to a closet under the winding staircase. The door is made up of two planks with a molded Gothic profile between them — something like a series of recessed beads — and with butterfly strap-hinges, one of which was found in the house.

Not the least interesting finds in the residence — though perhaps a bit technical to describe — were the two pieces of original window frames (p. 183) from different windows. One is an oak *sill* which once held a leaded casement, swung on hinges, in the middle, and *fixed* leaded windows on either side of it. Each sash must have been fourteen inches wide, and the mullion bars between them two-and-a-half inches.

The other piece is an oak *head,* sawn off at the left-hand end, but retaining sufficient traces to show that there were three fixed windows, of the same width in a row as in the other triple window.[6]

From this discovery it is clear that in the earliest houses the Nantucketers used very few openings in their window spaces, because they had to keep out terrifically strong winter winds, and besides the summers were so cool that they needed little ventilation in their homes.[7]

4 – Another Homestead Enclosing Simplest Beginnings

The other example of the one-room plan, two stories high, is the *Zaccheus Macy House,* later called the *Reuben Joy dwelling* (p. 245), built about 1700, and much expanded. This earliest portion is believed to have been moved before 1700 to its present site from somewhere else, probably the Capaum Pond area. Both floors have "gunstock" posts and summer beams with lamb's tongues. The reconstruction drawing of the chimney is based on the lines of the floor boards which exist today in the second floor passage and on the chimney opening through the roof sheathing. No trace remains of the old Great Room fireplace, which must have been at least seven feet in span. We have shown approximately on the drawing the large slope or weathering which the chimney must have once possessed.[8]

There are other one-room plan dwellings of this height in Town, but these two which we have briefly described in their original state are sufficient to demonstrate the type.

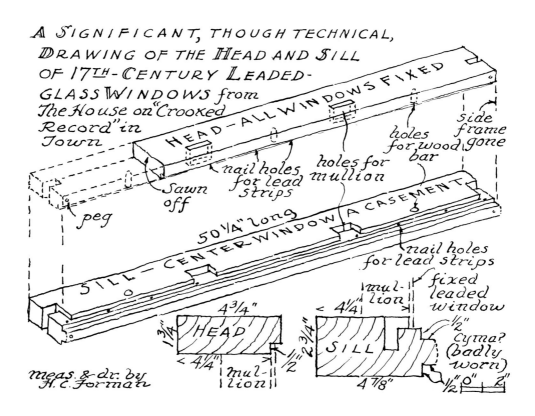

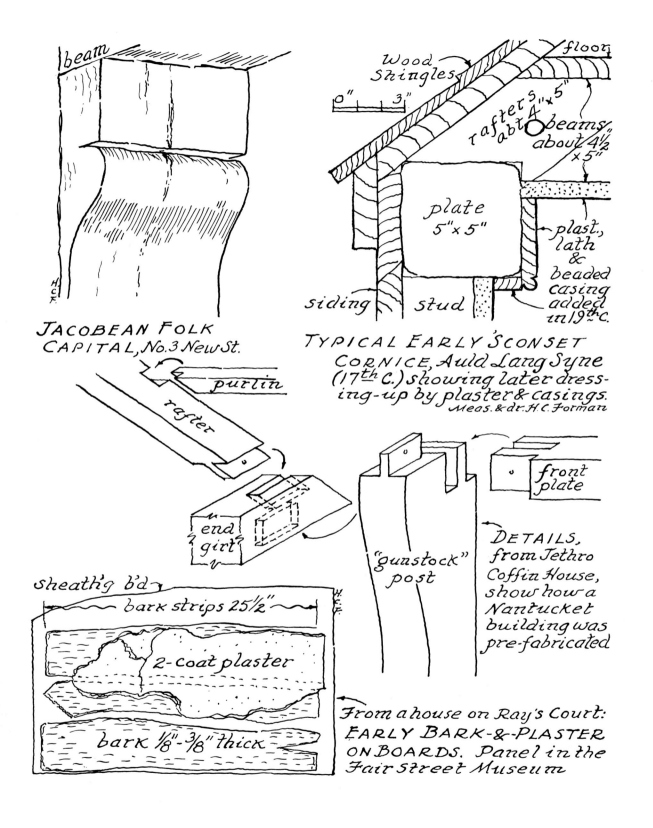

beam

JACOBEAN FOLK
CAPITAL, No. 3 New St.

Wood Shingles

floor

rafters abt 4"x5"

0" 3"

beams, about 4½" x 5"

plate 5"x5"

plast, lath & beaded casing added in 19th C.

siding   stud

TYPICAL EARLY 'SCONSET
CORNICE, Auld Lang Syne
(17th C.) showing later dress-
ing-up by plaster & casings.
Meas. & dr. H. C. Forman

purlin

rafter

end girt

front plate

"gunstock" post

DETAILS,
from Jethro
Coffin House,
show how a
Nantucket
building was
pre-fabricated

sheath'g b'd

bark strips 25½"

2-coat plaster

bark ⅛"-⅜" thick

From a house on Ray's Court:
EARLY BARK-&-PLASTER
ON BOARDS. Panel in the
Fair Street Museum

Taken soon after the Shurrocks repairs of 1928, this gives a good view of the horseshoe and catslide roof of the *Jethro Coffin House* in Town. BELOW: Stereoptican view of same building, about 1863, when part of the lean-to reputedly had been burned. *J. Freeman Photo.*

5 – The Twin-Gabled Jethro Coffin House

The one-room floor plan type of structure, flourishing on Nantucket, had its drawbacks. With only two areas, one for living, cooking and eating, the other for sleeping, it was poorly suited to the use of all but the smallest family of simple means. It is an axiom that family and furniture will increase in number, with the result that the early settler on Nantucket, when he did possess the means, would often plan a parlor next to his Great Hall, thereby making another standard domestic type, the medieval hall-and-parlor dwelling.

The finest example of such on the Island is the original section of the *Jethro Coffin House* (p. 230). But the type flourished elsewhere in New England, as in the well known *Parson Capen House* (1683), Topsfield, Massachusetts, and became well established in the American Colonies. In England, too, during the sixteenth and seventeenth centuries the hall-and-parlor abode was built by the thousands. The Great Room served for cooking and eating, and the parlor for a daytime living room and an overflow sleeping space. Upstairs were the Hall Chamber and the Parlor Chamber.

Over the years much has been written about the *Jethro Coffin House*, popularly known as the "Oldest House on Nantucket," and reputed to have been constructed in 1686. We take up the task of trying to brush away the erroneous cobwebs from the dwelling, which in its own right is an excellent example of early New England domestic architecture. There is no need for the misinformation which has grown up about the place in recent years. And after all, it has not had too good care during its long life: once it was used as a barn.

First, we come to the date of building. Worth wrote in 1906 as follows: "The date of its construction has been fixed at 1686 but upon what authority besides the assertion of Benjamin Franklin Folger in 1858 cannot be understood. In 1708 Jethro and Mary [Coffin] Gardner conveyed land and [the *Jethro Coffin*] house to Nathaniel Paddack, but no will or deed appears to show how either became owner of the same, nor is there any record of the marriage of these grantors. It is stated in the genealogies that their first child was born in 1687 and from this possibly it is inferred that the marriage took place in 1686 and hence that the house was built at that date. Such is the tradition in the family."[9] Even Dr. Will Gardner in his book, *The Coffin Saga* (1949), in the section devoted to Tristram Coffin's descendants, does not give any date for the marriage of Jethro Coffin (1663-1726) and Mary Gardner; and if a wedding date had been given, it would have proved little about the house.

Nevertheless just about every book and article written about Nantucket buildings in the last hundred years has given the date of the erection of the *Jethro Coffin House* as 1686. It is easy to copy off what another has written — to record hearsay. As to the date of construction, Mr. Frank Baldwin, one-time secretary of the American Institute of Architects, wrote an article which was reprinted (1928) in *The Inquirer and Mirror,* Nantucket, entitled "The Jethro Coffin House on Sunset Hill." Mr. Baldwin had an uncanny way of summing up the situation about the building date, which he did as follows: "The exact date of the house is somewhat obscure, but it may be placed between the years, 1685 and 1695. The Coffin family has selected the year 1686, and, perhaps to avoid unpleasant argument, that date is generally accepted.[10]

In 1686 Jethro Coffin was twenty-three years old. As far as the architecture of the original abode is concerned, it is perfectly possible that the dwelling was then built. But was it? No one really knows. Perhaps "1686 or soon after" should be true for the early portion of the homestead. That it is the oldest existing house on Nantucket is shown to be erroneous in view of three earlier buildings described in this work.

6 – Why the Coffin House Is a Partial Restoration

There are at least three events of interest in the known history of *Jethro Coffin's.* First, it was owned by the Paddacks from 1708 until 1840 — a span of 132 years; consequently it is much more a Paddack stronghold than a Coffin one. Second, it was purchased in 1881 by Tristram Coffin, of Poughkeepsie, New York, a descendant of the original Tristram of Nantucket. This new owner made repairs to the old home, thereby preserving it for posterity. Third, it came in 1923 into the possession of the Nantucket Historical Association. Under the aegis of Winthrop Coffin of Boston, the Association engaged the services of Alfred Shurrocks, the architect who renovated the *House on "Crooked Record."* Mr. Shurrocks measured the *Jethro Coffin House* in 1927 and, as far as he was able, renovated it in 1928. Assisting in that work was William Appleton, secretary of the Society for the Preservation of New England Antiquities, Boston.

It will come as a surprise to those who know the house that the restoration drawings (p. 234) of it by this writer little resemble the place today. But those diagrams are carefully based upon the Shurrocks blueprints and our recent study of the edifice. And in several instances the prints show the *framing* of *twin* gables on the front or south side.[11] There is not the slightest doubt that when first built the dwelling had these two gables side by side, like the *House of Seven Gables* and a few other seventeenth-century homesteads on the mainland. Why the gables were not put back in Mr. Shurrocks' work of 1928 is not known, but without these important frontal features there has been no real restoration. Mr. Shurrocks also measured the casement openings of the original building (Phase I), which proved to be somewhat smaller than those in the structure today. Our drawings illustrate the original casements.[12]

In Mr. Shurrocks' work most of the corner posts, girts, sills, rafters and diagonal braces had to be replaced. "So much repair," wrote Worth, "has been made to keep the structure standing that much of the original frame has disappeared."[13] Consequently he had a real job on his hands. The fireplaces were repaired or replaced. The part of the lean-to which had reportedly been burned before 1863 was rebuilt (p. 230) — that is, the Milk Room, and most of the kitchen and its fireplace. Wood casements with quarrels and calmes, or diamond panes and lead strips, replaced the later, eighteenth-century "guillotine" sash windows which had been inserted in the walls of the abode.

In 1927 there seems to have been one original corner post remaining from the second floor, and that was of oak with its top flared or tapered. A ship's knee (p. 236) was placed in the West Chamber — that is, the Parlor Chamber — sometime after the dwelling was built, in order to strengthen a weak corner post.[14]

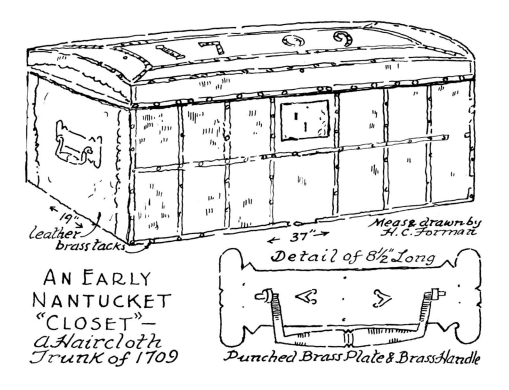

leather
brass tacks

19″

37″

Meas. drawn by
H. C. Forman

AN EARLY
NANTUCKET
"CLOSET"—
a Haircloth
Trunk of 1709

Detail of 8½″ Long

Punched Brass Plate & Brass Handle

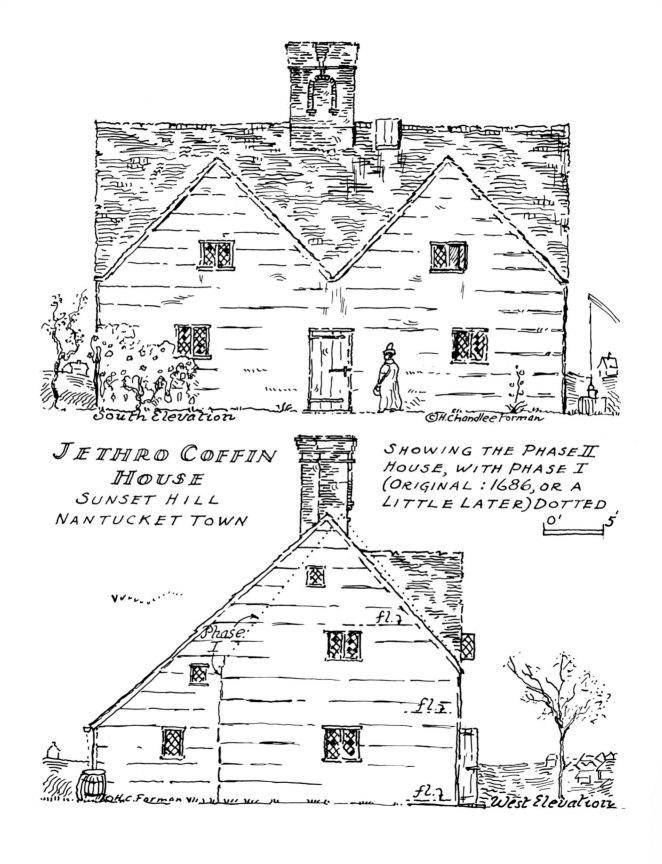

South Elevation ©H.Chandlee Forman

JETHRO COFFIN
HOUSE
SUNSET HILL
NANTUCKET TOWN

SHOWING THE PHASE II
HOUSE, WITH PHASE I
(ORIGINAL: 1686, OR A
LITTLE LATER) DOTTED
0'   5'

Phase
I

fl. 2

fl. 1

fl. 2

©H.C.Forman   West Elevation

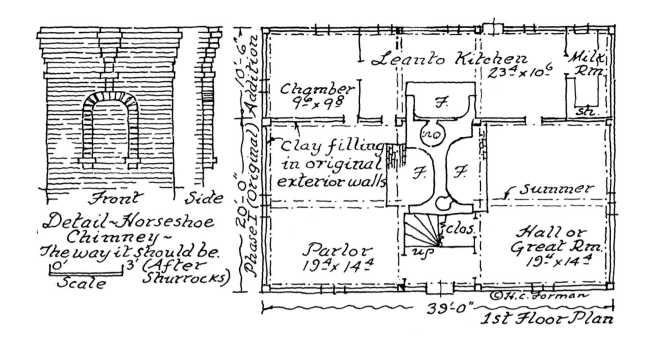

Detail~Horseshoe
Chimney~
The way it should be.
(After Shurrocks)

Front   Side

0'   3'
Scale

Chamber
9⁰ x 9⁸

Clay filling
in original
exterior walls

Leanto Kitchen
23⁴ x 10⁶

Milk
Rm.
Sh.

F.

no

F.   F.

Summer

clos.

up

Parlor
19⁴ x 14⁴

Hall or
Great Rm.
19⁴ x 14⁴

Phase I (Original) Addition

20'-0"   10'-6"

39'-0"

©H.C.Forman

1st Floor Plan

JETHRO COFFIN HOUSE
Nantucket Town

N.

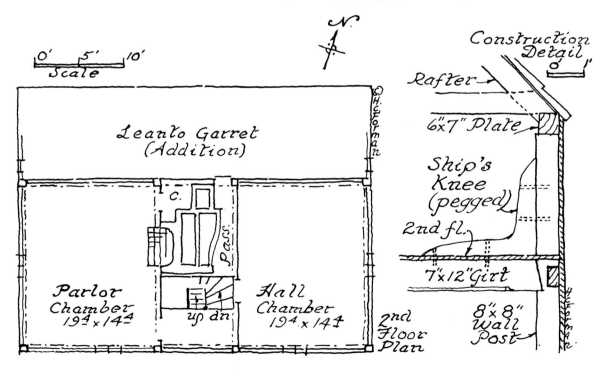

0'   5'   10'
Scale

Leanto Garret
(Addition)

C.

Pass.

Parlor
Chamber
19⁴ x 14⁴

up dn

Hall
Chamber
19⁴ x 14⁴

2nd
Floor
Plan

©H.C.Forman

Construction
Detail

0'   1'

Rafter

6"x7" Plate

Ship's
Knee
(pegged)

2nd fl.

7"x12" Girt

8"x 8"
Wall
Post

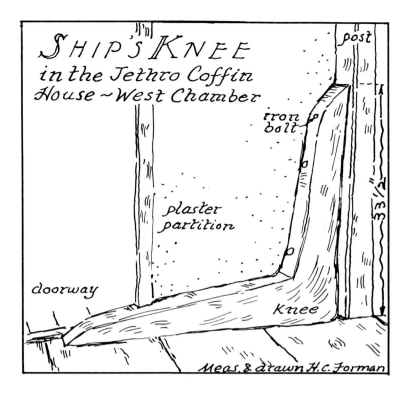

SHIP'S KNEE
in the Jethro Coffin
House ~ West Chamber

post

iron bolt

plaster partition

doorway

Knee

3'½

Meas. & drawn H.C. Forman

The architect's chief task was the raising of the chimney which literally leaned on the dwelling with age. It was found to be eight inches out of line at the west ridge. He also found a shallow cellar with stone walls about four feet deep, which extends along the whole front and some sixteen feet toward the rear.

In addition the Shurrocks blueprints show that the original house (Phase I) was a medieval hall-and-parlor dwelling of two stories and loft. At a later time, possibly around 1700, a lean-to addition was constructed on the rear, making Phase II — a development described in the next chapter.[15] It is interesting that the exterior walls of the first portion (p. 235), but not of the lean-to, have clay filling insulation. Also in his drawings of 1927 Mr. Shurrocks employed the correct terminology in identifying the two front downstairs rooms: that to the west being the "Parlor" and the other, possessing a larger fireplace, the "Hall." In the Old English vernacular the West Chamber was the "Parlor Chamber" or room over the "Parlor," and the East Chamber the "Hall Chamber."

These are some of the published myths about the *Jethro Coffin House*: it is the oldest house on Nantucket; it was built in 1686; it is primitive; both upstairs chambers have fireplaces; the West Chamber was the Bridal Chamber and has an "Indian" closet; there was no fireplace in the lean-to; there were originally five flues; there was no cellar; and there was at first a large porch on the front of the house.

7 – More Middle Ages Features in Town

Thus far we have found in early Town buildings that the following medieval features were used: steep roofs and gables, inclined at fifty-two degrees to the horizon, as in the *Jethro Coffin House*; casement sash and fixed windows of leaded glass; bevel-edged siding board walls with clay filling; exposed framework in the rooms, the beams sometimes with lamb's tongues; batten or board doors; break-your-neck or corkscrew staircases, that is, stairs in cases or boxes; eight-foot fireplaces with cooking ovens; and mud-and-clamshell mortars for chimney bricks. The types of roofing materials are the same as those illustrated (p. 101) for Siasconset.

But there is one very fine medieval detail in town which 'Sconset does not have: the brick chimney stack with "withes," which are vertical brick projections built to mark optically the partitions between the flues. Medieval stacks of this kind may be seen in England at Brinsome in Surrey, Petworth in Sussex, and other localities. However, almost all the "withes" in Town are Hangover Medieval, that is, they belong to a date after 1700; but the horseshoe withe on the *Jethro Coffin* chimney may be considered of Medieval Style. It is, by the way, a variation of the usual withe. Considering that all the good luck is running out, we believe that it is difficult to understand that the horseshoe was built to fight witches. On Nantucket the best withes are on the *Major Josiah Coffin House,* of a date well after 1700 (p. 252).

The only known leaded-glass window on Nantucket Island is also of the Hangover Medieval Style and is kept in the Fair Street Museum of the Nantucket Historical Association. It comprises a leaded, lattice sash, without styles or rails, which was fixed or non-sliding in the house framing, part of which is still attached to the sash. In fact, this piece of framing had been sawn out of a missing, larger house frame.

According to the ancient handwriting on the preserved frame which is more trustworthy than the extant typed museum label, it is a "window from the *Benjamin Brown House* on North S[t] Built in 1767 – on st—— by M. Barney." A reconstruction diagram (p. 235), based on a large-scale drawing made by this writer in 1962 for the Historic American Buildings Survey in the Library of Congress, Washington, shows this fixed, non-sliding, upper window as one of six units, with mullions between them. The lower sash were not fixed, but "guillotines," which slid upward, back of the fixed windows.

In this sash from the *Benjamin Brown House* of 1767 we have the remaining evidence of a transitional window – the halfway stage between the customary medieval, leaded, lattice casement on hinges, and the earliest type of "guillotine" sliding sash with rectangular panes, which was widely used after 1725 in New England. In other words, we have here, battered about in the Fair Street Museum basement, perhaps the most important example of a window sash in English America. It is the "missing link."[16]

While the standard early Nantucket exterior wall coverings were clinkers, board-and-battens called "muntin-and-plank work," and bevel-edge siding, there are some local variations which may be designated as medieval in inspiration. In the Fair Street Museum is a fragment from an early wall — a piece of horizontal wall sheathing board (p. 229) faced on the inside by wide bark strips to which plaster was affixed. Wattle-and-daub, or basket-work with clay, was probably used by the English on the Island and did not endure long because of the severe winter climate. The wattles would have become a sieve after the mud or plaster daubing fell away.

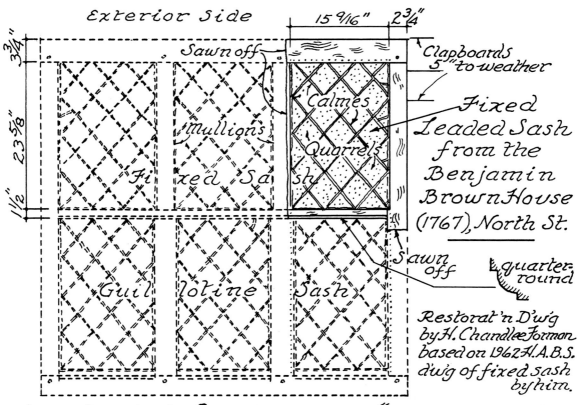

Nantucket Leaded-Glass "Guillotines"

8 – Following Through to a Weak Georgian

One of the noteworthy examples of Hangover Medieval Style is the *Old North Vestry* (p. 000) which was the Presbyterian Meetinghouse brought in 1765 from the North Shore of the Island where it was called the *North Shore Meetinghouse*. In that year, it appears, the Town granted the members of the church permission to store inside the Town House the "inside work of the North Shore Meeting House till it should be built during the coming summer." When re-erected, it was placed at the location where stands the Gothic-Revival *First Congregational Church* (1834) of Nantucket. A diary written in 1732 by one Judge Benjamin Lynde mentioned the *Old North Vestry,* thus: "Lord's Day, June 11, Mr. White preached very well at the new Presbyterian Meeting House." It would therefore be logical to assume that the edifice was constructed about 1730, and consequently the tradition that [it] was built in 1711 must be abandoned."[17] The claim that it was the first church building on Nantucket has no validity. The first Friends' meetinghouse was in existence as early as 1711, and besides, the American Indians with the help of Christian missionaries constructed the first churches on Nantucket Island.

In its physical aspects the *Old North Vestry* is two stories high and formerly had a gallery extending over the two main entrances in the front gable-end and along the two long sides of the structure. Today the interior has been much changed, since the gallery and box pews and high pulpit with sounding board have all vanished. In accordance with medieval fashion the oak beam-and-post construction is visible, and large diagonal braces, slightly bowed, strengthen the summer beams and the gunstock posts, two stories high. Originally the great meeting room was open to the rafters, but is now ceiled with plaster, leaving the summers exposed.

Other examples of the Hangover Medieval in Town were the row houses and row shops, with their gables facing the street — a *motif* widely known in England and in British possessions of the seventeenth century like Bermuda and the Bahamas. Row gables were used in Britain as far back as the time of the Anglo-Saxons in the fifth century. The well known view of London before the Great Fire (1666) shows many row-gabled streets. Further, the early lanes of Jamestown in Virginia and St. Mary's City in Maryland had row buildings with the gables to the fore.

In the old photograph from the *Old South Church* tower, Nantucket, is a number of row gables, contiguous one to another, with long valleys susceptible

OVERLEAF:

This photograph of the 1880s caught the beauty and serenity of the Nantucket harbor scene as it may have looked in colonial times. At far left is Commercial Wharf; in foreground, a fishing sloop.

to rain leakage. Two groups of elongated structures (p. 223), marked *a* and *b*, have party walls, and also false fronts, which were not always there. Across Main Street stood a two-story wooden store, *c,* carrying a double-gable, one being slightly larger than the other. And these buildings were constructed *after* the Nantucket Fire of 1846.

One of the surprising things about the Island to those who love to wander and look in the nooks and crannies of the Town is the evidence of continued Island hankering for things medieval even a hundred years and more after the Medieval Style had terminated. The chief sign of such reactionary work is the post-and-beam construction in many buildings of the 1750s and afterward. The corner posts, girts and summer beams persist widely into the era when the Georgian Style of architecture is supposed to hold sway. A few examples where the house framework is exposed in more or less degree are the *Maria Mitchell House* (1790), shown on page 256; the *Job Macy Dwelling* (1750s) on Mill Street; and the *Bunker-Dell House* of the early 1800s on Academy Hill.

Even if that last domicile is adorned with wooden quoins, a fanlight and a small Federal portico, there are inside plenty of exposed beams and posts. Because of medieval influence, the Georgian never got very strong on the Island. If Georgian mansions approximating *Mt. Vernon* and *Independence Hall* had been built on Nantucket, their rooms would have had summer beams, corner posts and lamb's tongues.

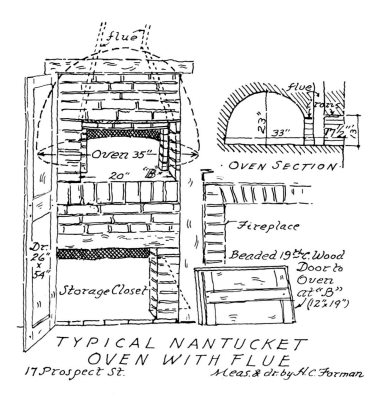

TYPICAL NANTUCKET
OVEN WITH FLUE
17 Prospect St.   Meas. & dr. by H. C. Forman

XV

Transitional Lean-Tos and Gambrels In and About the Town

1 – A Land of Catslides

ON NANTUCKET ISLAND a lean-to is *either* a large outshut or addition, with a roof of one slope, at the rear or side of a building *or* the whole edifice itself, including the long roof, called in Britain the "catslide," reaching close to the ground. And you may depend upon it — Nantucketers have been constructing lean-tos almost from the beginning of the white settlement.

The catslide was generally placed on the north side because the prevailing southwest wind tended to tear off fewer shingles than would be the case if the structure faced the other way. What Islander, besides, would wish to see his valuable shingles flying away like birds in the sky?

Inasmuch as the normal medieval building is *one* room thick or deep, any addition at the rear changes the character and the aspect of the design. And this rear outshut includes narrow "aisles" or "cells," which by a long, roundabout route were derived from the English medieval parish-church side aisles.[1] So slender were these rear cubbyholes and cuddies in old English homesteads that they resembled more than anything else aisles or passways.

Lean-to structures with catslide roofs and back aisles usually on Nantucket belong to the Transition — the Transitional Style of architecture, a style which is not very well known, but which is important for marking the halfway stage between the Medieval Style of the seventeenth century and the pseudo-classical Georgian Style of the 1730s through the 1790s.

243

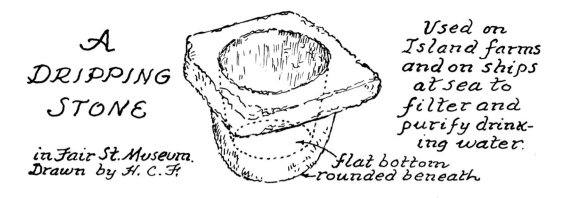

A DRIPPING STONE

Used on Island farms and on ships at sea to filter and purify drinking water.

flat bottom rounded beneath

in Fair St. Museum. Drawn by H. C. F.

On this Island the Transition flourished from about 1680 to about 1730; and there was also after that last date a strong *Hangover* Transitional Style, because the Nantucketer really loved the lean-to and hated to part with it. In a nutshell, the Transition was marked by a period of experimentation in building forms, like roofs, fireplaces and decorative details. To be more specific, we need mention, besides the catslide and the little back aisle, the gambrel roof — a roof of two slopes on two sides, the half-gambrel, the jerkin and hipped roofs and the catercornered fireplace. Then there are crude or heavy classical details, used sparingly, like cornice brackets or modillions, turned newels and flat pilasters.

It is interesting that in the Transition buildings were erected for the first time with aisle rooms at the rear, forming lean-tos. Eventually, of course, this kind of embryo floor plan blossomed out into the Georgian mansion, which was generally a full two rooms deep and a full two-stories-and-loft high, both front and rear. In the Georgian Style the lean-to disappeared.

Although the Georgian, a time of tea, china and good manners, was the favorite style of Nantucketers in the late eighteenth century, it should be realized that the Hangover Transitional Style flourished side by side with the Georgian, and in the number of examples was more prevalent and widespread than the Georgian. Because this Hangover Transitional represents an earlier era, which the Georgian does not, it is included here as rightly belonging to *Early* Nantucket. Consequently, Early Nantucket is not just a matter of time, but also of style, fashion and custom.

The Transitional lean-tos on the Island may be divided into two classifications, listed below; and it is not always easy to label them properly:
1. The Added Lean-to Type, like the *Jethro Coffin House* (Phase II, c. 1700?)
2. The Integral Lean-to- Type (*i.e.,* all built at once), like the *Thomas Macy House* (Phase I, before 1686) on Tattle Court.

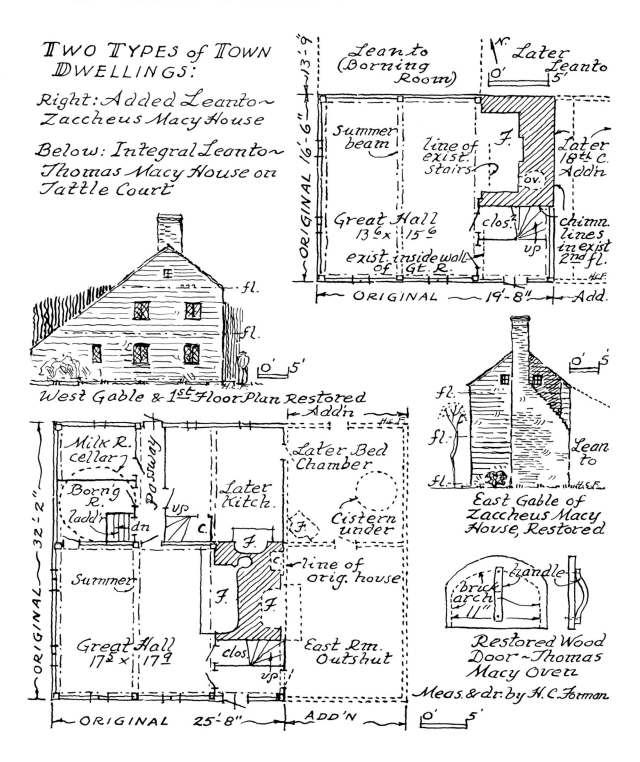

TWO TYPES of TOWN DWELLINGS:

Right: Added Leanto~ Zaccheus Macy House

Below: Integral Leanto~ Thomas Macy House on Tattle Court

Leanto (Borning Room)

N. Later Leanto

ORIGINAL 13'-9"
ORIGINAL 16'-6"

Summer beam

line of exist. stairs

F.

ov.

Later 18th C. Add'n

Great Hall 13'⁶ x 15'⁶

clos.

up

chimn. lines in exist 2nd fl.

exist. inside wall of Gt. R.

ORIGINAL ———— 19'-8" ———— Add.

West Gable & 1st Floor Plan Restored

Add'n

ORIGINAL 32'-2"

Milk R. cellar

Passway

Later Bed Chamber

Born'g R. ladd'r

dn

up

C.

Later Kitch.

F.

Cistern under

F.

Summer

F.

F.

line of orig. house

Great Hall 17'² x 17'⁹

clos.

up

East Rm. Outshut

ORIGINAL   25'-8'   ADD'N

East Gable of Zaccheus Macy House, Restored

Lean to

brick arch 11"

handle

Restored Wood Door ~ Thomas Macy Oven

Meas. & dr. by H. C. Forman

As in Connecticut the lean-to was at first usually an addition to the main structure, later to be constructed as an integral part of the edifice.[2] Such lean-tos in New England had the advantage of supplying a larger and more modern kitchen than the ancient Hall or Great Room and a newer fireplace built against the back of the old chimney.

At the *Jethro Coffin House,* the place was transformed into a Transitional habitation by the addition of three aisles or cells at the rear, making Phase II (pp. 230, 234). They are the borning room, to give birth; the kitchen; and the pantry or buttery — not named for butter but for bottles. Sometimes the pantry is called the milk room, a useful adjunct to the borning room.[3] Our restoration drawing (p. 235) indicated that the lean-to was added, the chimney stack with its horseshoe is a "T" in plan, and the ridge of the roof was moved a foot backward.

Another example of the Added Lean-to Type is the *House on "Crooked Record"* (p. 224), heretofore described as a dwelling of Medieval Style with Jacobean trimmings, but which finished up as a Transitional example when two narrow rooms — borning room and kitchen — were added to the rear. Now the normal procedure for a Nantucket owner in those days was to place a two-story addition on the other side of the chimney, as was done in a great many town examples. But in this particular Gardner lodging the place mushroomed horizontally on three sides. The East shed, by the way, was rebuilt using the existing mortise holes in the main-house framework as a guide for the rafters. The West shed, of unknown size, was never reconstructed.

2 – Some Integral Lean-tos

We find that some lean-tos were all built at once — one piece. The earliest of these seems to be the *Thomas Macy House* (pp. 245, 249) on Tattle Court in Town.

Elihu Coleman

Hidden away from the bustle and noise of summer living, this place later belonged to members of the families of Reuben Allen and Benjamin Robinson. Robinson used the premises as a carpenter shop and placed barn doors upon it. Recently the dwelling has been found by competent authorities to be older than the *Jethro Coffin House* (1686 or soon after). Their claims are backed up, it seems, by an old deed referring to the "Great Macy House," which stood in early Sherburne and was occupied by Thomas Macy I.[4]

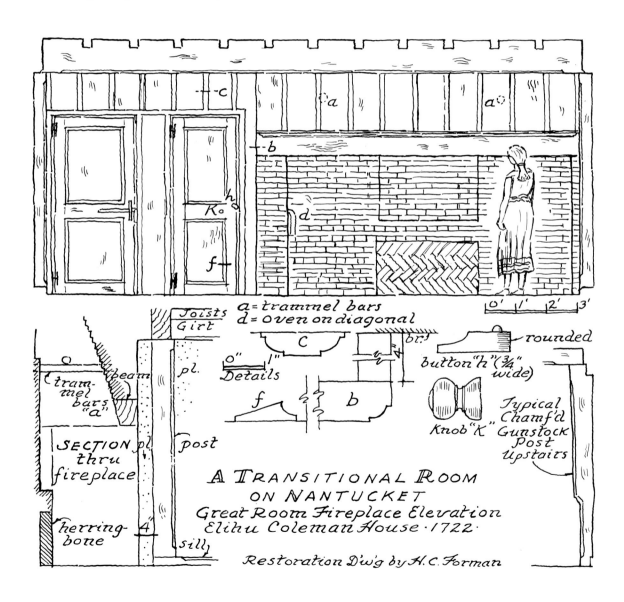

a = trammel bars
d = oven on diagonal

A TRANSITIONAL ROOM
ON NANTUCKET
Great Room Fireplace Elevation
Elihu Coleman House · 1722 ·

Restoration D'w'g by H. C. Forman

The *Thomas Macy House* on Tattle Court in Town, a lean-to of the Transition, was used as a carpenter shop in the 19th century. Renovated in 1949-50, this shows the Great Room fireplace. *Photo, author.*

The **Macy Great Room** is seventeen-and-a-half feet square with a chamber of the same size above it. The three back sides or cells are arranged differently from those in the *Jethro Coffin dwelling,* as may be seen in the plan (p. 245). When the *Macy House* was moved to Town, a round brick cellar about nine feet in diameter, used for storing vegetables, was put under the borning room. The loft is divided like those of early Siasconset by rafters into three bays, but instead of two purlins — the horizontal members between rafters — there are four. A few original bevel-edged siding boards, some nineteen inches wide, are still to be seen in the garret. At one time there were three pidgeon holes in a row on the west gable at loft floor level.

At the time of the renovation of 1949-50 in the *Thomas Macy House* there was found evidence which indicated on the first floor the existence of two sets of casement windows on the south and another couple of sets on the west. The bedchamber above had the identical arrangement. Those leaded windows — some of which may have been fixed, of course — have not been restored.[5]

The lean-to Kitchen of the *Elihu Coleman House* (1722) on Hawthorn Lane has a fireplace with a crane and a cooking oven shut by a green applewood door. Through doorway, right, may be seen a Bible or parson's cupboard. *HABS Photo.* BELOW: *Thomas Macy House. Photo, author.*

Probably the finest specimen of the Integral Lean-to outside the town is the *Elihu Coleman House,* built in 1722 on Hawthorn Lane in what was early Sherburne — a hall-and-parlor house with three aisles at the rear, borning room, kitchen and pantry. We find that the same old kind of medieval winding staircase (p. 249) hangs on here, even though it was designed at the end of the first quarter of the eighteenth century. The fireplaces include the largest one known on the Island — a little room in itself, having a ten-foot span — bigger than some 'Sconset staterooms (p. 247). The kitchen fireplace in the lean-to has a cooking oven, and the fireplace in the Parlor has beside it a "Bible" or "parson's" cupboard (p. 249), common to Nantucket. While most of the doors in the *Elihu Coleman House* are batten or board ones, there is an early use of the two-panel door, which became popular in the first half of the eighteenth century. Wooden latches and iron H-hinges with foliated terminations still persist from an earlier era. The straight posts downstairs and the flared, gunstock posts upstairs are sophisticatedly carved with chamfers and lamb's tongues — a decoration until this date usually reserved for beams and girts. At the rear of the abode is an ell called the "kitchen shed" (p. 251), which seems to date long after 1722, but nonetheless resembles the early 'Sconset whale house at the stage of being open to the rafters, after the wood chimney had been replaced by a brick one.[6]

Builder of the fine homestead in 1722 and occupant for over sixty years was Elihu Coleman (p. 246), a carpenter and venerated member of the Religious Society of Friends. He wrote in 1730 "A Testemony Against that Anti Christian Practice of Makeng Slaves of Men..." — the first tract against slavery published by a New England Quaker.

Very close in appearance to the *Coleman abode* is the *Captain Richard Gardner House,* erected about 1724 on Westchester Street in Town. On the front we find the same kind of chimney with withes as at *Coleman's;* on the other hand the front doorway has a five-pane transom, whereas *Coleman's* has none. Also the customary corkscrew staircase has gone, for here we meet with a typical Transitional open-well stairway (p. 226) — that is, a stair rising around the sides of a small square room and having thick turned newel posts and turned balusters on a closed stringer — an arrangement which when first used in England was criticized as a waster of space.[7]

On North Liberty Street stands another variation of the Integral Lean-to of the Transition. Built in 1724, two years after the *Elihu Coleman House,* the *Major Josiah Coffin House* (p. 252) has a more elaborate front façade and chimney stack than the previous example, and is considered on good authority to be "the finest specimen of ancient dwelling now standing on the Island."[8] Besides the added number of windows on the front, the really quaint feature is the use of

ABOVE: Interior of ell addition at *Elihu Coleman House* comes very close to 'Sconset type of medieval hall, opened to blackened rafters. *HABS Photo.* BELOW: *The Wood Box* in Town is a duplex, the right-hand part said to date from 1709. Probably one of first buildings to have lean-to roof raised a full two stories. *Photo, author.*

The *Major Josiah Coffin House* (1724) in Town, considered the "finest specimen of ancient dwelling" on the Island, belongs to the Transition even though it has medieval withes on chimney. *Photo, author.*

FACING PAGE: Quaint brackets in *Major Josiah Coffin House* show experimental nature of Transition. *Photo, author.*

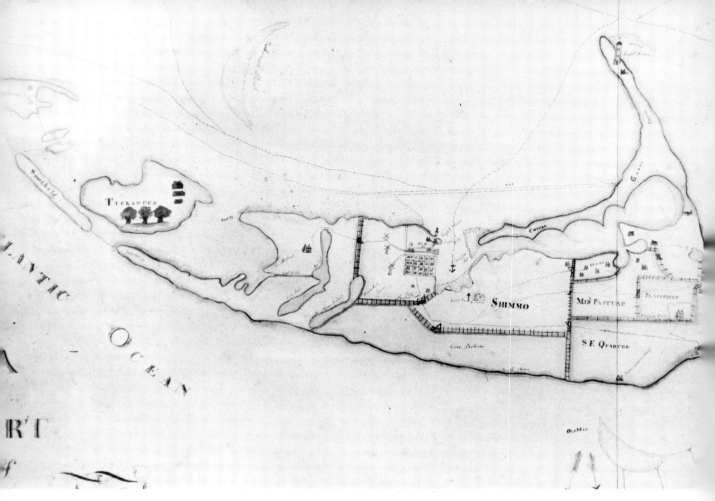

ABOVE: Simplified early map of Nantucket Island, painted Feb. 10, 1820, by Thomas F. Mitchell, shows that Sesachacha village was larger than 'Sconset. BELOW: Rear view of the *Nathaniel Paddack House* (c. 1720-25), showing its picturesque outhouses, now gone.

heavy wood consoles or "S"-shaped brackets under the main cornice except where the windows interfere, as may be seen in the detail (p. 253). The builder did not understand the nature of a modillion cornice and consequently placed his brackets picturesquely. As has been indicated, the Transition was a time of experimentation, when pseudo-classical decoration was sometimes fastened to a building without a true understanding of its function. As for the chimney stack, it has the finest withes on the Island.

There are several other Transitional lean-tos of note, like the *Nathaniel Paddack House* (c. 1720-25) (p. 254) on Sunset Hill; but once these edifices postdate 1730, they should be technically called Hangover Transitional, inasmuch as they no longer represent the halfway stage between Medieval and Georgian Styles, but only the slavish persistance of a style into later times.[9]

3 – Resistance to the Georgian Idea

On the Island there seems to have been much opposition to creating a Georgian-styled habitation by means of raising the lean-to roof to two full stories — making the rear as high as the front. There are at least three anecdotes current on the Island evincing antagonism to raising the catslide roof. The first story has it that certain Nantucketers compelled one house-owner to cut down the height of the rear posts of his home to keep to a "lean-to style," after it was discovered that the house-frame, manufactured on the mainland, had been shipped to the Island for a building two stories high front and rear. The second tale has to do with a legend coming out of the *Gull Island House* (1739) in Town, wherein it was claimed that the abode was the first building on Nantucket to be "built with the north and south sides of the roof of the same size" — which in effect means two stories high front and rear. The builder, Thomas Gardner I, it was reported, "was censured by the Friends for adopting such a fashionable design," meaning, of course, the roomier and fancier Georgian Style.

Best known of the three stories, the last concerns the deep-seated veneration of a Nantucket father, Richard Macy, who expostulated with his son Job when he learned that the plan was for Job to erect a domicile at the corner of Mill and Risdale Streets which was to be two stories in front and rear, without the customary lean-to. The father vowed that if the house were built in the new style, he would never in this world enter into it; and it is said that he never went into his son's home.

For that matter, lean-tos are not the only type of the Transitional Style to be found on Nantucket. There are gambrel-roof buildings, like the *Silas Paddock*

Late Nantucket Styles:

GEORGIAN
*Maria Mitchell
House 1790*

CLASSICAL REV.
*Atlantic House
'Sconset*

GOTHIC REVIVAL
*1st Congregat'l
Church 1833*

VICTORIAN
*Hotel in
'Sconset c. 1888*

House of about 1767 (p. 109) on India Street in town, the *Capt. Silas Jones House* (about 1774) at 5 Orange Street, and the *Seth Ray* or *Barrett dwelling* of about 1800 on North Liberty Street. There is that experimental example with combination of lean-to with gambrel roof, built about 1772 (p. 109) on Hussey Street, called the *Grindall Gardner House.* While the gambrel roof became popular on the mainland after 1700, Nantucketers appear not to have liked the form: there remain few examples of it on the Island; and anyway, most gambrels were built after 1750 and belong to the Hangover Transitional.

The "Dutch cap" roof is another experimental shape, of which there are two examples on the Island, one called the *Captain William Baxter House* (1790) on Main Street in Town, the other, of 1821 vintage, at 54 Centre Street. A "Dutch cap" is a pyramid or steeply hipped roof; and the one on the *Baxter mansion,* which may be designated as Hangover Georgian in style, is definitely an experimental affair — not having reached the ideal low-pitched hip roof, which the mainlanders liked very much. Perhaps the most famous of all "Dutch cap" roofs in this country stands on the *Governor's Palace* (c. 1710) in Williamsburg, Virginia.

At least we have come to realize that the Nantucketers hung on by tooth and by nail to the Medieval and to the Transition. With the advent of the Georgian Style about 1730, the "typical" Nantucket house came into being — if you mean typical of *existing* architecture.[10] But even when the Georgian was in its heyday on the Island, and even afterward, as exemplified by the *Maria Mitchell House* (1790) on Vestal Street, it was not pure Georgian. The front façade (p. 256) is unbalanced, and the chimney not on center. The stairway is carved with short, thin balusters on a closed stringer, not with full-length balusters set on the treads themselves. Further, the post-and-beam construction is still visible on the interior. Clothes are yet hung on wooden hanging strips, and wooden latches on batten doors are still predominant. The back staircase is a corkscrew, as ever dangerous. Then where is there evident the much vaunted Georgian? Its popularity on Nantucket was timid.

In closing, there is one final lean-to, no longer existing, which should be mentioned. After passing through a condition of decrepitude and desuetude for a number of years, this wind-blown abode by the name of the *Swain-Sevolle-Smith House* (p. 260), at Polpis, in 1902 succumbed to fire and was completely destroyed.[11] As may be seen from the reconstruction drawing (p. 257), the cottage went through four periods or phases of development, the first of which was presumably erected about 1704 and comprised only a Great Hall with loft above. When the abode was turned into a lean-to, a little back "aisle" was added to the rear, and a winding staircase was placed in that room. The three great summer beams or girders, with crude chamfers or beveled edges, were set parallel to the Great Room fireplace and possessed gunstock or flared posts. Of note in the house were the filling of clay and straw in the exterior walls, the ten-inch-long bricks and the small red Dutch bricks.

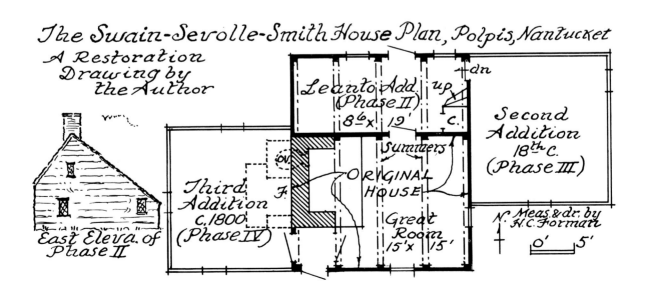

The Swain-Sevolle-Smith House Plan, Polpis, Nantucket

A Restoration Drawing by the Author

Leanto Add. (Phase II) 8⁶ x 19'

up
dn
c.

Second Addition 18th C. (Phase III)

Summers

ORIGINAL HOUSE

Third Addition c. 1800 (Phase IV)

Great Room 15' x 15'

N. Meas. & dr. by H. C. Forman

0'   5'

East Eleva." of Phase II

There must have been many details about this silver-shingled, weather-beaten, lonesome ruin which would have been worthwhile recording before its destruction. Its locale, Polpis, has come a long way from the days when the people of the Town thought of the farmers out that way as "Polpisy." It is safe to assume that the warning to children, "Don't act Polpisy," must have had some echo of Swains in it, for that hamlet would not have amounted to much without Swain buildings, such as the one here recorded. And the pity of it is that the *Swain-Sevolle-Smith dwelling* burned within the memory of persons now living.

This account of the early Island could be appropriately finished with the words found on a fireplace beam, covered over by ancient plaster, in a habitation of 1746 on Mooers Lane in Town:

When this you see, Remember Me.

12" high
36" long

*Crude Pine
Bench for Child
A Type used on Nantucket*

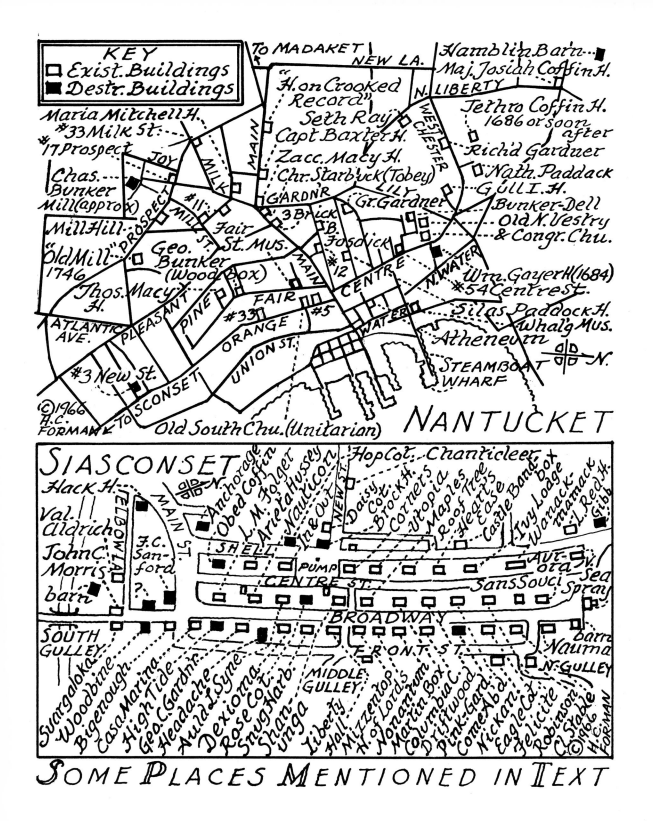

SOME PLACES MENTIONED IN TEXT

OVERLEAF: The north or back side of the *Swain-Sevolle-Smith House* shows a catslide roof. Built probably about 1704, it burned in 1902.

Notes

CHAPTER I

1. Austin, 1896, p. 227.

CHAPTER II

1. Ingstad, 1964; Pohl, 1952.
2. Forman, 1938, p. 12.
3. Macgowan, 1950.
4. Stockley, 1964.
5. Crèvecoeur, 1792.
6. Stackpole, 1953 (p. 17), indicated that the American Indian had to learn whale killing by European methods, because whaling was a European business before it became American.
7. Shurrocks and Shurrocks, 1940.

CHAPTER III

1. This Macy home site is believed to be near the place where stood in the 1880s the old Chase barn.

CHAPTER IV

1. Stackpole, 1953 (pp. 20-24), put forward the theory that the kind of fishing stage described by Crèvecoeur must have been the usual whale lookout throughout New England in an earlier time. Such lookouts also became common on the coast of Martha's Vineyard.
2. Underhill, 1888.
3. Forman, 1959.
4. The "Siasconset Path" went (1691) past a "great stone lying and being at old Siasconsett." This probably was the same big rock on the 'Sconset road marking in 1814 the first bound of Obed Mitchell's tract, Plainfield.
5. Underhill, 1888. Hussey, 1912, indicated *Shanunga* was built around 1682.
6. In 1775, 27 shares were laid out as one general field south of Siasconset with the Bank on the east. The western limit was to be eastward of the pond "quite to the [South] Gulley by Siasconset." Town Records, Nantucket.
7. In 1841 George F. Bunker erected another well and pump at 'Sconset by subscription. In drawing up the list he noted that "persons that do not pay must not use the pump."
8. New Street has been dotted on the plan of Siasconset because it was not laid out into lots until 1836, a year later, and should not be considered part of the original settlement.
9. In New England fish was usually dried or cured on "flakes," meaning brush or hurdles. McFarland, 1911, p. 96.

CHAPTER V

1. Underhill, 1888.
2. In the Nantucket Whaling Museum is a fine collection of scrimshaw, the most notable piece being a well-etched whale jaw pan about three feet long. The engraved lines, drawn and inked in with much realism, show a sperm whale being killed, cut up and boiled. The oldest known dated piece of scrimshaw which we have seen there is a tooth from the last whale caught by Joseph P. Sylvia in 1821 in the Nantucket ship, *Rambler*.

CHAPTER VII

1. Forman, 1948, p. 5.
2. *Ibid*, p. 86.
3. In 1632, "The Hall or Fier-house of the newe mansion house of the said John Parker." *Derbyshire Archaeological Journal*. Vol. 5, p. 45.
4. Braun, 1940, p. 59
5. Contrary to what Underhill and others have written about Siasconset, the staterooms were not additions in the sense of being a wing to the house.
6. Austin, 1896, p. 112.
7. Lloyd, 1931, p. 54.

CHAPTER VIII

1. Forman, 1948, p. 20.
2. Underhill and others have written that after wooden fireplaces came stone ones with clay mortar, but the probability is that there were few, if any, stone fireplaces, because stone was scarce on Nantucket. No early stone fireplace is extant in Siasconset.

CHAPTER IX

1. The *Thomas Macy House* on Tattle Court in Town is probably as old as, or older than, these two buildings; but at this writing is not known as such.
2. Hussey, 1912, p. 29.
3. If the brick fireplace had been *inside* the gable-end wall, but not touching it, in the manner of the usual early 'Sconset fireplace of masonry which we see today, there would have been a *brick* chimney or flue. But that was *not* the case at *Shanunga*.
4. This aperture extended out 34″ from the bevel-edged siding boards of the gable-end and was 9′-6″ long. In other words the brick flue must have come to 34″ inside the house. The summer beam extended out 3′-8″ or 44″ from the bevel-edged siding of the gable-end.
5. G. F. Worth, 1928, must have had Baxter's "lady" in mind when he described the "vague sense of some impending nautical experience" while approaching a 'Sconset cottage. "There on the grass plot which you crossed stands the wooden figure of a woman with flowing hair and garments, one hand raised as if urging on to speed the figure head of some vessel. The sole relic of some proud ship [Shanunga]? which met its doom on one of the treacherous shoals which lie in glistening white skirmish lines off shore to a distance of fifteen miles. Then, nailed above the entrance is a quarter-board bearing the name of another ill-fated craft."
6. Underhill, 1888. The writer's research has shown that *Auld Lang Syne* in 1835 was the property of a person whose initials were Z.H. In the latter part of the 19th century the dwelling was owned by Captain Henry Coleman, and in 1888 by heirs of Gorham Coleman.
7. Larger sash with twelve panes were installed on the Broadway front.

CHAPTER X

1. Underhill, 1888.
2. Chimneys against or inside the gable-ends of *Svargaloka* have disappeared. About 1900 a new fireplace was put in the middle of the east wall of the Sitting Room. The windows on the Ocean side and the interior two-panel doors are 18th-century. Old photographs show that the Broadway front had a narrow porch with four square Doric columns, a bal-

Wyer called this photograph "Three Fishers Went Sailing Out into the East," but the two men in the dory appear on the verge of landing.

Old view of fishermen at Quidnet. "Fishing's my line" is written all over them. Note two one-room huts and pent-roof outhouses for storage.

This view of Quidnet shows what remained of Sesachacha village, across Sechachacha Pond, in the 1880s.

ustrade, a roof carrying a Greek attic on three sides. Around 1910 the front porch blew away, for such things do happen there. The house was painted white or a very light color, except for the dark capping bands of the chimneys. The present fireplace crane came from *Hop Cottage*, 'Sconset.

3. In 1835 *The Woodbine* property was owned by a man with the initials O.B. See drawing of ocean side in Forman, 1961. On the site of this cottage was built after 1884 a large, barnlike home, *Big Sunflower*, of Victorian style.

4. On the authority of Underhill, 1888, *Big-enough* stood in position in 1814 on Broadway and was owned by Abijah Swain, later by Henry Paddack, and in 1888 by a Mrs. Reynolds. This writer has found that the place in 1835 belonged to Joseph Sheffield and probably was used for cod "fish flakes."

5. The front, which faced north up Broadway, had four windows and some Greek elements: a pilastered doorway, surmounted by a wide, white frieze and crude, low-pitched pediment. The west gable window was large, and when one of the photographs was taken of it, appeared to have had no sash, but only one shutter, and the curtains blowing outward.

6. The *Casa Marina* lot was owned in 1835 by Job Coleman, the "contents of this piece being a barn." It would appear therefore that the house was actually brought to this site after 1835 and perhaps should not be included in our restoration drawings of the Broadway street. Our restoration drawings of the house are based on measurements of the structure and on several fine old photographs. It was *Casa Marina* which Miss Eva Channing before 1877 drew in a sketch of Broadway from the upper north window of *Svargaloka*.

7. Underhill, 1888, stated that in 1814 Charles Nichols owned *High Tide*, and that Charles Mitchell bought it before 1820. This writer has found that the place in 1835 was owned by Job Coleman and

had a "House" upon it. In 1888 the abode was held by Mrs. Harrison Gardner and was known as the *Harrison Gardner House*. Hussey, 1912, took note that old *High Tide* had an owner, Franklin Folger, before the Gardners came into possession. In 1880 a renter of this cottage was Judge A. J. Northrup, of Syracuse, N.Y. — see Northrup, 1881. In the rear of the dining room at *High Tide* was a new kitchen with sink, hand pump and small coal range. Against the east wall of the kitchen stood a necessary house. There were two other outhouses joined to the dwelling on the east side. At the south end of the Great Room, then the Parlor, was a single bedroom, the remnant of the original twin staterooms. This room in the 1880s and '90s was always kept dark with the blinds drawn. The space was just large enough to contain a double bed. (Given by Miss Mildred Burgess.)

8. This writer's research has confirmed that in 1834 the lot was owned by Peter Chase and was part of the sheep common aforesaid.

9. Later this box was ceiled across, and a smaller door, only 15″ high, was placed under the ceiling to gain access to the hanging loft.

10. In recent years *Nauticon* was owned by George Sheffield Davis, whose mother was a Sheffield. At the rear of the dwelling, facing Centre Street, a yard was later formed by an "ell" off the kitchen and by a quaint stable or barn, made out of odds and ends — both structures 19th-century.

CHAPTER XI

1. This writer's research has revealed that this property was owned in 1834 by Barker Burnall, where "the south corner of his house" was noted. See also Forman, 1961, note 19. The *Gardner House* loft is much larger than most 'Sconset garrets, partly because the top of the plates on which the rafters rest are 24″ above the floor. There was but one win-

dow to light the loft, that in the south gable; and as far as existing known records show, was a 12-pane window, not a little square casement. The chimney was built 4″ inside gable-end for fire protection. At one time the kitchen addition was extended eastward to enclose a "bathroom." On the other hand the early necessary was a separate outhouse. Note twin sash window facing Broadway: in the 18th century there was probably one window only. Over each of the two openings is a heavily molded cornice of the 19th century. The window on the ocean side is wider and taller than any in the building and dates from 19th century. It may be noted that window of west stateroom is not original.

2. A photographic glimpse of what purports to be this house is shown on page 37. It is possible that all or part of the George C. Gardner barn was made out of *Headache House.* At any rate, when Miss Mildred Burgess built her modern cottage on this site, she had torn down a section of a shed, all that remained of the Gardner barn and perhaps of *Headache House.*

3. According to Underhill, 1888, *Dexioma* was conveyed by Stephen Hussey to Sylvanus Ewer. In 1835 the property was owned by one "S.E." Note that the little wart forming a vestibule for the later, present front door on Broadway is an addition of the late 19th century. In the 1920s the Greek attic boards on the roof were removed. The present stepladder to loft has been moved slightly northward from the position shown on the floor plan. The original board-and-batten partitions are still to be seen: the battens are 1½″ strips with ⅜″ beads. The purlins are saplings set just below the mid-point of each rafter; and the roof sheathing runs up and down in the usual manner.

4. Underhill, 1888, stated the cottage was owned in 1814 by Seth Folger and may have been built by his father. This writer found that the lot on which *Snug Harbor* was built was held in 1835 by

John H. Shaw and had a "house" upon it. In the Victorian era an oriental latticed small porch was built over the Broadway front doorway.

5. We have found that in 1835 the land on which *Rose Cottage* stood was owned by W. P. Our restoration drawing of the cottage is based on (1) studying and measuring existing structure on Morey Lane, much as the house has changed; (2) incorporating the little piece of the house sticking out from behind *Auld Lang Syne* as shown in the Channing sketch of before 1877; (3) examining the crude sketch of the cottage in the 1881 "Bird's Eye View of Nantucket Town."

6. Underhill, 1888, declared that the *Liberty Hall* property belonged in 1814 to Griffen Barney, while this writer has found that in 1835 it was owned by G.B. — probably the same person. In 1888 it was known as "Mr. Redell's house, opposite the post office."

7. These are some of the later changes to *Mizzentop*: (1) Phase IV, 1840s-60s: kitchen shed changed into large kitchen under main roof extended; eaves raised 22″; inside entryway on Broadway side incorporated; Broadway front door had freize above it; Gothic Revival crenelated "attic" added to main eaves and wart eaves; narrow clapboards put on walls. (2) Phase V, between 1865 and 1879: warts removed; garret roof raised over the *original* house, making a gable facing Broadway; crenelated "attic" removed except for a small section immediately over front door. (3) Phase VI, 1906 and after: east wing, roof of which unesthetically projected above main roof, was added to kitchen; another wing later added on the east.

8. This writer has found that a person with the initials B.C. owned the *Eliza Mitchell House* in 1835. She was probably Betsy Cary. Note that the outside siding of this house comprises bevel-edged boards. That the original abode dates from the early 18th century, not the 17th, seems to be indicated by beaded,

instead of plain, corner posts on the inside. The wall plate is also beaded. As the floor plan shows, additions and alterations, including a "colonnade," were made during the 19th and 20th centuries.

9. Underhill, 1888, gave out that *The Martin Box* was then owned by Mrs. Aaron Coffin, that it was built by Obadiah Folger and that its origin was a single room. He incorrectly stated that the little bedrooms, or staterooms, were then added. According to this writer's research, this property was owned in 1835 by a person with the initials R.F. Note that in Phase III a small kitchen was added to the north end; and then an old boat house was added to that kitchen. Curiously the roof of the boat house reached higher than the main roof. Traces of the double doors of the boat house may be seen in the discolored shingles shown in the old photograph, entitled "Fisherman's Cottage, Siasconset" (p. 170). The nine-foot-wide Great Room proved much too narrow, so that in Phase V the whole Broadway front was projected outward some four feet, to almost line up with the early wart addition on the east stateroom, and likewise the twin staterooms themselves were extended southward for almost five feet. The roof over Kitchen and Parlor was also raised some four feet.

CHAPTER XII

1. The Nantucket *Inquirer and Mirror* (August 20, 1887) stated that "many years ago there were three hermits living at 'Sconset. One cottage named 'Nonantum' was the home of Franklin Folger..." This dwelling has mushroomed in all directions: there are now three floors, and two large rooms have been added to the Broadway front, making an entirely new façade.

2. Underhill, 1888, presented the wild guess that *Columbia Cottage* is "more than 100 years old, was built by Benjamin Bunker who died 40 years ago [*i.e.,*

c.1848] at the age of 90," and in the date of construction seems to be off by two or three decades. This writer has found that in 1835 the property belonged to William Coffin, who was called "president" because he had that office in a local insurance company. The northwest corner of the lot was situated 39/100 of a rod from the southwest corner of John C. Coffin's house. Other, later owners were Edward Kelley, Robert Coffin, Capt. William Cash and (1888) Mrs. Cash.

3. Before the Broadway front of *Columbia* was extended out some six feet, there was a front porch with small, square columns, and a Greek boarded "attic" on the main eaves and those of the wart. Still later photographs illustrate in the same spot a Victorian front porch with turned columns and an "attic" with balusters between square posts. Gaily striped hammocks and awnings decorated the verandah.

4. Referred to by Underhill (1888) as "the dilapidated little house...now owned by Mr. Cromwell G. Macy of New York." In 1835, we have found, it was John C. Coffin's house. Before that time, according to Underhill, it belonged to Eben Gardner in 1814, and before that jointly to Tristram Pinkham and Eben Gardner.

5. Underhill, 1888, stated that *Eagle Cottage* was in its present site in 1814 and that "in 1879 Capt. William Baxter was inclined to sell it for $200 including its furniture, but on second thought he changed his mind, and four years after he sold it for $900." In 1835, as this writer has learned, the property was the home of Samuel B. Folger. The front of the cottage has been pushed out some eight feet on the Broadway side, and the south gable-end has been extended about three feet; and there were further additions at the rear, as shown on the floor plan. Benjamin Ferris (b. 1780, d. 1867) was a native of Wilmington, Del., and in 1804 married Fanny Canby. He was the author of a number of books, including *A History of the Original Settlements on the Delaware* (Wilmington, 1846).

6. This writer has found that *Clark's Stable* was owned in 1835 by E.C. — presumably Elisha Clark. Underhill, 1888, declared that at one time Mr. and Mrs. F. J. Crosby used to come from Town and occupy the upper portion — that is, the part having the Victorian octagonal bay — on Sundays, and keep their horse in the barn, which was part of the building to the north. At last Mr. Crosby saw that there was trade enough in Siasconset to warrant a store, and he enlarged the south end.

7. In 1835 the property belonged to one U. F. By 1881 the front stateroom wart had been taken away. In 1893, Mr. H. C. Gardner purchased the dwelling and extended the kitchen area northward and eastward, raised the roof in 1909, and ended by adding to the rear or west side.

8. This writer found that in 1835 *Nonquit* was the "Timothy M. Gardner House lot." There was a barn in the northwest corner. In the 1880s the property belonged to Captain Charles C. Mooers. After 1881 the cottage was enlarged by a second story and by a porch and porch chamber, in Victorian style. Later the front porch became enclosed. Note that the 1881 "Bird's Eye View of the Town of Nantucket" indicates that two outhouses, a small one and a large one, stood on the north side of *Nonquit*. They had gable-ends to Broadway, the smaller one in front of the larger. An old photograph of *Felicité* also seems to prove their existence.

9. Underhill, 1888, stated this cottage was then in possession of a Captain McCleave, and that about 1868 the second story was added — a time which corresponds closely with the date of 1865, or soon after, when Joseph Mitchell placed a "Broadway gable" on top of the *Mizzentop*. The old photograph of *Felicité* in the 1860s-70s shows that a door once stood in the middle of the big gable-end facing Broadway.

10. See 1881 "Bird's Eye View of the Town of Nantucket." An unattractive two-story addition to *None Too Big* cottage was built across the gable-end facing Broadway, the downstairs portion of which structure was used for a grocery store by Richard Burgess & Sons in the 1910s-20s. Underhill, 1888, forgot to mention this building, and Hussey, 1912, confused it with *Felicité*.

11. This arrangement can perhaps be explained by assuming that the original wall had the customary bevel-edged siding exposed on the inside as well as the exterior; that the occupants dressed up the interior by placing lath and plaster directly on siding between studs — a common method in 'Sconset; and that when more insulation was needed, a new layer of lath and plaster was placed across the studs in the usual manner.

12. Underhill, 1888, stated that it was then owned by Mrs. J. H. Belcher. This writer has found that *Sans Souci* in 1834 was "William Brown's House at Siasconset." This same Brown also owned the empty lot across the road to the north of this cottage. In our drawings of Phase IV we have succeeded in locating eleven of the thirteen windows mentioned in 1879. Also in this Phase IV was a large shed, or outshut, 23' long and 8' wide, which fitted nicely against *Sans Souci* and the lower portion of the boat house roof. Additions since 1930 have spoiled the quaint appearance of the dwelling.

13. A distinctive feature is the incipient or embryo "freestanding" brick chimney, built in Phase III to run up the outside of the gable-end.

14. This cottage was not called *Nauma* by Underhill or anyone else; it is possible that in 1888 it had no fancy name. Probably the name came from a sign "Nauma," found half a century ago in the barn on this property. The sign "Marion Street," tacked on this house, was found in the barn by this writer when he was a child. This writer has discovered that in 1835 the Nauma lot on which the house stands was owned by a person with initials O.S. and the ocean or front portion of the lot by one

R.M. The *Robinson House* was squatted down upon a corner of the Nauma lot, but that appears to be the way in which many 'Sconset cottages were erected.

15. Underhill, 1888, declared *ex cathedra* that *Nauma* was used "as a public house [tavern] and was kept by Rachel Paddack, the widow of Jonathan Paddack, and a Quaker woman." Did Underhill mean that both Rachel and a Quaker woman kept tavern there? Few Quakers would get satisfaction from that interpretation. In the 1860s the house belonged to Mrs. George Richardson, whose heirs, the Mitchells of *Mizzentop*, sold the property in 1910 to this writer's father, Horace Baker Forman, Jr. The photograph of the front of *Nauma*, taken in 1910, probably shows the Mitchell gentleman who sold the abode to our family, which held it forty-one years.

16. In Phase IV the rear wart, located on Broadway, was removed, possibly because it interfered with increased horse traffic up the lane. This writer has held a hunch that this rear wart was moved to the ocean or east side of the dwelling, was enlarged and was attached to the kitchen. Also in Phase IV the eaves were raised three feet to gain headroom in the loft, and the twin bedchambers or staterooms were removed, the Parlor then becoming 16½ feet square. Like similar changes at the *Mizzentop*, the main front had its face lifted: larger windows, a front doorway of 1870-type panels and trim, shingled walls, a Greek "attic" on the roof, and an inside entryway which was partly taken off the kitchen. Some of the interior doors were grained with ochre to make a pattern, and floor boards were spattered to make a criss-cross design.

17. The *Nauma* barn, made of driftwood and various old timbers from other buildings was brought in 1866 from Shimmo by Mr. George F. Mitchell. In 1881 this stable appears to have had an ell which projected out into Broadway. At *Nauma* Elizabeth Chandlee Forman wrote several of her poems, notably "The Little Grey Lane," obviously referring to Broadway and this cottage (Forman, 1919). In her second volume (Forman, 1951), there is a poem, "Rose of Sharon," which undoubtedly refers to the great althea trees in the front yard of *Nauma*. Since the Samuel Murrays bought *Nauma* in 1951 the property has been appreciatively renovated. Old split-tree-laths in east bedroom are shown through a glass panel to visitors; the Parlor beams have been uncovered; the "Escape Scuttle" is unchanged.

18. See 1881 "Bird's Eye View of the Town of Nantucket."

CHAPTER XIII

1. In 1888 this well gave the name to the only daily newspaper ever printed on Nantucket — "The Sconset Pump."

2. See "Bird's Eye View," *q.v.*

3. This writer's research indicates that the owner in 1834 was Z. C., probably another Coffin. The *Arietta House* does have one mark of distinction: the two tall stateroom warts. The west wart must have been built since the 1870s because it does not show in a photograph of that time; it could have replaced an earlier wart.

4. "The little yellow cottage called 'Sunnyside'... belonging to the heirs of Capt. Charles P. Swain, is very old. Capt. Swain told the writer [Underhill, 1888] that he knew the house in 1806, and that then it was known to very old." According to our research the property in 1835 was owned by one J.M.

5. In 1835 *The Corners* was possessed by one N.B., possibly Nathaniel Barnard. One of the forgotten points of interest about this lot is the tiny property which stuck out into the Pump Square which was held by G.U., the initials of George B. Upton. When New Street was laid down in 1836, it is possible that little piece of ground became part of the Square.

6. In 1834 *Utopia* was the "House Lot" of Thomas Barney. The highest part of the

house was probably added in the 1780s-90s, and the north shed about 1890.

7. Named *Irving House* because it was the summer home of Mrs. Billy Thompson, the noted actress called Isabel Irving. Our own research has revealed that in 1834 it was owned by Sylvanus Coffin. Underhill, 1888, stated it then belonged to old Captain Obed Bunker.

8. Underhill, 1888, mentioned also that *Hearts Ease* was then held by Capt. Edward B. Hussey, and that for many seasons was occupied by Mr. and Mrs. J. Ormond Wilson and family of Washington, D.C. In 1835 the owner was one S. F., whoever that was.

9. A few four-pane-wide sash, which were later insertions, help to give distinction to the dwelling. About 1815 Frederick Mitchell is believed to have bought the place. In 1834 it was called the "Benjamin Worth House at Siasconset."

10. In 1833 *Wanackmamack* was the "Susan E. Elkins House." Although the writer's drawings from an old, faded watercolor of the 1880s by J. B. Reid shows a west wart, there was no corresponding east wart. See 1881 "Bird's Eye View of the Town of Nantucket." In later years the house has added huge Victorian diamond-pane windows, capacious glass verandahs and other features which have completely destroyed the picturesque cottage of the 1880s and before.

11. "The late Josiah Macy enlarged it and put on clapboards so that its characteristic features as a fisherman's cottage were lost, and it has been further enlarged" (Underhill, 1888). In 1835, according to our research, the "villa" was owned by one I. N. At that time Centre Street crossed Broadway and extended northward the length of one lot, and then came to a dead end. That was the lot of William Brown, and in 1881 there was a house there.

12. Old photographs show that *The Anchorage* had a central chimney and a small ell at the rear. There was a 19th-century Greek "attic" board, punctuated by dark squares.

13. According to Mrs. Julia Macy Urann, *Hop Cottage* was popularly known as the oldest building in the village and was believed to antedate *Auld Lang Syne*. With the cottage now gone, there is no way to check on this tradition for accuracy. According to this writer's research, *Hop Cottage* is not shown on the 1835 plan of Siasconset.

14. By 1881 a small one-story building replaced the *Brock House*, and formed the "hangout" of *Uncle Nat's Shanty*. It had vertical board walls, wide and overhanging eaves and large windows — all Victorian. One old photograph shows it as an "Ice Cream Saloon," where "grandmother" Folger made and sold ice cream.

15. In 1834, the "Castle" was owned by W. Joy. It seems to the writer that the shop which was brought from Mooers Lane in Town formed the Great Room or Parlor, to which were added the three chambers, the unfinished kitchen addition and the outshut back of the kitchen. Some time after 1814 the three staterooms were enlarged four feet to the southward.

16. In 1835 the property was owned by S. G., presumably Samuel Gibbs. Apparently the two staterooms at *The Little Red House* were removed from the south end of the Great Room and shuffled around to the west side of that room, as may be seen in the floor plan. There may have been a third or "closet" stateroom inserted between these two chambers. The post construction shows in the early kitchen addition, and the two-panel doors and thin wooden latches indicate an early 18th-century date.

17. Samuel B. Swain owned lot number 1, where stood the *Thomas Brock House* formerly. There were altogether 20 lots, as well as three additional which did not border on the highway.

18. The "S. C." marked on a lot in the 1835 village plan probably refers to Stephen Coleman and possibly shows where part of the *Valentine Aldrich* house came. Two other structures saved in the gale

This old photograph of a rutted, sandy road at the back of Nantucket Town evokes wraithy visions of ancient Sherburne, the first town on the Island.

of 1841 were the *Captain George W. Coffin House* on the north side of New Street and part of *George C. Macy's abode* on Main Street in the village. See Underhill, 1888.

CHAPTER XIV

1. Worth, 1928, p. 257.
2. Kelly, 1924, fig. 1.
3. Worth, 1928, p. 228. The original house does not appear to have been a lean-to, because summer beams do not carry through into rear additions.
4. Macy, 1929.
5. Forman, 1948, figs. 94, 99. Each of the buildings which went into the erection of *Mill Hill*, a recent homestead near the *Old Mill* in Nantucket, had the rounded bracket capital. These were the *Hamblin House* (c. 1696 ?) and *No. 3 New Street*, and a dwelling on the Madaket Road near Town.
6. The Great Room and the chamber above it were restored with triple wooden casements with leaded glass and mullions. Other casements were put in the later additions to give an overall harmony. Some time after the reconstruction work by Mr. Shurrocks in 1927, two pieces of original frames from different windows in the dwelling came to light and have been drawn by the writer. No vertical members of these frames were found, so that their heights will probably never be known. Note that in the case of the fixed window, there was no style or rail: the lead perimeter was nailed securely in a rebate or recess in the heavy framework of the windows.
7. Wooden shingles were placed over the bevel-edge siding boards for their protective qualities. From Joseph Gardner the house descended to his son, Caleb Gardner, who later sold it to George C. Gardner. After 1800 the place was no longer occupied as a home.
8. The chimney stack cut through the ridge almost on center. A drip board must have been nailed to the siding of the chimney gable in order to cover the

steep rake of the brick weathering, so that the rain would not infiltrate at that point.
9. Worth, 1928, pp. 225, 226.
10. Coffin, 1911, declared that there used to be in the loft the figures "1686" on a piece of mortar, which was destroyed. Now that bit of information is about as reliable as the account of the brick at *St. Luke's Church*, Virginia, having the date "1635" upon it. In the *Jethro Coffin House* Mr. T. Coffin did not state who saw the numerals and when; or whether the figures were clear or ambiguous; or who eradicated the figures; or whether they were old or modern style numerals; or when they disappeared.
11. One print illustrates a "Section at Middle Rafter Showing Former Front Gable." In the Shurrocks' upstairs plan he showed all the rafter mortise holes of the two "old front gables." On a drawing of the front framing he presented the rafters of the two front gables in place.
12. The present modern casement sash on first floor are 16″ by 3′-4″ in size. Shurrocks showed in his prints a conjectural reconstruction of the raised brick emblem, called a horseshoe, on the stack. This writer has redrawn this reconstruction, even though it was never built.
13. Worth, 1928.
14. A puzzling feature about the place is that certain authors, like Worth, indicated the exterior boards were originally nailed vertically upon the·building, as was done elsewhere on the Island. Shurrocks' floor plans show the usual posts and studs to which horizontal siding boards were nailed. And his West Elevation actually shows horizontal boards in place from ground to ridge. These were bevel-edged boards.
15. Proof of the Jethro Coffin lean-to being an addition is shown in Mr. Shurrocks' measured drawings, such as "West End of House," where early siding boards on lean-to are slightly narrower than those on original structure; or as "Elevation of Lean-to," where lath and plaster are shown on top of the original horizontal

siding boards on lean-to side of the rear wall of original house.

16. This leaded, fixed, upper sash, was labeled "casement" by Duprey (1959, p. 24). Its original height was 24″, but the leadwork has been sunk in a groove in the frame at the top. The leadwork is attached to ½″ rebate in frame by small rose-headed nails. Quarrel size: 4¾″ x 6″ and about ¹⁄₁₆″ thick. The calmes are ⁵⁄₁₆″ wide, and the small lead ribbons about ³⁄₁₆″ wide. Oak saddle bars are ⁷⁄₁₆″ square.

It was Mr. J. Marshall Whiting in the summer of 1962 who discovered on the interior of the window framing evidences of 1) flat wear on the left frame, and 2) a long channel on right mullion, presumably worn down by a peg of the lower or "guillotine" sash.

Note that F. J. Kelley (1924, fig. 94) illustrated a lattice leaded sash from Guilford, which he called "double-hung" — although it was never hung. He found no traces of the window framing, nor did he know whether the sash slid upward, like a "guillotine," or horizontally, as was often done.

See writer's H.A.B.S. drawing of 1962 for further details of this Nantucket leaded window.

17. Worth, 1928, pp. 235, 236. In spite of this historic reference the church issues pamphlets declaring that the Congregationalists claim the distinction of having erected on Nantucket the first church building, the *Old North Vestry*, in 1711.

CHAPTER XV

1. Forman, 1948, p. 90
2. Kelly, 1924, p. 12.
3. Mr. Shurrocks called the borning room "the Leanto Chamber." If the original house was constructed in 1686 or soon after, then the lean-to may very well date from around 1700.
4. In a letter to the writer dated at Nantucket October 6, 1958, Dr. Will Gardner stated that the *Thomas Macy House* on Tattle Court was older than the *Jethro Coffin House*, a discovery based on the findings of the craftsman who both restored the *Thomas Macy House* and located "a very ancient deed of the house which refers to it as 'the *Great Macy House.*'"

This deed has not yet been made available to the writer, but it is clear that the *Thomas Macy House* was built before 1686.

Further, the architecture of that house is older than the date, 1717, when the Fish Lots, on which the building stands, were laid out in the Town of Nantucket. In 1717 the house stood facing south, with its chimney-gable standing end to Fair Street, because at that time Tattle Court did not exist. In 1949-50 the house was completely restored by the above craftsman.

5. The *Thomas Macy House* was erected as a lean-to house if the evidence on the lean-to side of the rear wall of the Great Room may be believed: no bevel-edged siding boards, but only old lath and plaster. It is interesting that the corkscrew staircase, upon nearing the loft, turns into zigzag steps, as may be seen in the floor plan. An old photograph of the house shows that the brick chimney was an ell in plan and had a handsome cap and a plaster necking band — much like those found in Maryland and Virginia. About 15 to 20 years after the house was finished, the East outshut was attached to the chimney gable-end in the same manner as that at the *House on "Crooked Record."* The East room has a small fireplace; at the rear of this room there was once a first-floor bedchamber with small catercornered fireplace. Under that bedchamber was a cistern of curved, cut brick.

6. The bricks in the fireplace are smooth and late in date; they measure only 7½″ long. The breasts of the fireplace are not at an angle as wide as those at Siasconset. The round brewing copper pot, 25″ in diameter and with stubby little flue to main chimney, is not found at 'Sconset.

7. In Duprey, 1959, p. 8, there is put forward the hypothesis that the existing stairway is so unusual that it might have been replaced by an earlier, corkscrew stair.

8. Worth, 1928, p. 231.

9. Also to be included in a list of Transitional lean-tos should be the *Christopher Starbuck dwelling*, or *Tobey House*, opposite the Civil War Monument — a home embodying parts of an earlier structure brought from early Sherburne which perhaps dates from 1690 and having round lights, instead of square ones, over some interior doors — the embryo of what have been called "Nantucket lights"; the *Sarah Turner House* (c.1750) at 86 Centre Street; *Dr. Will Gardner's abode* (1760) at 33 Orange Street, a one-sided lean-to; the *Benjamin Fosdick homestead* (1740-50), Liberty Street; and in Siasconset, the original *Lucretia M. Folger House* and *Svargaloka*. It has been indicated recently that the lean-to was typical of Nantucket architecture *until* the second quarter of the 18th century (Fowlkes, 1959, pp. 24, 31); while on the contrary, the usual building in the 17th century was a medieval structure, one room in depth — not a lean-to.

10. Duprey, 1959, p. 74.

11. Forman, 1962. A painting of the *Swain-Sevolle-Smith House* showing a wood door high up on the right-hand side of the Great Room fireplace was made in 1919 by J. Walter Folger and hangs in the Fair Street Museum.

Selected Critical Bibliography

Addy, 1933	Addy, S. O. *The Evolution of the English House*. London, 1933.
Ashley, 1926	Ashley, C. W. *The Yankee Whaler*. Boston, Mass., 1926.
Austin, 1896	Austin, J. G. *Nantucket Scraps*. New York, 1896. A delightful, anecdotal, yet sentimental description of Victorian Nantucket.
Baird, 1873	Baird, H. M. "Nantucket," in *Scribner's Monthly Magazine*, vol. 6, no. 4. August, 1873.
Braun, 1940	Braun, H. *The Story of the English House*. London, 1940.
Bullen, 1947	Bullen, R. F. and Brooks, E., "The Squam Pond Indian Site," in *Bulletin*, Massachusetts Archaeological Society, Andover, Mass., vol. 8, no. 4, 1947.
Bullen, 1949	Bullen, R. F., and Brooks, E., "The Herrecater Swamp Site, Nantucket," in *Bulletin*, Massachusetts Archaeological Society, Andover,, Mass., vol. 10, no. 4, 1949.
Coffin, 1911	Coffin, T., ed. *The Oldest House on Nantucket Island*. 2 vols., 3rd ed. Poughkeepsie, N. Y., 1911. About Coffins and Gardners — partly sentimental.
Crèvecoeur, 1782	deCrèvecoeur, J. H. S. J. *Letters of an American Farmer*. 1782. Reprinted from the original edition: New York, 1904. The most detailed account of early Nantucket, by a visitor to the Island.
Crosby, 1937	Crosby, E. U. *95% Perfect, The Older Residences at Nantucket*. Nantucket, 1937. Drawings and photographs of a few Town buildings.
Douglas-Lithgow, 1911	Douglas-Lithgow, R. A. *The Nantucket Indians*. Nantucket, 1911. Written entirely from the point of view of an historian.
Douglas-Lithgow, 1914	Douglas-Lithgow, R. A. *Nantucket, a History*. New York, 1914. A good general history of the Island.

277

Dow, 1925   Dow, G. F. *Whale Ships and Whaling.* Salem, Mass., 1925.

Drake, 1944   Drake, T. E. "Elihu Coleman, Quaker Antislavery Pioneer of Nantucket," in Brinton, H. H., ed., *Byways in Quaker History.* Wallingford, Pa., 1944.

Duprey, 1959   Duprey, K. *Old Houses on Nantucket.* New York, 1959. Picture book of 51 dwellings, with attention to furnishings, both old and modern, and with measured drawings of typical 18th-century Town house, of two basic plans.

Fairburn, 1945   Fairburn, W. A. *Merchant Sail.* Center Lovell, Maine, 1945-55. Vol. 2, pp. 980-1000.

Forman, 1919   Forman, E. C. *King of the Air and Other Poems.* Boston, Mass., 1919. Includes a few poems about Nantucket.

Forman, 1951   Forman, E. C. *The Singing Day and Other Poems.* New York, 1951. Also has poems about Nantucket.

Forman, 1938   Forman, H. C. *Jamestown and St. Mary's: Buried Cities of Romance.* Baltimore, Md., 1938. Includes story of the founding of earliest English settlements in America.

Forman, 1948   Forman, H. C. *The Architecture of the Old South: The Medieval Style, 1585-1850.* Cambridge, Mass., 1948.

Forman, 1959   Forman, H. C. "Vanished 'Sconset Houses on Nantucket," in *Historic Nantucket,* Nantucket, Mass., vol. 6, no. 3. January, 1959.

Forman, 1961   Forman, H. C., ed. *Underhill's The Old Houses on 'Sconset Bank.* Nantucket, Mass., 1961. In this volume referred to as "Underhill."

Forman, 1962   Forman, H. C. "Swain's Burnt-Out Polpis Lean-to," in *Historic Nantucket.* Nantucket, Mass., vol. 9, no. 3. January, 1962.

Fowlkes, 1959   Fowlkes, G. A. *A Mirror of Nantucket.* Plainfield, N. J., 1959. A short, superficial architectural history of the Island.

Guba, 1964   Guba, E. F., "The Sheep's Commons Fight," in *Historic Nantucket,* Nantucket, Mass., vol. 12, no. 1. July, 1964.

Guba, 1965   Guba, E. F. *Nantucket Odyssey.* Privately printed, Waltham, Mass. 2d ed., revised, 1965. A popular history of the Island, brought down to present times.

Hanaford, 1890   Hanaford, P. A. *Heart of Siasconset.* New Haven, Conn., 1890. Of little significance.

Hare, 1937   Hare, L. C. M. *Thomas Mayhew, Patriarch to the Indians, 1593-1682.* New York, 1937.

Harper's, 1860   "A Summer in New England," in *Harper's New Monthly Magazine,* vol. 21, no. 126, p. 745. November, 1860.

Hart, 1872   Hart, J. C. *Miriam Coffin or the Whale-Fishermen.* San Francisco, Calif., 1834; republished, 1872. Good for sheep-shearing business, as well as the seafaring life on Nantucket.

Hinchman, 1926   Hinchman, L. S., compiler. *Early Settlers of Nantucket.* Philadelphia, Pa., 1926.

Historic Nantucket   *Historic Nantucket,* Quarterly of the Nantucket Historical Association, Nantucket.

Hussey, 1912   Hussey, R. B. *The Evolution of Siasconset.* Nantucket, 1912; reprinted 1954. A short account of the village, mostly taken from Underhill's writings, especially E. F. Underhill's "Old Houses on 'Sconset Bank" (1888). See Forman, 1961 (above).

Ingstad, 1964

Ingstad, H., "Vinland Ruins Prove Vikings Found the New World," *National Geographic Magazine,* vol. 126, no. 5. Nov., 1964. This article outdates Pohl, 1952.

Gardner, 1949

Gardner, W. *The Coffin Saga.* Cambridge, Mass., 1949. Story of one of the Nantucket proprietors, his origins and his descendants.

Godfrey, 1882

Godfrey, E. K. *The Island of Nantucket.* Boston, Mass., 1882. The most inclusive history of the Island to that date.

HABS

Historic American Buildings Survey, Library of Congress, Washington, D.C.

Kelly, 1924

Kelly, J. F. *The Early Domestic Architecture of Connecticut.* New Haven, Conn., 1924. The standard work on the subject.

Kobbé, 1888

Kobbé, G. "'Sconset Scenes," in *Inquirer and Mirror,* Nantucket, Mass., August 4, 1888, and September 1, 1888.

Leach, 1950

Leach, R. J. "The First Two Quaker Meeting-Houses on Nantucket," in *Proceedings of the Nantucket Historical Association,* Nantucket, Mass., 1950, p. 24.

Lloyd, 1931

Lloyd, N. *A History of the English House from Primitive Times to the Victorian Period.* London, 1931.

Macgowan, 1950

Macgowan, K. *Early Man in the New World.* New York, 1950.

Macy, 1835

Macy, O. *The History of Nantucket.* Boston, Mass., 1835. The standard early history of the Island.

Macy, 1915

Macy, W. F. *The Story of Old Nantucket.* Nantucket, Mass., 1915.

Macy, 1929

Macy, W. F. *Nantucket's Oldest House.* Nantucket, 1929.

Macy and Hussey, 1916

Macy, W. F., and Hussey, R. B., *The Nantucket Scrap-Basket.* Nantucket, Mass., 1916. Best collection of folk anecdotes on the Island.

McFarland, 1911

McFarland, R. *A History of the New England Fisheries.* Philadelphia, Pa., 1911.

Nantucket, 1892

Nantucket Characters, photographs by H. S. Wyer. Nantucket, Mass., 1892.

N.H.A.B.

Nantucket Historical Association Bulletins, Nantucket, Mass.

Northrup, 1881

Northrup, A. J. *'Sconset Cottage Life: A Summer on Nantucket Island.* Syracuse, N. Y., 1881.

Oldest House, n.d.

The Oldest House, 1686. Nantucket Historical Association, Nantucket. N.d. Pamphlet about Jethro Coffin House which continues some of myths about the dwelling, like date of erection, into the mid-twentieth century.

Pohl, 1952

Pohl, F. J. *The Lost Discovery.* New York, 1952. A thought-provoking book, with errors.

Poor, 1932

Poor, A. E. *Colonial Architecture of Cape Cod, Nantucket, and Martha's Vineyard.* New York, 1932. Attempt to make a photographic record of some early buildings.

Schweinfurth, 1913

Schweinfurth, J. A. "Nantucket for an Architect's Vacation," in

The American Architect, vol. 103, no. 1932. January 1, 1913. Contains some elementary measured drawings.

Schweinfurth, 1917   Schweinfurth, J. A. "The Early Dwellings of Nantucket," in *The White Pine Series of Architectural Monographs.* Boston, Mass. Vol. 3, no. 6. December, 1917. Has a few Georgian and Classical Revival buildings.

Shurrocks and Shurrocks, 1940   Shurrocks, A. F., and Shurrocks, A. A., *Nantucket Indian Artifacts.* Nantucket, Mass., 1940. Interesting booklet on Island tools.

Spears, 1908   Spears, J. R. *The Story of the New England Whalers.* New York, 1908.

Stackpole, 1953   Stackpole, E. A. *The Sea-Hunters; the New England Whalemen during Two Centuries, 1635-1835.* Philadelphia, Pa., 1953. Essential work on the subject.

Starbuck, 1924   Starbuck, A. *A History of Nantucket.* Boston, Mass., 1924.

Stark, 1959   Stark, L. *The Story of Tuckernuck.* Nantucket, Mass., 1959. Booklet with indifferent photographs of buildings on that island.

Stevens, 1936   Stevens, W. O. *Nantucket, the Far-Away Island.* New York, 1936. Most popular, but not too accurate, modern book about the Island. Shows high standard of English.

Stockley, 1964   Stockley, B. H. "Archaeology and History," in *Historic Nantucket,* Nantucket, Mass., vol. 12, no. 1. October, 1964.

Thayer, 1919   Thayer, H. B. "Hereditary Architecture," in *Proceedings of the Nantucket Historical Association.* Nantucket, Mass., 1919.

Town Records   Town Records, on file in record office, Nantucket, Mass.

Underhill, 1885   Underhill, E. T. & Co. *A Picture Booke of Ye Patchworke Village, 'Sconsett by Ye Sea.* New York, 1885. It was Underhill who coined the word "Patchwork Village" — taken over by later writers.

Underhill, 1886   Underhill, E. T. & Co. *The Credible Chronicles of The Patchwork Village: 'Sconset by the Sea.* New York, 1886.

Underhill, 1887   Underhill, E. F. "'Sconset Then and Now — A Retrospective Glance at the Patchwork Village," in *The Inquirer and Mirror,* Nantucket, August 20, 1887.

Underhill, 1888, or "Underhill"   Underhill, E. F. "The Old Houses on 'Sconset Bank," in *The 'Sconset Pump,* Nantucket, summer of 1888. Reprinted in Forman, 1961 (above). Referred to in our text as "Underhill."

Underhill, c.1893   Underhill, E. T. & Co. *'Sconset by the Sea.* New York. N.d., but probably c.1893.

Wailes, 1931   Wailes, R. "Notes on Some Windmills in New England," in *Old Time New England.* Boston, Mass. January, 1938. Best article on subject of Nantucket mills.

Waterman, 1950   Waterman, T. T. *The Dwellings of Colonial America.* Chapel Hill, N. C., 1950.

Worth, 1904   Worth, H. B. "Early Houses at Nantucket," in *Proceedings of Nantucket Historical Association.* Nantucket, Mass., 1904. Of little value — simply a re-hash of earlier descriptions.

Worth, 1928

Worth, H. B. "Nantucket Lands and Land Owners," in *Nantucket Historical Association Bulletin*. Nantucket, Mass. Vol. 2, no. 5. 1906; republished 1928. An essential handbook for Town streets and buildings.

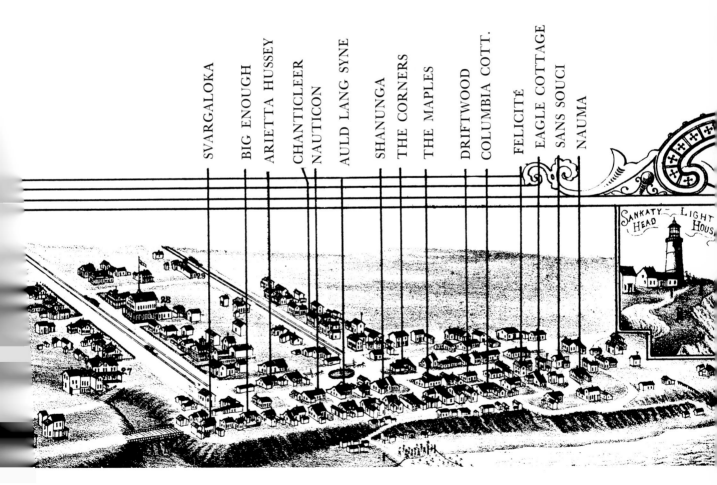

SVARGALOKA
BIG ENOUGH
ARIETTA HUSSEY
CHANTICLEER
NAUTICON
AULD LANG SYNE
SHANUNGA
THE CORNERS
THE MAPLES
DRIFTWOOD
COLUMBIA COTT.
FELICITÉ
EAGLE COTTAGE
SANS SOUCI
NAUMA

SANKATY HEAD LIGHT HOUSE

Siasconset in 1881, with some early dwellings identified by author. (Insert from "Bird's eye View of Town of Nantucket . . . Looking Southwest," 1881.)

Index

ACADEMY HILL, 242
ACCAWA, 19
AFRICA, Central, 6
AGRICULTURISTS, Indian, 6
AISLES ("Cells"), description of, 243
ALGONQUIAN group, 6
ALLEN, Reuben, 247
ALLEY, Elijah, H., 132
ALLEYWAY, off Shell St., 213
ALMY, Mrs., 138
ALTAR Rock, 10
AMERICAN Independence, 42
AMERICAN Indian, age of, 6; description of, 6. *See* Indian.
AMERICAN Institute of Architects, 232
AMERICAN Revolution, 1, 34, 53, 78
ANCHORAGE, The, 212; illus., 175
ANGLO-SAXONS, 239
APPLETON, Wm., 232
AQUIDNET Point, 32
ARBORS, medieval, 10
ARCHAIC peoples, 6
ARCHITECTURAL STYLES, 79, 80; lag in, 222; outline of, 110; Early Nantucket, illus., 109; Late Nantucket, illus., 256
ARCHITECTURE, American Indian, 9; Georgian, beginning of, 28. *See also,* Medieval Style, Jacobean Style, Transitional Style, Georgian Style, etc.
ARIETTA HUSSEY House (Cathcart House), 198; illus., 200, 211
ARTIFACTS, Indian, 6, 13, 16
ASA P. Jones House. *See* Ivy Lodge.
ASTON, Benjamin, 64
ATHEARN'S House, 44
ATHENAEUM, 110

ATLATL (throwing stick), 6
AULD Lang Syne, 34, 109, 111; description of, 126; illus., frontispiece, 106, 125, 127, 128, 129
AURORA Villa, 211; illus., 155
AUTOPSCOT, Chief, 7, 18

BAHAMAS, 239
BALDWIN, Frank, 232
BANK (Bluff) Highway, 43
BARN, of Mrs. Cathcart, 198; of Nauma, 271; at The Corners, 213
BARNABY Lodge (General Quarters), 154
BARNARD, Eben, 216; Nathaniel, 26, 271; Robt., 24; Shubael, 202; Thos., 21
BARNEY, Cromwell, 181; Griffin, 268; Mathew, 209; Thos., 46, 202, 271
BARTHOLOMEW, W. M., sketch of, 225; illus., 223
BATTEN STRIPS, 104
BAULK, meaning of, 90. *See* Hanging-loft
BAXTER, William, 114, 269
BEAN HILL, 19
BEARD, John, 114, 121
BECKFORD, Samuel, 52
BED, wainscot (box), 82, 84. *See also* cots, X-cot
BED screw for rope beds, illus., 202
BELCHER, Mrs. J. H., 185, 270
BENJAMIN Brown House, 237
BENJAMIN Fosdick House, 276
BERMUDA, 239
BETSY CARY House (Saint's Rest). *See* Shanunga

283

BIG Sunflower, 135
BIGENOUGH (Tuckernook), 135, 160; illus., 114, 139
BIN, cobblestone. *See* Dexioma
"BIRD'S Eye View . . . Siasconset in 1881," 268; illus., 281
BOAT house, 153, 165, 185, 269
BOAT'S crew, whaling shelter for, 81
BOOKS, in early Siasconset, 53
BORNING room, 246, 275
BOND Castle (Md.), 227
BOWEN, Billy, 220; illus., 172; house of, illus., 120
BOWLING alley, 46
BOX-carts (tip-carts), 58; illus., 59, 61
BOX-wagons, 58; illus., 20
BRITAIN, 1; whaling off, 12
BRITTEN, Henry (Indian), 16
BRICKS, Dutch, 257
BRIDAL Chamber, 236
BROWN, William, 270, 272
BROADWAY (Siasconset), 4, 34, 45; *passim*; illus., 45, 68, 132, 144, 175, 180
BRUSH-EVERARD House (Va.), 102
BUILDING idiosyncrasies, 221; Indian, 11
BUNKER, Benjamin, 174, 269; George, 174; Obed, 272; Uriah, 71, 216; Wm., 25
BUNKER house, 24
BUNKER-DELL House, 242
BUPTON, George, 160
BURGESS, Mildred, 267, 268
BURYING ground, circular, 8; Quaker, 25
BUTTERY, 96, 246

CAERNARVONSHIRE (Wales), 87, 95
CALMES, size of, 275
CANDLE water heater, illus., 161
CANOES, Indian, 12
CAPAUM Harbor, 23, 24, 25, 27, 74; Pond, 12, 228
CAPE COD, 49; whaling from, 29
CAMBRIDGE Farm, 25. *See also* Upper Cambridge, Lower Cambridge
CAPTAIN'S Walk, 62
CARRIAGE-HOUSE, 225
CARTER, Edward, 75
CARY, Betsy, 76, 122, 268; illus., 77
CASA Marina, 136; illus., 137, 138, 140
CASEMENT windows, 106, 108, 227; at Jethro Coffin House, 223; at Shanunga, 118
CASH, William, 269; Cash's Fish Market, 45
CASTLE Bandbox, 109, 160, 213; illus., 215, 217
CATHCART House. *See* Arietta Hussey House

CEDAR Park (Md.), 102
CELLAR, round, 248
CELLS ("Aisles"), 134, 243
CENTRE St. (Siasconset), 42; illus., 211; (Town), 256, 276
CHAISE house, 216; chaises (chairs), 58
CHANNING, Eva, 133
CHANTICLEER, The, 216; illus., 216
CHASE, Benjamin, 42; Jonathan, 151; Peter, 145, 267
CHEROKEES, 7
CHESTER St., 12, 25. *See* Westchester St.
CHIMNEYS, brick, 98, 221; freestanding, 108; horseshoe, 237; necking band on, 275; with withes, 237, 250; wood, 97, illus., 83, 100
CISCO, 31
CISTERN, curved, 275
CLAMBAKE, 55
CLAPP, Joe, 151
CLARK, Elisha, 181; Nancy, 202; Uriah, 202; Clark House. *See* Utopia
CLEATS to loft, 178
CLIFTON Cottage. *See* Driftwood
CLINKERS, 62, 209, 221; meaning of, 102
CHILD'S closet room, 127, 161, 184, 209
CHRIST'S Cross (Va.), 227
CHRISTOPHER STARBUCK (Tobey) House, 276
CHURCH, English parish, 243; first, on Nantucket, 239; Indian, 9, 10; timber-framed (1698), 11
COATUE, 13; timber on, 26
CODFISH Park, 45, 101
COFFIN, Elizabeth, 43; Dionis, 24; James, 23; James Josiah, 198; Jethro, 231; John C., 269; Levi, 134; Mary Gardner, 231; Michael, 126; Mrs. Aaron, 269; Nathaniel, 216; Obed, 145, 198; Richard, 75; Robt., 269; Stephen, 74, 272; Sylvanus, 213, 272; Tristram, 21, 24, 25, 231, 232; Winthrop, 232
COFFIN Saga, The, 231
COFFIN, George W., House, 274
COLEMAN, Elihu, 250; Gorham, 266; Isaac, 23; Job, 267; John, 24; Obed, 220; Sarah, 136; Stephen, 213, 216; Thos., 21
COLESWORTHY, Jonathan, 145
COLUMBIA Cottage (Willow Harp), 87, 88, 174; illus., 87, 176
COME ABOARD (Nonquit), 183; illus., 184
COMMONS, Town, 65
COMMERCIAL Wharf, building on, illus., 68
CONNECTICUT, 225, 246
CONSANGUINITY, 54
COOF, meaning of, 2
COOK, Sam (Indian), 75

COOKING outdoors, 96
COPPER plate, of Siasconset, 43; illus., 39
CORNERS, The (Meeresheim), 134, 202; illus., 177, 199, 203, 204
CORNICE, modillion, 255; illus., 253
COSKATA, 8; whaling station at, 31
COTTON MATHER, 9
COTS, canvas, 50; illus., 51
COUNCIL Chamber, 8, 9, 11
COURT, Nantucket, 13, 18, 25, 26, 52, 57
CREDIBLE Chronicles, The, 104
CREVECOEUR, 11, 21, 28, 38, 40, 42, 50, 53, 54
CRIMES, Indian, 18
CRIMINAL Cases, 75
CROGLOFT. *See* Hanging-Loft
CROOKED Lane, 25
"CROOKED RECORD," House on. *See* House on the "Crooked Record"; Richard Gardner II House.
CROSBY, F. J., 270
CUDDY, 30, 76
CUPBOARD Bible, 250; illus., 249
CURTAINS (claddings), 105
CUTTYHUNK, 5

DANCE, Nantucket, illus., 219
DAVIS, George S., 267
DEEDS, Indian, 16
DEXIOMA, 109, 153; illus., 159
DISHES, 52
DIVIDEND land, 63
DOORS, two-panel, 250; Siasconset, 105
DRAY, Nantucket, 217
DREW, Gershom, 163
DRIFT whales, 31
DRIFTWOOD (Clifton Cottage), 181; illus., 182
DRIPPING stone, illus., 224
DUGOUTS, Indian, 11
DUKE St., 25
DYER, James (Indian), 28

EAGLE cottage, 179; illus., 180, 181
ELBOW Lane, 42, 216
ELIHU COLEMAN House, 24, 250; illus., 249, 251
ELISHA CLARK'S Stable, 181; illus., 181
ELIZA MITCHELL House. *See* The Maples
ELIZABETH Islands, 5
ELKINS, Chas., 211; Geo. B., 46; Susan E., 211
EMMETT, John, 183

EVER-GREEN Park, 110, 141
EVOLUTION Chart of Siasconset Whale Houses, 130
EWER, Sylvanus, 268

FACTORY, twine, 185
FAIR English house, 80
FAIR Street Museum, 19, 42, 238, 276
FELICITÉ, 183; illus., 167, 183
FENCE, Town, 16, 24; Siasconset, 213
FERRIS, Benjamin, 170, 180, 269
FIGUREHEAD, ship, 266
"FINS" (half-gable projections), 135
FIREPLACES, central, 81; early, 47; hoods of, 97; largest on Island, 250; stone, 266; wood and brick, at Shanunga, 112, 112, 118
FIRST buildings in Town, 221
FIRST Congregational Church, 239
FISH house (Siasconset), illus., 102
FISH Lots (1717), 275; racks, 32; illus., 35
FISHING family (Siasconset), 38, 39; off Siasconset, 33, 34
FISHING Stages, Indian, 13; Long Island, 31; Nantucket, 31, 32, 33, 34; private, 31; map of, *see* Title page
FLAKE, fish, 3; illus., 197; meaning of, 46, 256
FLAKE lot, 46; yard, 3, 46
FLOCK bedstead, 52
FLOORS, types of, 95
FLOUNDER wing, 202
FOLGER, Abiah, 24; Barzillai, 173; Benjamin Franklin, 173, 231; Chas., 134; Felix S., 211; Franklin, 267; George, 181; J. Walter, 276; Obadiah, 269; Peter, 9, 19, 24, 25, 79; Samuel B., 269; Seth, 268; Solomon, 213; Sylvanus, 42
FOLGER'S Crow's Nest, 204
FORMAN, E. C., poems by, 271
FRANKLIN, Benjamin, 9, 24
FREDERICK C. SANFORTH House, 135; illus., 137
FREDERICK M. PITMAN House (Sea Spray), 193, 194; illus., 194
FRIENDS burial ground, 25; meeting, first, 24, 25, 26. *See also* Quaker
FRONT St., 34
FULL loft, Siasconset whale house, 88, 90, 118
FURNITURE, of poorest Islander, 50; of richer homes, 52; wall, 82

GALE (storm) of Oct., 1841, 213

GALLOWS Field, 28, 74
GAM, 56, 58
GANGS, 56
GARDENS, 74
GARDNER, Annie, 208; Brown, 163; Caleb, 274; Daniel, 28; Eben, 178; Eliza, 11; George C., 156, 274; H. C., 270; Harrison, 143; John, 11; Joseph, 225; Latham, 165; Mrs. Harrison, 267; Prince, 149; Richard, 32, 225; Ruth, 3; Sylvanus, 28; Thomas, 28, 255; Timothy, 46, 270; Will, 231, 275; Wm., 199
GARDNER, Roland, Shop Book of, 2
GARDNER St. (Town), 225
GAYER House, 24, 53
GEORGE BUNKER House. See The Wood Box
GEORGE C. CHASE House, 195
GEORGE C. GARDNER House, 109, 149, 213; illus., 123, 150, 156
GEORGE WILBUR House. See Dexioma
GEORGIAN architecture, 28; characteristics of, 28; mansion, 244; Style, 3, 239, 242, 243
GIBBS, Geo., 213; Samuel, 213, 272; Swamp, 8
GIRLS, pretty, 2; characteristics of Nantucket, 55
GOSNOLD, Bartholomew, 5
GOTHIC Revival Style, 80, 110
GOVERNOR'S Palace (Va.), 256
GREAT MACY House, deed, 275
GREAT Point, 8, 187
GRINDALL GARDNER House, 256
GUILFORD (Conn.), 275
GUINEA (Town), 194
GULL Island House, 255

HACK-HOUSE, 220; illus., 220
HALL (Great Room), 80; meaning of, 52
HAMBLIN House (Town), 274
HANGING-LOFT (baulk, crogloft), closing off of, 87; development of, 86; first described, 4; in England, 90; in Siasconset, 84, 85; in Wales, 84, 85; illus., 83, 85, 86, 87
HANGOVER Georgian Style (Persistence of Georgian), 110, 256
HANGOVER Medieval Style, 80, 149, 221, 237, 239; meaning of, 80
HANGOVER Transitional Style, 110, 244, 255
HARDWARE, door, 105
"HARPER, The," 68
HARPOON, bone, 12; illus., 4
HARVARD College, 9
HAWTHORN Lane, 132, 250

HEADACHE House, 151; illus., 37, 155
HEALTH, of Islanders, 54
HEARTHS, central, 90
HEARTS Ease, 108, 208; illus., 205, 206, 208
HENRY COLEMAN House. See Shanunga
HIACOMMES (Indian), 9
HIGH TIDE, 141; illus., 132, 143
HIGHWAY along Bank Edge, 34. See also Bank Highway
HILL St., 135
HINGES, wood, 105, 106, 202; illus., 106
HISTORIC American Buildings Survey (HABS), 112, 237, 275
HONORABLE, Dorcas, 19
HOP Cottage (Waldorf Astoria, Jr.), 212, 213; illus., 211
HORACE FOLGER House. See Utopia
HOUSE, arbor, 10; at Rye, Sussex, 104; but-and-ben, 79; chaise, 216; English or "fair" English, 10, 11; fire, 80; first hall-and-parlor, on Nantucket, 52; Great Macy, deed of, 246; hall-and-bower, 79, 90; at Rhiw, Wales, illus., 84; hall-and-parlor, 231; in Pembrokeshire, 83; "L"-, 153, 202; Lancashire, twin-stateroom, illus., 82; oldest, on Nantucket, 111; Maryland twin-stateroom, 91; of Lords, 163; of Seven Gables, 232; on the "Crooked Record," 225, 226, 227, 246, illus., 224; row, in Town, 239, 242, illus., 223; Saxon, 90; Siasconset, furnishings of, 53; "T"-, 97, 81, 149; "tan," 11; "the Unknown," 135; timber-framed, 11, 23, 80; typical fisherman's, 43. See also Whale Houses
HOUSEHOLD furnishings, 52
HUDIBRAS, 53
HUMMOCK, Head of, 24; Pond, 8, 16, 23, 26, 64
HUSSEY, Christopher, 24; Edward B., 272; R. B., 111; Stephen, 26, 75, 153

IN and Out (Sunnyside), 198; illus., 171, 201, 204
INDEPENDENCE Hall (Penna.), 242
INDIAN encampments, 32; lands, 16; language, 19; manufactures, 13; plague, 18; population, 18; villages, 8; whales, 16. See also American Indian
INDIANS, contributions of, 7
INNIS, Katherine, 52
INQUIRER and Mirror, The, 232
INSULATION, clay, 236. See also Wall
IRELAND, 90
IRVING House. See Roof Tree
IVY Lodge (Ivy North, Ivy South), 208, 209, 213; illus., 206, 209, 210

JACOBEAN decoration, 225; Style, 221, 227; folk capitals, 225
JAIL, 25, 70
JAMES ATHEARN House. *See* Frederick M. Pitman House
JAMESTOWN (Va.), 5, 239
JENKINS, Jonathan, 208
JETHRO COFFIN House, 24, 103, 227, 231, 232, 246; illus. 229, 230, 234
JOB MACY Dwelling, 242
JOEL, son of Hiaccomes, 9
JOHN C. MORRIS House, 135
JOHN (Johm), P. (Indian), 16; stone of, illus., 17
JOSIAH COFFIN House, 237, 250; illus., 252, 253
JOY, Edward, 136, 145, 160, 188, 198, 213; Reuben, 188; W., 272

KELLEY, Edward, 269
KITCHEN, Nantucket, 48; utensils, 95. *See also* Porch

LADDER ("stee"), to crogloft, 84, 90, 91
LAMP, petticoat, illus., 48
LANCASHIRE (England), 81, 90
LATCHES, wood, 105, 250
LATHS and plaster, 127. *See also* Plaster
LEADED window. *See* Windows
LEAN-TO, 53, 145, 243; added, 244; integral, 244, 246, 250; not typical of Nantucket, 276; Transitional, 244, 276
LEIF ERICKSON, 5
LIBERTY Hall, 155; illus., 162
LIBERTY St., 276
LIFE, pioneer, on Nantucket, 47, 48, 49
LILY Pond, 25
LIQUOR business, 75
LITTLE Red House, The, 213; illus., 203
LLAINFADYN House (Cardiff, Wales), 83
LIFT, full-, 118; half-: *see* Hanging-Loft
LONDON (Eng.), 1; Great Fire of, 239
LONDON Tower. *See* Liberty Hall
LONG Island (N.Y.), fishing stages on, 31; whaling at, 29
LONG Pond (Nantucket), 13
LONG Woods, 26, 64
LOOKOUTS, 13, 31. *See also* Fishing stages
LOOMIS House (Conn.) 103
LOUVRES, Medieval, 148
LOWER Cambridge, 24
LUCE, Keziah, 213
LUCRETIA M. FOLGER House, 80, 145, 276; illus., 140, 147, 172, 211

MACON (Ga.), 11
MACY, Arabella Coffin, 62; Cromwell, 269; Geo. C., house of, 274; James, 136; Job, 255; Josiah, 272; Richard, 255; Obed, 44; Thos., 16, 21,, 23, 74
MACY, Thomas, House. *See* Thomas Macy House.
MADAKET, Road, 274; settlement at, 16, 23
MAGNALIA, Cotton Mather's, 9
MAIN St., mansions, 3; in Sherburne, 25; in Siasconset, 45; in Town, 225, 242, 256
MAINE, 21
MANNING, Denny, 52
MAP, of Island (1820), 254; of Sherburne, 22, 120, 121; of Siasconset (1835), 40, 41; of Siasconset (for visitors), 259; of Three Villages, 38; of Town (for visitors), 259
MAPLES, The (Eliza Mitchell House), 165; illus., 162, 168
MARIA MITCHELL House, 242, 256; illus, 256
MARRIAGES, 53, 54
MARTHA'S Vineyard, 5, 8, 9 16; wigwams on, 10
MARTIN Box, The, 165; illus., 170, 171
MARYLAND version of Welsh twin-state-room cottage, 91
MASKOTUCK Neck, 26
MAYHEW, Thos., Jr., 9, 13; Thos., Sr., 16, 19, 24
MEADER, George, 194; Nicholas, 194
MEDIEVAL Style, 28, 43, 178, 221, 225, 227, 242; characteristics of, 80, 237; in Siasconset, 109; meaning of, 3
MEDIEVAL town plan, 25; village, 3, 46
MEERESHEIM. *See* The Corners
MEETINGHOUSE, Friends, 26; Indian, 18; North Shore, 239
MIACOMET, 11, 16, 64; Pond, 31; Sheep Pens, illus., 66
MIDDLE Gulley, 34, 45; illus., 37; Pasture, 69
MILK Room, 233, 246
MILK St., No. 33, 110
MILL, fulling, 70; grist, 25, 70; Hill (house), 274; Hills, windmills on, 71; horse, 71; Round-Top, 71; tidal, 25, 71. *See also* Old Mill
MILL St., 242, 255
MISSIONARIES, 9
MITCHELL, Charles, 267; Frederick, 272; Geo. F., 271; Joseph, 160, 270; Obed, 183, 265; Thos. F., map by, 254
MIZZENTOP, 160, 161, 184; illus., 85, 162; boat-house of, illus., 100
MOOERS, Chas. C., 270; Lane, 213, 258
MOREY Lane (Siasconset), 154, 220
MORTAR and pestle, Indian, 7, 16

MORTAR, mud and clamshell, 237
MT. VERNON (Va.), 242
MULATTO, 28
MUNTIN-AND-PLANK partition, 104
MYRICK, Geo., 133; Peter, 136
MYSTICETA, 29
MYTHS, about Jethro Coffin House, 236

NANTUCKET, became an island, 6; County records, 2; discovery of, 5; summary of, 2; fishing off, 13; Harbor, 12, 16, 24, 25, 27; meaning of, 1
NANTUCKET (Town), 16, *passim;* Fire (1846), 242; Hotel on Brant Point, 110; "lights," 276; naming of, 27
NANTUCKET Historical Association, 11, 19, 232
NATHANIEL PADDACK House, 255; illus., 254
NATTICK, 9, 53
NAUMA, 8, 31, 34, 188, 271; illus., 188, 189, 190, 191, 192
NAUTICAL expressions, 58
NAUTICON Lodge, 34, 85, 98, 99, 145; illus., frontispiece, 45; casement, illus., 107; hanging-loft, illus., 86; yard, illus., 197
NEGROES 19, 28
NEVER, Jack (Indian), 75
NEW Dollar Lane, No. 4, 110
NEW England, first known white settlement in, 5
"NEW Guiney," 28. *See also* Guinea
NEW North Cemetery, 71
NEW Street (1836), 213, 216; illus., 217; in Town (No. 3), 274
NEW Town Gate, 28
NEW York, 21
NEWBURY (Mass.), 24
NEWFOUNDLAND, 5
NICHOLS, Chas., 267
NICKANOOSE, Chief, 13 19; House 34, 194; illus., 155
NO Bottom Pond, 24, 25
NOBADEER, 8
NONANTUM, 173; illus., 170, 174, 175
NONE Too Big, 184
NONQUIT. *See* Come Aboard
NOPQUE, 8
NORTH Gulley, 34; Liberty St., 256; Shore Meetinghouse, 239; Street, 237
NORTHRUP, A. J., 267
NORWAY, 5
N'YUM N'Yum Hut, 55

OBLONG, Place Called, 74

OCCAWA (Agawam), 8
OCMULGEE Mounds (Ga.), 11
OFF-ISLANDERS, 2, 5
OLD MILL, 274; North Vestry, 239; South Church, 239
OLDEST Known Buildings on Nantucket, 111
ORANGE St., 256, 276
OUTHOUSES, in Sherburne, 25
OUTSHUTS (Outshots), 96
OVEN, 250; illus., 249; wood door of, at Polpis, 276

PADDACK, Benjamin, 154; Chas., 216; Henry, 135, 267; Ichabod, 31; Jonathan, 271; Latham, 212; Nathaniel, 231; owners of Jethro Coffin House, 232; Rachel, 271
PAINTING, red ochre, 209
PALIS (Screen), 83
PARKER, Fred, illus., 35; Owen, 134
PARLIAMENT House, 24, 25, 26
PARSON CAPEN House (Mass.), 231
PARTITION (parclose), 81; ("scaffo'd"), 90. *See* Wall
PARTY, colonial kind of, 133
PEAT Houses, 46
PEDEE Village, 38; Whaling station, 31
PENN, William, 34
PEWS, box, 239
PHILADELPHIA (Pa.), 34
PIDGEON holes, 248
PINKHAM-GARDNER House, 178; illus., 178
PINKHAM, Tristram, 178
PITMAN, Frederick, 45, 194
PLAGUE (1763), 18
PLAINFIELD, 34; map of, 38
PLAN, the one-room, 225
PLASTER and lath, unusual, 183. *See also* Laths; Plastering
PLASTERING, 104, 177, 208, 238
PLEASANT St., 28
POCHICK, Bluff, 8; Rip, 34; St. development, 109
POCOMO, 8
POLPIS, 6, 11, 32, 53, 70, 257; amusements in, 54
PORCH, cooking, 95, 96; inner, 99; kitchen, 199, 208, 209
POST (S), and beam construction 242; gunstock, 227, 228, 239, 250, 257
POST OFFICE, Siasconset, 122
POTCONE (Sachem), 7
POTTERY, 6, 13
POUND, for animals, 25, 74

PRESBYTERIAN Meetinghouse, 239
PRISON, 25. *See* Jail
PROPRIETORS' early town, 21; records, 43, 44
PUBLIC House, 76, 211, 271
PUMP Square, 213; 271; illus., 177, 197, 199, 204
PUNCHEON, meaning of, 23

QUAISE, 8
QUAKER (S), 9; fined, 57; first meetinghouse of, 25; organization of, 56; records, 49; served as magistrates, 57. *See also* Friends
QUAKERISM, 222
QUANATA Beach, 33
QUARREL size, 275
QUEEN (Ship), 185
QUIDNET (Aquidnet), 8; fishermen at, illus., 262; fishing stage, 32; hermit of, illus., 35; oak-tree stump at, 26; view of, 263; whaling station at, 31
QUOINS, wood, 242

RAGLAN, Monmouthshire, cottage at, 89
RAM'S Pasture, 8
RAMSDELL, Reuben, 220
REDELL, Mr., 268
REED Pond, 23, 74
REID, J. B., watercolors by, 178, 209
REREDOS, meaning of, 98
REUBEN JOY House. *See* Zaccheus Macy House
REVOLUTIONARY War. *See* American Revolution
RHIW, Caernarvonshire, hanging-lofts at, illus., 84, 88
RICHARD GARDNER House, Capt., 250; illus., 226
RICHARD GARDNER (II) House, 225, 228. *See also* House on the "Crooked Record"
RICHARDSON, John, 26; Mrs. Geo., 271; Richard, 24
ROBINSON, Benjamin, 247; family, 205; House, 34, 194
ROCKER, barrel, illus., 222
ROOF TREE (Irving House), 208; illus., 207, 209
ROOF (S), catslide, 134, 243; clinker, 102, 103; Dutch cap, 256; gambrel, 244, 256; pitches of, 103, types of, 102; up-and-down board, 103, illus., 102, 103; whale-house, types of, 101
ROOM, the Inner, 52; East, 53

ROMAN numerals, on house timbers, 23
ROPE Walks, illus., 27
ROSE Cottage, 34, 155
ROYALL House (Mass.), 53
RUG pattern on floor, 122
RULE, Chas. H., 154
RUSSELL, Daniel, 71; John, 136

SALISBURY (Mass.), 16
SANFORD, Frederick C., House, 43, 45
SANS Souci, 108, 159, 185; illus., 159, 186, 187
SANKATY Head, 5, 8, 33; Light, 184; Road, 188
SARAH TURNER House, 276
SAUL'S Hills, 10
SCHOOLHOUSE, 25
"SCONSET Pump, The" (newspaper), 271
SCREEN ("palis"), 83
SCRIBNER'S Monthly Magazine, 1
SCRIMSHAW, 62, 266
SEA, influence of, 22
SEA Shell. *See* Hack-House
SEA Spray, 44, 193. *See also* Frederick M. Pitman House
SESACHACHA, 4, 8, 34, 134, 188, 194, *passim;* on a map, 38; medieval plan of, 46; size of, 33; view of, illus., 263; whale station, 32. *See also* Sesachacha Beach
SESACHACHA BEACH, Indian, 32; whaling station at, 4, 31, 32
SETH RAY House (Barrett House), 256
SHANUNGA (Betsy Cary House), 34, 76, 109, 227; discoveries at (1955), 111; fireplaces, archaeological drawing of, illus., 113; four stages of, 117, 118, 119; full loft at, 118; hanging-loft, 88, illus., 85; later history of, 122; parlor, illus., 122; wooden fireplace at, 97, 98, 99, illus., 100
SHANUNGA (ship), 122
SHAW, John H., 153, 268
SHAWKEMO Chapter, Massachusetts Archaeological Society, 8
SHEEP business, 69; common, 64, 145; earmarks, 69; shearing picnic, 68, illus., 67, 210; pens, 64
SHEFFIELD, Josiah, 145, 148; Lane, 148
SHELL St., 42; illus., 211
SHELTERS, thatched, 31
SHERBURNE (town), 12, 33, 41, 47, 52, 70, 74, 247, 250, 276; building of, 23; maps of, 22, 120; roads in, 25; warehouses in, 25
SHIMMO, 8
SHINGLES, wood, on walls, 103
SHIPBUILDING, influence of, 222

SHIP'S Knee, 62, 222, 233; illus., 236
SHURROCKS, Alfred, 225, 232, 274
SHUTTERS, 107
SIASCONSET ('Sconset), 12, 18, *passim;* cliffs, 7; ethic, 208; first summer resort in America, 76; founding of, 34; from the south (1860s), illus., 175; gridiron plan of, 41; hill, 43; hut, described by Crèvecoeur, 38, 39, 40; importance of, 4; in 18th century, 32, 41; map of, 40, 41; meaning of, 8; medieval plan of, 43, 46; nucleus of, 34; on map, 38; square on Front St., illus., 17; small plantations of, 46; view from across South Gulley, illus., 125; whale cottage trappings of, 79; whale station, 32; whaling village, 33. *See also* Siasconset Bank
SIASCONSET BANK, 31, 34, 78, 185; illus., 37; Lot, 34; Pasture, 74; Road, 74; Roots, 8; Well (1776), 42, 195; Well (1841), 265
SIDING, bevel-edged, described, 103
SILAS PADDACK House, 256
SINKER, Indian, illus., 12
SKILLET, illus., 49
SLAVES, 38. *See also* Elihu Coleman House
SLICER-SHIPLAP House (Md.), 103
SLOOPS, 30
SMITH'S Point, 8
SMOKING Field, The, 74
SNUG Harbor, 153; illus., 160
SOAP making, 48
SOCIETY for the Preservation of New England Antiquities, 232; of Friends, Religious, established on Nantucket, 56. *See also* Quakers
SOUTH Gulley, 41, 42, 45, 216; Bridge, 133
SOUTH Pasture, 69
SOUTH Well, 41, 42, 43
SPANISH coin, 153
SPEER ("Spur"), meaning of, 99
SPERM whaling, 34
SQUAM, 11; excavations at, 10, 108; latten spoon from, 48; wigwams, 10
SQUANTUMS, 55
SQUARE, on Front St., Siasconset, illus., 17
ST. ANTHONY (Newfoundland), 5
ST. MARY'S City (Md.), 97, 239
STACKPOLE, E. A., 265
STAIR, closed-stringer, 257; open-well Transitional Style, illus., 226
STARBUCK, Edward, 21, 23, 24; Nathaniel, 24; Nathaniel, Jr., 26; Reuben, 208
STATEROOM, 47, 84
STATIONS, whaling. *See* Fishing stages
STEPLADDER ("Stee"), 81
STONY Brook, 70
STORAGE bin, 153

STORE, provisions in, 76
STORMS of 1835, 1841, 34
STORY, Thos., 11
SUMMER resort, first in America, 3
SUNNYSIDE. *See* In and Out
SUNSET Hill, 24, 255
SURFSIDE, 7, 10
SURREY (England), 237
SVARGALOKA, 80, 133; illus., 133
SWAIN, Abijah, 135, 267; Anna, 149; Chapman, 11; Chas. P., 271; John, 11, 16, 24, 69, 75; Richard, 24, 25, 202; Samuel B., 272; Uriah, 122. *Also* furnishings of John Swain, 53; stage of John Swain, 31; Old Mill of Timothy Swain, 71
SWAIN-Sevolle-Smith House, 257, 258; illus., 257, 260
SYLVIA, Joseph P., 266

TABLE board, 52
TABOO, Nantucket, 3
TAKITEZIE. *See* Arietta Hussey House
TAN (English hut), 11
TASHMA, Benjamin, 18; "Tashmy's House," 19
TATTLE Court, 246
TEA-HOUSE, 174
"TESTEMONY" (against slavery), 250
TETOUKEMAH Lots, 74
THOMAS BROCK House, 213; illus., 211
THOMAS LEE House (Conn.), 225
THOMAS MACY House, 246, 247, 248; illus., 245, 249
THOMPSON, Mrs. Billy (Isabel Irving), 272
THOROUGHGOOD House, Adam (Va.), 102
THORN Lot, 25
THREE Bricks, 110
"THREE FISHERS WENT SAILING" (Wyer), illus., 262
TIMBER-FRAMING, 11
TIPI (Indian house), 10
"TIS TEW I CAN'T," 63, 68
TOM Nevers Head, 122
TOOLS, Indian, 13
TOWN building, 221
TOWN house, 25, 44
TOWN Pump (Siasconset), 42
TRADER'S Lane, 185
TRAILS, Indian, 11
TRANSITIONAL Style, 221, 255, 256; characteristics of, 243, 244
TRENCHERS, 48, 52, 55
TRUMPERY month, meaning of, 1
TRUNK, Haircloth, illus., 233
TRY-KETTLE, 48
TRY-WORKS, 30

TUCKERNOOK (House), illus., 114. *See also* Bigenough
TUCKERNUCK (Island), 7, 8, 11, 23, 53

UNCLE Black's Cave, 11; illus., 10
UNCLE Nat's Shanty, 204
UNDERHILL, Edward F. ("Underhill"), 33, 49, 80, 87, 95, 98, 103, *passim*
UNDERHILL'S Ever-Green Park, 110, 141
UPHAM, Jonathan, 126
UPPER Cambridge, 24
UPTON, Geo. B., 271
URANN, Julia Macy, 172, 272
URBAN architecture, 221
UTOPIA (Clark House or Horace Folger House), 202; illus., 205, 207

VALENTINE ALDRICH House, 216; illus., 125, 175
VERANDAH House, 24
VESTAL Street, 257; illus., 20
VESTRY, Old North, 239
VILLAGES, map of 17th-century, 38; six Indian, 8
VINLAND, 5

WAINSCOTING, in England, 104
WALDORF-ASTORIA, Jr. *See* Hop Cottage
WALES, origins of Siasconset whale huts in, 90
"WALKING SANKATY," 211
WALL(S) bark strip and plaster, 238; board-and-batten, described, 104; clay and straw, 257; horizontal board-and-batten, illus., 100; muntin-and-plank, 238; types of, 103, 238; wattle-and-daub, 238. *See also* Insulation; Partition
WANACKMAMACK (Lodge), 209, illus., 155; (Sachem), 7
WANNACOMET, 8, 23, 25
WAREHOUSE, Mr. Coffin's, 74
WARTS (Outshuts), 97
WASHING Pond, 64
WATER Supply, 48, 49
WAUWINET (place), 8; (Sachem), 7, 9, 13
WELL. *See Siasconset* Well
WELSH National Folk Museum (Cardiff), 83
WESCO, 16, 25, 28, 74; early buildings in, 25; Lots, 27; meaning of, 23; move to, 27; Pond, 71
WEST Chamber, 233, 236
WESTCHESTER St., 25, 250
WEWEEDER, 8, 31

WEYMOUTH, 12
WHALE houses, first in Siasconset, 34, 38; first Nantucket, 31; imitation, 149, 198, 208, 209, 213; prototypes of, 81; characteristics of Siasconset, 80
WHALE tail, 12, 16
WHALEBOAT, crew, 31, 32; description of, 29, 30
WHALERS, first American, 12
WHALES, drift-, 13, 14, 15, 16; kinds of, 29
WHALING, companies, 31; Indian, 12; Museum, 266; off-shore, 12, 13, 29, 220; sperm, 63; stations, 29, 31, 32
WHIPPEY, Benjamin, 71
WHIPPING, 18, 75
WHITE Stone, The, 23
WHITING, J. Marshall, 275
WIGWAM Ponds, 10
WIGWAMS, characteristics of, 10; size of, 11
WILBUR, Nathan, 71
WILL GARDNER'S House, 276
WILLIAM BAXTER House (Town), 256
WILLIAMSBURG (Va.), 256
WILLOW Harp. *See* Columbia Cottage
WILSON, family, 205; J. Ormond, 272
WINDOWS, Anglo-Saxon, 106; casement, 248; "fenestral," 106; glass, at first Friends' Meeting, 25; guillotine, 108, 237; leaded, 227, 248; leaded, but not a casement, 275; leaded, perhaps most important in English America, 237, 238; lie-on-your-stomach, 85; transitional type of, 237, 238; Nantucket, 237. *See also* Casement
WOOD Box, The (George Bunker House), illus., 94, 251
WOOD chimneys, 97; importation, 26; supply, 25
WOODBINE, The (Thornycroft), 134, 135
WOODLAND people, 6; lodges, 11
WOODS, at Parliament House, 26; at Long Woods, 26; on Coatue, 26
WOOL trade (sheeping), 63
WOOLMAN, John, 213
WORTH, Benjamin, 213, 272; G. F., 266; H. B., 221, 231, 233; Wm., fishing house of, 32
WYER, Nathaniel, belongings of, 52
WYER'S (Maxcy's) Pond, 23, 24, 25, 52, 64

X-COT, canvas, 50; illus., 51

YORK St. (Town), 28
YORKTOWN (Va.), 1

ZACCHEUS MACY House, 225, 228; illus., 245